# PIONEER URBANITES

# PIONEER URBANITES

A Social and Cultural
History of Black San Francisco

*Douglas Henry Daniels*

*Foreword by Nathan Irvin Huggins*

TEMPLE UNIVERSITY PRESS
*Philadelphia*

Temple University Press, Philadelphia 19122
© 1980 by Temple University. All rights reserved
Published 1980
Printed in the United States of America

Publication of this book has been assisted by a grant
from the Publication Program of the National
Endowment for the Humanities

*Library of Congress Cataloging in Publication Data*
Daniels, Douglas Henry.
 Pioneer urbanites.
 Bibliography: p.
 Includes Index.
 1. Afro-Americans—California—San Francisco—
History. 2. San Francisco—History. I. Title.
F869.S39N43     979.4′6100496073     79-25602
ISBN 0-87722-169-3

*For my parents,*
*Henry Edward*
*and*
*Eleanora Louise Washington Daniels,*
*who inspired me,*
*and for Doris*

# Contents

# Map and Tables

# Foreword

"The land was ours before we were the land's." So began Robert Frost's poem read at the inauguration of President John F. Kennedy, and the poet went on to describe how "we gave ourselves outright . . . To the land vaguely realizing westward." In such words, Frost alluded to the single most dominant feature of the American experience and of American character. We are a created nation and a created people, continuously renewed by a conceptually renewable frontier, yet continuously exhausted because our roots—never going very deep anywhere—fail to sustain us for long in any place. We are, thus, forced to seek the next place in order to rediscover ourselves as Americans, as "new men."

The frontier, as metaphor, remains the essential and distinctive symbol in the American experience and imagination. It is a metaphor, however, which has been the stuff of myth making, sustained and reinforced by literature and popular culture. The images are both complimentary and contradictory. It is sometimes, as with Hector St. John Crèvecoeur, a wilderness to be tamed, an anarchic man to be controlled and civilized. It is the forest wilderness of James Fenimore Cooper, where man's innate nobility survives free from the corruption of civilized artifice. And, as Frederick Jackson Turner would have it, it is the crucible for the shaping of American character and democratic institutions.

Whatever the contradictions, there is a common thread running through it all: the American experience is one of renewal. The person, in nature, brought into touch with his innate being, is reborn. Society, forced to reconstitute itself, is improved in the process. At each new settlement, the social compact is reenacted by an aggregate of individuals rediscovering the necessity of community, making it stronger because of the deliberate choice. The myth, thus, merely articulates the American faith in possibility—in the individual, society, and nature—which has been the ground on which our chronic optimism and faith in progress has rested.

Like all myths, however, this one has more to do with faith and our will to believe than it does with actual experience. The myth would have us always think of the frontier as rural and "natural"; those who peopled the

frontier as remarkably Anglo-Saxon or northern European. Aside from
Mexicans and Indians, who in the myth are merely part of the wilderness to
be overcome and tamed, the rest were Yankees or southern whites with an
occasional Swede or Irishman for comic relief. Reality was something
altogether different. The West's urbanizing was almost simultaneous with
its settlement, and it was everywhere more heterogeneous than we have
imagined. Certainly, blacks have been part of the pioneering force developing America from the seventeenth-century colonies to the Indian Wars at
the end of the nineteenth century. Professor Douglas Daniels, in this
remarkable study of blacks in San Francisco, breaks ground in two ways:
He brings to our consideration the city as part of the frontier experience,
and he obliges us to pay attention to race as an element of new community
formation. We are made to ask how renewing the experience really was;
especially for blacks.

When I read Professor Daniels's work and pondered these questions,
two different ironies pressed themselves on me. The first came from the
observation of how quickly something new becomes something old. And
the second had to do with the paradox which, until the mid-twentieth
century, perplexed Afro-Americans: to become part of the mainstream one
would minimize racial identity, submerge difference, become invisible; but
to gain the power and political leverage to demand fair treatment and
respect, one needed conspicuous numbers and racial identity. *Pioneer
Urbanites* brings these to mind with great intensity.

Thinking about the first of these questions, I recalled some mental
ramblings of mine from a year I spent in Berkeley. I lived in a house, high in
the Berkeley hills, which had a spectacular view of San Francisco and the
entire Bay. From my window I could see from the Golden Gate, Marin
County stretching north to the Richmond–San Rafael Bridge and beyond. And from San Francisco south, I could see the San Francisco–
Oakland Bridge, the airport south of the city, and as far as San Jose when
smog from industrial waste did not come too far up the Bay. Such a grand
panorama, such a perspective, pressed upon me the grand human achievement of engineering, building, and design everywhere to be seen. But, then,
even more compelling was the sense of breathtaking natural beauty which
had been there to start with, which survived more in hints and fantasy than
in actual reality.

Often, as I gazed out my window, I wanted to peel back that human skin
to see what it had been once. I tried to imagine the thoughts of those first
European sailors who chanced to come through the fog bank always
masking the estuary, through the Golden Gate into the sun-swept, glisten-
ing bay. Were they not stunned? Were they not seduced by the land,
realizing itself forever eastward? Did it not come to mind that this was a

new Eden, a new chance to start the human story all over again? That, too, is part of the American myth, and we have at each new landfall dreamed the dream again.

When San Francisco was settled by Yankees and southerners, black and white, it quickly became old. Professor Daniels's discussion of changing race relations makes that clear. In the early days circumstances would not allow the old, Eastern ways to persist. Blacks were not equal with whites, some indeed were slaves, but frontier necessity did not permit the luxury of applied racism. There was more freedom and more opportunity, and men tended to succeed in terms of their character and ability. Even black men and women were "making it." It was as if Frederick Jackson Turner was writing the script. If you could freeze the action, stop the story in the decade following the Civil War, you might imagine that race relations in San Francisco would take a course quite different from what it had in the East.

With development came familiar institutions—schools, churches, labor unions. The city wanted to be "civilized," and that meant mimicking old practice, not venturing the new. As the pressures of necessity abated, the luxuries could be indulged, including that of presumed racial privilege. As white workers formed unions, they would assert this privilege by denying membership to blacks and Chinese, claiming a difference between white men's work and labor for others, protecting themselves from competition thereby. Ironically, with development, the relative status of blacks in the work force fell. It was hardly a story of progress.

San Francisco wanted to be a city like familiar Eastern cities, except for being new. As in the western movie, everyone knew what the signs of success were. Anarchic tendencies needed to be curbed; law and order would be the byword. The city had to be safe for decent white women—typified by the schoolmarm and the churchgoing matron. There needed to be an opera house where one could hear recitals of music and readings of Shakespeare. There needed to be a social register and other such distinctions of class. Above all, social etiquette had to be observed, including acceptable manners in race relations. These were as much signs of "civilization" as anything, and white Americans would consider themselves wild and barbarian were they lax in any particular.

So San Francisco, like all frontier settlements, from Jamestown and Plymouth to Fairbanks, Alaska, was as eager to become like the old as to become something new. In the most narrow sense, it was a rebirth—a re-creation, a renewal—of what had been before. Still, it could never be quite the same as the cities and settlements from which its inhabitants had come. It was West, it was more open and more free. One had choices of lateral mobility unavailable in the East. And for blacks, since there were so few of them until the second world war, they suffered discrimination but they were never perceived as a threat by whites. It was a relatively benign and comfortable place, so whites and blacks could indulge a kind of complacency.

One is struck, in reading *Pioneer Urbanites,* by this ironic complacency of black residents of San Francisco before 1941. I was struck by it especially, because as a child I was one of the 4,846 blacks listed in San Francisco's census of 1940. I was in junior high school then, but I remember well how small a community we were, especially in relation to what we would become by the time I graduated college. I remember the black bourgeoisie of redcaps, porters, waiters, the occasional civil service employee, and the one or two professionals. How self-satisfied everyone was, despite discrimination in almost every line of employment, pervasive restrictive covenants, and powerlessness in city politics. How ambivalent everyone was about the wave of blacks from the South, brought in to man new jobs in the war industries.

Perceptions were often wrong. The old residents saw the new as crude, rough, and boisterous. They lacked the manners and sense of decorum San Francisco blacks had come to see as signs of accomplishment and good taste. Still they were often skilled and semiskilled workers, whereas the older residents had been largely servants. They made a lot of money in the shipyards and, with wartime restrictions on consumer goods, like most Americans they spent wildly on parties, and whiskey, and fun. Some saved and formed the basis of black business in the city.

The older residents, quite self-conscious of the image of blacks, were often embarrassed by them. In those days, the great teenage recreation was going to dances at Sweet's ballroom in Oakland, where the big bands played. Duke Ellington, Jimmy Lunceford, Chick Webb, Count Basie, and the others would come through town, playing two successive nights at Sweet's. The first night was for whites and the second for blacks. I don't know how that came about; I never saw a written rule. But whites never went on the second night, and blacks never went on the first.

The older residents of the Bay Area had been going to dances like that for years. During the war it continued, but now the Zoot Suit craze was on, and there was always some violence. There was sure to be at least one knife fight at every dance. The older residents liked to say that it was because of the newcomers, who hadn't yet learned how to behave.

With greater numbers, blacks in San Francisco could not be ignored, so much of the ground for complacency disappeared. Racial tensions rose. Certainly not like Detroit, New York, or Los Angeles, but it was palpable. There were now incidents of police brutality, something the older residents had not remembered. There were white as well as black newcomers—most from the South—and no one seemed to know how to behave as San

Franciscans. There were not a few older black residents who expressed the wish that they would all go back where they came from.

Numbers, a significant racial presence, made a difference. The character of San Francisco's black middle class changed as the black population could support black business and professional people. Doctors, lawyers, dentists, and later teachers supplanted the redcaps and porters as a new bourgeoisie. But numbers meant potential political clout, not much realized until the 1960s. Blacks became difficult to ignore. Racial tensions rose from benign indifference to antagonistic cooperation. Few would regret it.

One event sticks in my mind as symbolic of that shift from old black San Francisco to new. During the height of the war, the San Francisco papers broke a curious story. A young man had been hired by the Municipal Railway as a streetcar motorman. He had joined and been accepted by the union, no one had identified him as an Afro-American, because he looked white. And he did not make it known until after he had been hired. It was something of a scandal. It brought public attention to what had always been known: blacks were excluded from even the most ordinary city employment. The union's loud protest at the man's "deception" exposed its own racism. White workers would not work with blacks as equals, it was said—as it had been said for over a century. White people would feel uncomfortable and refuse to ride on a streetcar driven by a Negro. The war and not the western frontier made such cliches obsolete. The man kept his job, and in a short time blacks were being generally hired on the Municipal Railway.

Douglas Daniels's *Pioneer Urbanites* makes us rethink community formation in the United States. Cliches about the frontier melting pot can no longer abide. The emerging community that Daniels describes is one of multi-ethnic diversity and tension. Equally important, this is a rare study of the birth, development, and transformation of an Afro-American community.

NATHAN IRVIN HUGGINS

# Preface

—————•·•⟨⟩⟩•·•—————

*We have the record of kings and gentlemen ad nauseum and in*
*stupid detail; but of the common run of human beings, and particu-*
*larly of the half or wholly submerged working group, the world has*
*saved all too little of authentic record and tried to forget or ignore*
*even the little saved.*

*W. E. B. Du Bois*

This work focuses on the quality of life and the urban identity of the
Black residents of the San Francisco Bay Area from 1850 to World War II,
mainly from the vantage point of San Francisco, the first west coast
metropolis. When the East Bay municipalities of Oakland and Berkeley are
considered, they are regarded primarily as organically related to the oldest
city, and only secondarily as cities in their own right. This focus highlights a
phase of Black city life that has been neglected because of a scholarly
preoccupation with the mass migration of Black southerners and the
development of the modern ghetto. While justifiable, this preoccupation
ignores a pioneer period that is probably not unique to San Francisco,
thereby preventing a clear understanding of the history of all Black city
dwellers and of their successes before the ghetto. Study of San Francisco
clarifies the import of the pioneer phase, because in that city it was long
lived—from the emergence of the city in the 1850s to the development of
the ghettos around World War II.

This is not the typical Black urban history, which invariably titillates
the reader with the squalor of ghetto life, the carnage of the race riot, or
both. The San Francisco and Oakland ghettos developed a full generation
later than in the northeast; riots involving Blacks are rare and fairly recent
occurrences in the Bay Area. Nor is this an examination of social mobility,
social class, or working-class culture.

Until the 1940s, Black San Francisco had no large proletarian class,
which in itself prevents the usual working-class emphasis. Moreover, the
city's Afro-Americans were servants, porters, chambermaids, cooks, and
waiters, rarely professionals or businessmen. They developed close personal ties with the city's leading citizens and, consequently, frequently

expressed the political and economic ideas of the elite—not those of the proletariat. They considered themselves cultured, in the particular sense in which the term was used by Eurocentric nineteenth-century Americans.

But this is not a study of a Black middle class, either. I have tried to envision new ways of viewing Black citizens that do not rely on old conceptual cliches. It is a mystery to me that scholars can use a term derived from analysis of white Europeans and Americans, making it inapplicable in discussion of a people who experience race segregation and job discrimination to a degree that is unique in history. Nor is this a quantitative history, but rather a qualitative one. I am more concerned with what should be counted than with the actual enumeration. Because of its age and unusual history, San Francisco's contingent of Afro-Americans was the largest on the Pacific slope until the turn of the last century. Oakland's Black community also emerged early in this century, becoming numerically superior to San Francisco after the earthquake and fire of 1906. But the East Bay can still be regarded as an adjunct of the metropolis, because many East Bay residents were former San Franciscans who moved to Oakland, beginning in the 1890s, to become suburbanites and to dominate the East Bay's social and cultural life. While there is something to be said for considering Black Oakland as an independent urban area in its own right, that is for another study.

I have analyzed the Afro-San Franciscans topically, rather than chronologically. This is in part because the pioneer urbanites remained much the same for more than five decades. Also, there is little of the rich evidence such as one finds in U.S. political and economic history that makes possible close attention to minute change. As Lawrence Levine and various Black folklore scholars indicate, the Afro-American experience remained consistent during drastic changes in the rest of the nation, for example in the jobs available to Blacks. The history of Blacks in the U.S. might be comparable to that of African and other peoples whose records do not permit chronological analyses such as scholars of this nation prefer.

It should be pointed out that after 1900, changes did occur. The pioneer urbanite became a suburbanite in the outlying neighborhoods of San Francisco or in the East Bay. He mingled with Black newcomers who foreshadowed the mass migration, but who still had more in common with the pioneer than with the contemporary ghetto dweller. After 1910, southerners, married couples, and families made up a larger proportion of the Bay Area population (Black and white), particularly in Oakland. But the more familiar changes that Harlem and Chicago's South Side underwent did not occur in the Bay Area for another generation.

My use of ethnic terms may disturb or confuse readers. I have employed *Afro-American, Negro, Black,* and occasionally, *colored* because at various times they have all been current. Even in my short life each has passed in or out of use. I wish to draw upon this rich heritage—not because I am unaware that some designations are more acceptable in certain circles, but because I appreciate what the debate means. It is related to the search for identity that has been vital to the American, and especially the Afro-American, experience for centuries. Moreover, it is also relevant to the central theme of this work, the urban component of Black identity. My use of the different terms should remind us of the distinctive history which gave us these words.

Several diverse sources were necessary to construct a unified portrait from fragmented evidence. Neglect and fires destroyed documents of Negroes as well as many of the city's written records. In the Appendix I present brief biographies of my informants, so the reader can view them as individuals, each with a personal history but all sharing a number of qualities in common. (Two informants did not wish to be included in the Appendix.) Hopefully this study may help in the construction of a national history which incorporates ordinary individuals, neglected social groups, and the so-called inarticulate masses, as well as elite political and business leaders.

In the course of researching and writing this book, I became indebted to scholars and institutions. Professors Gunther Barth and Lawrence Levine read and criticized each draft of the work beginning with the dissertation, and I wish to thank them for their patience and the insights they provided. Professors Nathan Huggins, Winthrop Jordan, Raymond Kent, Leon Litwack, Henry Nash Smith, and John Ralph Willis influenced my thinking on social and cultural history. Professors Lawrence B. de Graaf and Roger W. Lotchin read a version of the manuscript and suggested revisions to improve it. Dr. Donn G. Davis and Melvin Wade helped me to clarify my thoughts at the University of Texas at Austin, and so have students in several classes and members of other audiences. Tom Stoddard permitted me to read his manuscript on Black musicians in the Bay Area and gave Chapter 9 a critical reading. James de T. Abajian was most cooperative and encouraging from the very beginning, and he very generously permitted me to consult his voluminous files, which was quite an aid to me, particularly before the publication of his bibliography and guide to Afro-Americans in the west.

I also owe a special debt to the eighteen individuals who were kind enough to allow me to enter their homes and interview them for several hours. I would like to express my special gratitude to the late Ethel Terrell, the late Walter L. and Veola Gibson, Mrs. Eleanor Carroll Walkins, and the officers of the East Bay Negro Historical Society, Eugene and Ruth Lasartemay, and Royal E. Towns, in particular.

In addition, I would like to thank the staffs of the Bancroft Library, the California State Library, the California State Archives, and the California Historical Society for their cooperation. I am grateful to my typists, Debra Jene Williams and Margaret Schockley, who readily transcribed tapes, prepared the manuscript, and brought some errors to my attention. Margarita Valencia, my research assistant, gave the manuscript a close reading, detected some errors, and suggested improvements, and for this I am grateful. Michael Ames and Bill Day of Temple University Press also deserve credit for helping me to improve the work's organization and the quality of its prose.

I conducted the research and found time to write while funded by a number of grants, including National Defense Education Act (Title IV), John Hay Whitney, and Ford Foundation fellowships. The Newberry Library, the National Endowment for the Humanities, as well as the African and Afro-American Studies and Research Center, the Dora Bonham Fund of the History Department, and the University Research Institute of the University of Texas at Austin also funded my research and provided support during the revision.

Part of Chapter 1 appeared in *Discovery* I (June 1976). A version of Chapter 5 appeared in *Umoja: A Scholarly Journal of Black Studies* I (1977), 2.

# PIONEER URBANITES

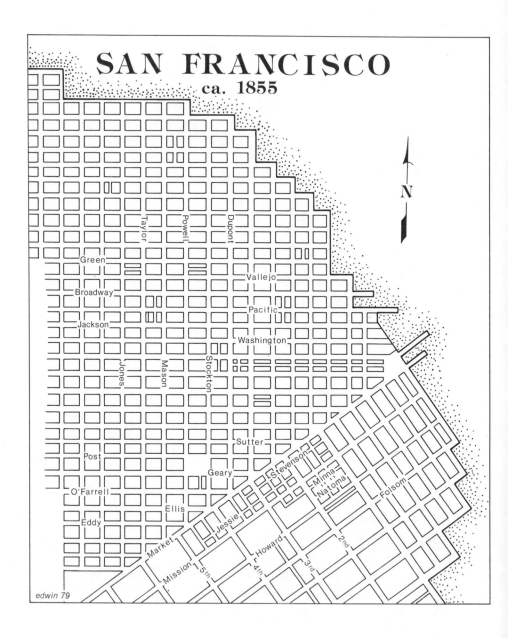

SAN FRANCISCO
ca. 1855

N

Taylor
Powell
Dupont
Green
Vallejo
Broadway
Pacific
Jackson
Washington
Jones
Mason
Stockton
Sutter
Stevenson
Post
Minna
Natoma
Geary
Folsom
O'Farrell
Ellis
Eddy
Jessie
Market
2nd
Mission
5th
Howard
4th
3rd

edwin 79

# 1

# Introduction

*Neither words nor yet the most detailed painting can evoke a moment of vanished time so powerfully and so completely as a good photograph.*

*Beaumont Newhall*

The writings of nineteenth-century antislavery people, humanitarians, and reformers are part of the intellectual heritage that emphasizes the ways in which society mangles Afro-Americans, turning them into drones or rebels. Black social scientists of the present day—Dr. Kenneth B. Clark, for example—and many liberal historians are heirs to this tradition. They wish to arouse the nation's reformers by calling attention to the injustices of American racism, industrialization, and urbanization. This point of view finds expression in literature and autobiographies, as well as in scholarly works. Richard Wright, particularly in *Black Boy* and *Native Son*, and *The Autobiography of Malcolm X* focus on the humiliation, degradation, and oppression of Afro-Americans in the rural south and the urban north.

Richard Wright stated the assumptions underlying this emphasis in *Twelve Million Black Voices:* "This text assumes that those few Negroes who have lifted themselves, through personal strength, talent, or luck, above the lives of their fellow-blacks—like single fishes that leap and flash for a split second above the surface of the sea—are but fleeting exceptions to that vast, tragic school that swims below in the depths, against the current, silently and heavily, struggling against the waves of vicissitudes that spell a common fate."[1] The problem with this particular perspective is that it robs Blacks of those qualities which enable them to survive, despite and in defiance of the system. It reduces them to pitiable creatures, if not to things. Wright refers to them as the "countless black millions," "teeming black millions," "legions of nameless blacks," and "terrified black folk."[2] Like the abstractions of social scientists—"dehumanization," "deperson-alization," "tangle of pathology," "disorganization"—Wright's terms show nothing if not the distance of the observers and their difficulty in regarding Afro-Americans as humans like themselves. Portraits of ghetto life—of dilapidated housing, broken families, streetcorner men, matriarchal women, and deserted children—accomplish similar objectives by depicting Afro-Americans as blues people with little chance of changing their condition.

A second tradition comes out of the slave narratives and histories written by Afro-Americans after the Civil War and in the early twentieth century. It emphasizes the heroic aspects of Black life, and the successes of the people who, like "single fishes," leap out of the sea of suffering;[3] it can be found in popular versions of Negro history, and in *Ebony, Jet,* and other contemporary sources. The authors write of unknown and unheralded Negro inventors, scientists, cowboys, soldiers, race leaders, and of proud and distinguished politicians, lawyers, teachers, and ministers. Unlike Richard Wright, these writers do not view the success tales as exceptions, but either as the rule or as representations of the potential of Black folk.

To many observers, this kind of history is a self-inflation or glori-fication of a few successes that overlooks the impoverished and oppressed conditions characteristic of Afro-American life. Meanwhile, the critics of the ghetto pathology school maintain that the social scientists and social workers overlook the pleasanter aspects of life and the strengths of Black folk.

I find both criticisms worthy of serious reflection. The vitality of Afro-Americans and their culture is all the more impressive when we appreciate the unceasing attempts to control, modify, and destroy Black culture and its creators. Focusing on their documents and struggles emphasizes Negroes as actors; it also permits us to consider the point of view of Afro-Americans themselves, whose thoughts and analyses are far more impor-tant than those of outsiders—census-takers, social workers, and well-meaning reformers and scholars. The problem with the alternative, as exemplified by Richard Wright and many others, is that it sees Afro-Americans as mere reactors to vast impersonal forces—like Bigger Thomas.

These different perspectives affect policy. We know that such concerns played a greater role in motivating nineteenth-century reformers than did any consideration for the human being. Abolitionists, antislavery people, and politicians were concerned with abstractions: democracy, free soil, free labor, the union; and it was for these reasons that they denounced slavery or the south. In the twentieth century, reformers and politicians care more about the reputation of the nation as a leader of the free world than they do about the oppression of Afro-Americans, and so once again the "Negro revolution" or "movement" is a means to another end. They believe they need only to tinker with their system by passing civil rights laws or "preparing" Negroes for integration to make all right with their world.

Those who stress Black pride and accomplishments are rarely more critical of the system. They emphasize the importance of individual efforts, rather than questioning the basic nature of American society. While giving Afro-Americans a measure of humanity and the ability to improve their condition, they ultimately blame the citizen rather than the system for his failings. Like Booker T. Washington and today's conservatives, they hold the victim responsible for his poverty, if not for the crimes of his oppressors.

These thoughts resulted from a look at the early urban experiences of Blacks in San Francisco. Along with other assumptions, I began research convinced that the documents of Negroes need to be consulted and given priority over government reports, census data, court testimony, and the records of bureaucrats. In addition, while I believe that written documents of the Afro-Americans should be used when available, scholars must tap the most appropriate sources, which are not always recorded on paper or even preserved in archives. Oral, musical, and photographic records are as significant in Black history as the traditional kinds of written documents. I have tried to give primary consideration to Afro-San Franciscans' views of themselves. Politicians, proscriptive legislation, and race relations, which have all figured largely in a number of Black history works, are tangential. Only after careful consideration of Afro-American life, culture, and views can we undertake comparisons of ethnic groups and formulation of social policy.

Rather than treat the destructive impact of the city, or merely glorify the accomplishments of the pioneers, I tried to relate the pioneers' experiences to the central theme of Black American history. The remoteness of San Francisco, and the racism of capitalists, of unions, and of its citizenry, prevented many Afro-Americans from migrating west. White westerners, through deliberate actions or as a result of apathy, aided those individuals and institutions who sought to keep Afro-Americans in the south, shackled to the plantation system during slavery and to sharecropping and tenant farming after emancipation. The successful efforts of a few thousand Blacks to reach the city, to find jobs, to combat discrimination, to form their own institutions, and to create images of themselves represent the creative and heroic aspects of Black history. The successes of early Negro Bay Area residents gain in significance when we realize the enormity of the obstacles they faced.

Thinking on these matters and on Black urban history is hindered by two factors. Given the lack of research on the topic, one must be very speculative or willing to generalize from data based entirely on northern and some southern cities, mainly after 1900. Our lack of understanding of the history of the Black urban dweller also results from scholars' preoccupation with notions of ghetto pathology used to describe changes wrought by the Great Migration of World War I. While northeastern and midwestern cities have received attention, southern and particularly western cities have been neglected. An accurate portrait of Black urban life is lacking for other reasons. Scholars have focused on the present century, often ignoring the nineteenth-century Black urban experience. Also, there are few studies of the small town life of Afro-Americans. Those that exist— for example, Hortense Powdermaker's *After Freedom: A Cultural Study in the Deep South*—are anthropological or sociological, not historical. Consequently, scholars lack a comparative dimension to clarify the quality of Black urban life.

Until quite recently, studies based on exhaustive and sympathetic examinations of Black city dwellers were poorly received because of an unwillingness or an inability to appreciate the humanity of Black folk, and because of the tendency to view the urban existence of Negroes as chaotic and pathetic. W. E. B. Du Bois's *Philadelphia Negro* and St. Clair Drake and Horace Cayton's *Black Metropolis* were overlooked until the 1960s. Both studies are particularly insightful because the authors immersed themselves in the communities, conducted interviews, and analyzed social activities and family life as participant observers. Using written records as well, these Black scholars provided an important human dimension to citizens who were usually regarded as unworthy of attention except as objects of social policy. Recent historical studies of Herbert Gutman and Nathan Huggins also offer a much-needed humanism. They represent departures in that they regard Afro-Americans as actors instead of subjects. But their works are not specifically urban histories. Richard Wade's *Slavery in the Cities* illuminates our perceptions of the peculiar institution, and does analyze the essence of Black city life. Along with John Blassingame's *Black New Orleans*, it constitutes one of the few studies of the urban history of Black southerners.

Regrettably, historians of Afro-America have not been alone in neglecting urban developments in the northwest, far west, and southwest. Historical monographs on Seattle, Portland, San Francisco, Oakland, and Los Angeles are rare. Emphasis on different ethnic groups or a history of one of them in a specific city is still more rare. An analysis of Black city life in a far western city inevitably suffers because of the lack of work on the topic. Studies of different cities in various areas of the United States must sooner or later shed light on regional differences and create an accurate national perspective. For Blacks in the nineteenth century, the Pacific slope was far different from the south, where most Afro-Americans resided. West-coast Negroes invariably inhabited cities or towns, whereas until quite recently most southerners lived in rural areas. Also, the far west lacked a heritage of entrenched slavery, so the entire society was not committed to placing onerous burdens and humiliating restrictions on Afro-Americans. Of course, its citizens' barbaric treatment of colored people, Chinese, Japanese, native Americans, and Mexicans, means the Bay Area does not deserve its reputation for being free of the race problems of southern and northern cities.

Proud and resourceful Black pioneers inhabited San Francisco as early as the Gold Rush. At home in the city, they had a basis for self-esteem and pride that is rarely associated with Black urban dwellers. They survived in a competitive metropolis at a time when most of the nation's whites and Blacks avoided that setting. Their experience as pioneer city dwellers also invalidates the common notion that whites were the first and only significant, urbanites in the United States. As city dwellers, the Black pioneers mastered elements of the new urban technology. Their literary records and a number of family photograph albums indicate the degree to which they, like all urbanites, depended on two popular forms of communication—print and photography.

I had to develop strategies suitable for my sources: methods for the traditional written sources, others for oral evidence, and others for visual material. My need for several approaches resulted from the evidence in the various kinds of records—not from any preconceived ideas; sources and methods both reflected the unique history of Blacks in San Francisco.

I began with the traditional documents because of their ready availability and my familiarity with the necessary approaches. These included the unpublished Manuscript Censuses from 1860 to 1900, published censuses, and the City Directories. Another primary source, the Black newspapers, offered Negro San Franciscans' own views of themselves, their work, the issues that concerned them, and the social and cultural events that figured in their lives.

I began interviewing aged Black residents of the Bay Area one year after I started collecting written evidence. Informants' names were offered by knowledgeable individuals, local historical societies, and eventually by respondents themselves. I questioned residents about their lives and knowledge of the Bay Area and its Black population. Some responded as if they had been waiting years for someone to record their impressions and insights. I appreciated the opportunity to see them where they were most comfortable, in their own homes.

The historical consciousness of the residents needs to be researched and analyzed in some depth before the contours of Black urban life on the entire Pacific slope can be presented and before comparisons can be made among Afro-Americans and with other ethnic groups. Aside from a WPA project in the 1930s, there has been little use of oral history techniques—especially by historians—among Negroes. This is particularly unfortunate given the strength and vitality of the Afro-American oral tradition. Oral history is especially appropriate for Black urbanites, because most moved to cities in this century, and many migrants survive today, waiting for scholars to record their testimony.[4]

Because of the bias of white-dominated newspapers and the paucity of written records from representative Black sources, oral history is particularly important for revealing the identities and concerns of anonymous Negroes. It also permits a Black citizen to have a role in interpreting history. However, it is more than simply a matter of asking questions and recording testimony, because San Franciscans—like other people—did not always carry their ideas through. Moreover, they presented a highly developed sense of protocol. Their concern with appearances should be evaluated in its own right, instead of being viewed as a barrier to understanding.

While my knowledge of the history of the area and of the leading personalities facilitated my entrance into San Francisco's Black world, this rapport was even more readily established with photographs. After conventional documents and interviews, this medium was the third stage in my analysis of the Black pioneers' social history. When I began, I could never have anticipated I would find many photographs because of the dearth of written records in the libraries and in informants' households. After four years of research, I discovered that the Black urbanities were more likely to possess photographs than traditional written records.

Karen Becker Ohrn, a professor of journalism, is aware of the value of these visual documents. She observes, "The family photograph collection serves as an 'archives' of family life—a way of remembering the way people and events used to be, and also a way of passing on these memories to other members of the family."[5] Eventually I realized the worth of these records for aiding a failing memory, for checking the accuracy of someone's recollections, or for simply starting a conversation. More than twenty years ago, John Collier, a photographer trained in anthropology, found photographs to be valuable for interviewing and conducting research: "Photographic probes sharpened [the informant's] . . . memory, reduced the area of misunderstanding, and compelled him to stick to the truth." They not only stimulate, but "help to overcome the fatigue and repetition often encountered in verbal interviews." They also "opened doors of memory and released emotions about forgotten circumstances, which allowed a second interview to be as rewarding as the first." Particularly important for people whose verbal abilities vary, when used as a research aid, photographs "function as a language bridge." I did not realize this at first, nor did I encounter Collier's work until recently. I had to depend on my intuition as I groped for a way to deal with these fresh sources.[6]

Eventually I understood the importance of photographs for both families and historical research. For old and young alike, "the memories that are sustained by looking through the old pictures are the memories of earlier selves." A family collection provides "a concrete link with past lives, and going over the collection is a way of communicating with the past" for both the informants and the scholar. Among old-timers, photographs "seem to provide a continuous thread with . . . [their] own past." For younger generations, "the pictures provide a way to discover the past and link . . . oneself to it."[7]

Photographs are especially appropriate for a people who grew up in an urban area during a period of unprecedented technological change. Affected by popular photography, pioneer urbanites were image- or photo-conscious, in that they valued pictures and relied on them to present their best selves to the world. In a period of rapid change, they sought to stop time. Many photographs were also published as illustrations in newspapers and on handbills. The photographs dramatically contradicted the cruel stereotypes of the popular press. To me, a historian and interpreter of Black culture, it was as if they left the photographic documents so that the world could assess their prosperity and note their pride.

The images of poised, well-dressed nineteenth-century urbanites were unlike what I usually encountered in published accounts of the metropolitan ghetto experience. Recent histories of New York's Harlem and Chicago's South Side used photographs and other records to portray wretched conditions and broken lives. The contrast with my findings suggested different conditions in the north and the far west, and reflected the simple fact that it is easy to find evidence of oppression among Afro-Americans, particularly when that is the main interest. What is significant from my research is that despite social and job discrimination, the pioneers managed to find a basis for self respect. Their photographs are evidence of this proud and unique heritage.[8]

While historians have used literary documents to depict Blacks as helpless subjects, photographs allow us to see many of them as confident human beings. Occupation, income, education, and similar variables are important for assessing accomplishments and status, but I would also emphasize the public image or self-image that is presented. Scholars can use photographs to study historically "inarticulate" segments of our population. Since most ordinary Americans leave few, if any, written records—diaries, autobiographical memoirs, or letters—historians and others must start taking seriously such seemingly inconsequential material as family photographs, snapshots, and albums. Nearly every family keeps such mementoes as part of its own historical record. For understanding the self-image of Blacks, photographs are especially useful when they are portraits approved by the subjects because they find the likenesses flattering.

For the nineteenth and twentieth centuries, photographs are at least as appropriate as written records for documenting the social history of ordinary citizens. This popular medium touches more lives, in a more personal manner, than written literature. Uneducated urban dwellers were extremely literate, in terms of their ability to read and appreciate photographs, and historically sophisticated, considering their successful preservation of these documents. Photographs of Black pioneers are significant as images with the power and vitality to stir the imagination and to give the subjects an immortality they rarely achieved through written records.

It is important to note possible objections at this point. One has to be careful not to read too much into stylized studio portraits. Photographers often furnished subjects with clothing and asked them to pose in a particular way. This does not diminish the value of the photographs, but it means we must analyze the relationship between photographers and their clientele. As Richard Chalfen notes, "photographic events include inter-actions between people using cameras and people on camera."[9]

Along these same lines, we can view the photographs as cultural artifacts like letters, works of art, or other objects. "Interactions between people looking at pictures and the content of the pictures per se" should also be our interest. Scholars can ask informants what they see in photographs and study how they use them—in albums, in wall displays, and to accompany letters to distant families and friends.[10]

By interviewing and photographing the aged, we can assess their vision of the past, compare it to information gleaned from traditional sources, and understand connections between past and present. Elderly people, I came to see, embody specific historical traditions that can be analyzed, comprehended, and some day compared to other accounts. This reali-zation was especially important for a young historian trained to view history as an academic discipline and an impersonal abstraction. Oral history and photography taught me to view the pioneer urbanites through their own eyes, by their own standards, and as a result of their own words and the visual images by which they wished to be remembered. None of them expressed the ideas or myths of Negro pathology presented by scholars. Then too, the personal quality imparted to history by my approach suggests its usefulness in making the discipline meaningful to laymen.

Amateur and professional resarchers can benefit from the use of visual images. In "Photography and Sociology," Howard S. Becker argued that scholars should continuously refine "not only their concepts and measures, but also their basic imagery, relying on that refinement more than they have to clear up theoretical and technical muddles." The photographs of the Black San Franciscans enabled me to visualize individuals' dress, posture, and bearing, and to compare these images with the stereotypes found in popular and scholarly literature, in cartoons, and in their written records.[11]

Tools like the printing press and the camera allowed Blacks to participate in urban life when labor unions and discrimination excluded them. The Black pioneers fashioned their own likenesses to record, to learn, and to project their history, their identity, and their visions and dreams of modern urban life. The Black pioneers reminded me of contemporary city dwellers of various ethnic and racial groups who similarly depend upon newspapers, magazines, pocket cameras, and lavish color photographs. By focusing upon these nineteenth-century predecessors we might better understand the uses of popular technology and, ultimately, ourselves.

It might be said that, just as we are approaching a true understanding of Black history, I am claiming that we actually know very little about the history and needs of Afro-America. But considering the three centuries of conscious and unconscious efforts to deny the history and humanity of the Black race, it seems natural and inevitable that, today, we are just making a beginning.

# 2

# Pioneers

*Colored men are destined to perform an important part in the future history of California, as well as in the older States of this Republic. Here as there, they have been among the pioneers of civilization: they have assisted in developing the great resources of the country; the mineral and agricultural wealth of the land have been brought forth by their labor equally as by that of white men. In every department where labor, industry and integrity are required they have been employed, and in higher positions, where genius and skill are essential, their aid and assistance have been eagerly sought.*
San Francisco Pacific Appeal, *May 23, 1863*

The Black residents of nineteenth-century San Francisco were much like frontiersmen: they were robust mature adults, predominantly single male workers with few dependents. They were also unmistakably urbanites, boasting high literacy rates, cosmopolitan origins, small families with few children, a fascination with technology, and a willingness to sacrifice present material comforts for future economic gain or for a desired style of life. These demographic characteristics resulted from the peculiar conditions attending migration and the city's unique history, location, growth, economy, and competition with other Pacific slope cities. Potential Afro-American residents with different characteristics seem to have avoided San Francisco.

The quality of life in San Francisco retained many of these characteristics in the early twentieth century, although the percentage of northern-born Blacks decreased considerably by the early twentieth century, and the proportion of married couples increased significantly after World War I. The number of Afro-Americans in San Francisco proper did not increase considerably after the 1860s, and in fact declined between 1890 and 1910. Oakland's Black population grew significantly in the late nineteenth century, and this trend continued, but still the Bay Area's Negro contingent was relatively small. Meanwhile, Black Los Angeles mushroomed between 1890 and 1940 (see Table 4).

In Los Angeles and northeastern cities, the phenomenal rise in the Black population was part of the Great Migration. This mass movement of Blacks to urban areas around World War I formed a picture of Black urban America that is usually accepted as standard. But it did not affect San Francisco, Oakland, Berkeley, or Richmond to any considerable degree until the 1940s. It is difficult to understand why the Bay Area, which held so much promise in the 1850s, did not support a large Black population until well into the twentieth century.[1]

San Francisco's growth rate during the 1850s marked its dramatic emergence as a metropolis over a few short years (see Table 1).[2] Despite steady increases, the Black population remained proportionately small. Significantly, while the total population continued to increase after 1900, the number of Negroes declined between 1890 and 1910. Before accounting for this phenomenon, we must first explore the reasons for the metropolis's emergence, and the features that drew and held the Black pioneers.

The city's economic life sustained dramatic changes. Beginning as a hamlet, San Francisco became an entrepôt for the gold fields, then dominated both the mining country and the agricultural hinterland. By 1870 it was the ninth-largest American city. As a port, San Francisco rivaled New York, Boston, and New Orleans. In 1850, its exports amounted to nearly five million and its imports to more than seven million dollars. By 1890, its trade equaled thirty-five million dollars in exports and

*Table 1*
*Growth of Population in San Francisco and Oakland, 1852–1900*

| Year | San Francisco | | Oakland | |
|------|-------|-------|-------|-------|
| | Total | Black | Total | Black |
| 1852* | 34,776 | 464 | | |
| 1860 | 56,776 | 1,176 | 1,543 | 11 |
| 1870 | 149,473 | 1,330 | 10,500 | 55 |
| 1880 | 233,959 | 1,628 | 34,555 | 593 |
| 1890 | 298,997 | 1,847 | 48,682 | 644 |
| 1900 | 342,782 | 1,654 | 66,960 | 1,026 |

*Based on the state census of 1852; the federal census was lost.
SOURCE: U.S. Census.

forty-eight million in imports; the combined total for the other California ports was less than half a million dollars.[3]

Manufacturing was insignificant at first, but by the end of the century investment in this sector exceeded the combined worth of exports and imports. In 1860 more than twenty-two million dollars were invested in California manufacturing, the vast majority of which was situated in San Francisco. By 1904, San Francisco's manufacturing output reached $137,788,233, while Oakland's amounted to only $9,014,705.[4]

Other factors besides population growth and increases in commerce and industry indicated the nature and wealth of this unusual urban milieu. The assessed valuation of the city serves as an index of its good fortune in the nineteenth century (see Table 2). By 1890 San Francisco ranked seventh in population among United States cities and third in commercial importance (see Table 3). Its one-third million citizens supported a multitude of hotels, saloons, restaurants, and theatres, one hundred and fourteen churches, twelve daily newspapers, and about one hundred weekly, semiweekly, and monthly journals.[5]

To better understand why the Black population was as small as it was— despite the city's resources—we need to account for its presence at mid-century. San Francisco drew Black sailors and maritime workers, such as Richard Dalton, from St. Thomas in the West Indies. Dalton came west in 1847 on the *U.S.S. Flint* and served as a steward on the steamer *Brother Jonathan*. He was one of a number of Afro-Americans toiling on the vessels that plied the Sacramento and San Joaquin rivers to Sacramento and Stockton, respectively.

Pioneers often continued to work on the boats after becoming residents, while others found new jobs, sometimes related to their former work. Blacks who started out as ordinary mariners found San Francisco an excellent place to advance. Abraham Cox, a ship's waiter in 1860, ran a

*Table 2*
*Assessed Valuation of San Francisco, 1860–1890*

| Year | Valuation (Dollars) |
|------|---------------------|
| 1860 | 35,967,499 |
| 1870 | 116,375,968 |
| 1880 | 253,520,366 |
| 1890 | 291,583,668 |

SOURCE: John P. Young, *San Francisco: A History of the Pacific Coast Metropolis,* 2 vols. (San Francisco, [1912]), I: 272–73.

*Table 3*
*U.S. Cities and Their Black Population, 1900*

| City | Total | Black | Percentage |
|------|-------|-------|------------|
| New York | 3,437,202 | 60,666 | 1.8 |
| Chicago | 1,698,575 | 30,150 | 1.8 |
| Philadelphia | 1,293,697 | 62,613 | 4.8 |
| St. Louis | 575,238 | 35,516 | 6.2 |
| New Orleans | 287,104 | 77,714 | 27.1 |
| Washington, D.C. | 278,718 | 86,702 | 31.1 |
| Atlanta | 89,872 | 35,727 | 39.8 |
| San Francisco | 342,782 | 1,654 | 0.5 |
| Oakland | 66,960 | 1,026 | 1.5 |
| Berkeley | 13,214 | 66 | 0.5 |
| Alameda | 16,464 | 144 | 0.8 |

SOURCE: U.S. Census.
NOTE: Percentages have been rounded.

sailors' boarding house in 1862. Later it was taken over by a West Indian mariner, John T. Callender.[6]

Even after the nineteenth century, a number of young Black residents went to sea to gain employment. Aurelious Alberga, a San Francisco native, worked on a ship that took him to the Arctic at the turn of the century. In the 1920s, Eugene Lasartemay, from Hawaii, went to sea because he found it impossible for a Black worker to obtain a good job in San Francisco.[7]

Other transportation workers labored on the trains. The transcontinental railroad guaranteed the development of stronger trade connections with the eastern states after 1869. The Central Pacific Railroad employed Blacks, but usually only as cooks, dining car waiters, or Pullman porters. In the late nineteenth and early twentieth centuries, Moses Freeman and Samuel E. Young secured positions catering to millionaires who frequently journeyed by rail from coast to coast. Around the turn of the century, Black railroad men often settled in Oakland, the terminus for the Central Pacific, Southern Pacific, and Western Pacific railroads. Many informants worked on the trains at some time in their careers; this employment made it possible for quite a few to inhabit the Bay Area, particularly the East Bay.[8]

Sailors, boat workers, and railroad men were essential to the settlement and residency of Black folk in a distant metropolis, even if they were not vital to the economy itself. They were among the first English-speaking migrants to become San Franciscans, largely because of their physical mobility. Moreover, they frequently adapted to the metropolis by opening boarding houses or restaurants. Proprietors and patrons discussed their successes and informed other Blacks of opportunities on the west coast.

Some Black Americans moving to the Pacific slope depended on ties with entertainment to visit and inhabit its major show town. One such itinerant showman, John E. Smith, exhibited trained horses in the Pacific states. He advertised his arrival and his talented horses before coming to San Francisco in the early 1860s. Another Afro-American, John "Jack" Fisher, held an important position as the horseshoe specialist for Elias J. "Lucky" Baldwin, a millionaire whose hobbies included racing prize horses. Oakland Blacks also worked as hostlers and jockeys and, along with prize fighters and athletes, became part of the sporting world.[9]

Black musicians, some respectable and others shady, also played in San Francisco and Oakland. The "Black Nightingale," Anne Pindell, performed in the Bay Area and in California cities and towns. She was accompanied by a group of Afro-Americans who entertained westerners with dramatic and comic routines. The Hyers sisters, Anna Madah and Emma Louise, also sang in the popular European tradition. They performed in the Bay Area and in California cities after the Civil War before leaving to tour the United States and Europe.[10]

Some show folk followed an entirely different musical tradition and appealed to a broad spectrum of urbanites. Originally working as minstrels, Egbert "Bert" Williams and George Walker, the famous New York comedy, song, and dance team, met and launched their careers in San Francisco in the 1890s. Twenty-five years later, Ferdinand "Jelly Roll" Morton, Creole composer and self-proclaimed "inventor of jazz," ran a San Francisco night club. His integrated policy and lack of a license for dancing caused police to crack down and forced him to leave town.[11]

The city occasionally sheltered a contingent of soldiers in the Presidio, the military garrison. During the Spanish-American war, Black cavalry and veterans of the Caribbean campaign were stationed there. Around World War I, the Twenty-Fourth and Twenty-Fifth Regiments of Infantry, made up of Black soldiers and white officers, stayed in San Francisco. Afro-Americans with similar temporary ties to the city included strike-breakers and other transient workers.[12]

Black service workers with more permanent connections labored in households, hotels, and restaurants. John Hanson Butler served as "a kind of valet" when he came west with his employer. Afro-American caterers such as Charles Smith and Thomas Taylor provided delicacies and utensils for parties, weddings, balls, and dinners. Other Blacks were butlers, coachmen, cooks, and servants. Negroes' tradition of excellent service accounted for the presence of nearly two hundred Black employees at San Francisco's famous Palace Hotel from 1875 to 1889.[13]

Afro-American churches, Masonic lodges, newspapers, and schools (for fifteen years) offered positions, but they were neither numerous nor lucrative, so leading settled Negroes usually depended upon other pursuits for their livelihood. They worked as barbers, seamstresses, and janitors, speculated in real estate and mining stock, and depended on their ingenuity. But even the leading Blacks of San Francisco and Oakland never commanded positions of power in the city—as elected officials, judges, heads of labor unions, captains of industry, or bankers. Nor were many Black pioneers skilled craftsmen or ordinary laborers, as these jobs were monopolized by whites from the 1850s.

A number of factors kept the Black population small in the nineteenth and early twentieth centuries. The Blacks' lack of power and influence in San Francisco and the distance from the south accounted for the size of the population before 1880. After 1880, powerful white labor unions prevented Negroes from winning jobs, while white immigrants took many of their traditional service positions. Industrialists and financiers rarely lent aid to the Black community and did not promote its growth through migration schemes. They only used Blacks occasionally as strikebreakers, the last kind of situation to lead to permanent residency or power. Finally, by 1900 Oakland grew and attracted Blacks, including San Franciscans, but then other new Pacific coast cities offered more opportunities to Afro-Americans and other migrants.[14]

For Blacks, San Francisco was perhaps more of a paradox than its boosters would admit. It offered economic opportunities for only a few—those with physical mobility, ties with leading citizens, and considerable independence, versatility, and perseverance. Even these opportunities were largely limited to the mid-nineteenth century, World War I, and World War II, as the growth of the Black population indicates. The decrease in population from 1890 to 1910 was contemporaneous with and affected by the emergence of Oakland and the earthquake and fire of 1906, when San Francisco refugees settled in the East Bay. The political power of white labor unions increased during these same years, forcing some newly-unemployed Blacks to leave the Bay Area. Increases in the Black population between 1910 and 1940 were significant indications of new possibilities, but the numerical increments were matched or outstripped in several other cities during the Great Migration (see Table 4).[15]

The origins of the Black urbanites indicate as cosmopolitan a group as one could find in any American city. San Francisco was the United States city with the largest percentage of foreign-born residents in 1880. Correspondingly, from 1860 to 1910 approximately one in seven of its Afro-Americans was born abroad. Only New York City had as large a percentage of foreign-born Blacks. San Francisco's foreign-born Negroes came from the West Indies, especially Jamaica; a few migrated from

*Table 4*
*Growth of U.S. Cities and Their Black Population, 1900–1940*

| City | Total Population | | Black Population | |
|---|---|---|---|---|
| | 1900 | 1940 | 1900 | 1940 |
| New York | 3,437,202 | 7,454,995 | 60,666 | 458,444 |
| Chicago | 1,698,575 | 3,396,808 | 30,150 | 277,731 |
| New Orleans | 287,104 | 494,537 | 77,714 | 149,034 |
| Detroit | 285,704 | 1,623,452 | 4,111 | 149,119 |
| Washington, D.C. | 278,718 | 663,091 | 86,702 | 187,266 |
| Los Angeles | 102,479 | 1,504,277 | 2,131 | 63,774 |
| Memphis | 102,320 | 292,942 | 49,910 | 121,498 |
| Seattle | 80,671 | 368,302 | 406 | 3,789 |
| Oakland | 66,960 | 302,163 | 1,026 | 8,462 |
| San Francisco | 342,782 | 634,536 | 1,654 | 4,846 |
| Berkeley | 13,214 | 85,547 | 66 | 3,395 |
| Alameda | 16,464 | 36,256 | 144 | 249 |

SOURCE: U.S. Census.

Canada, Central America, and Latin America; some came from as far away as the Cape Verde Islands, off the coast of Africa; and a handful originated in Africa. The Blacks with Spanish, Portuguese, French, British, and other backgrounds imparted a cosmopolitan quality to Afro-San Francisco.[16] The city drew mobile Blacks from throughout the diaspora, and these select few took advantage of the opportunity to travel to the city and survive in it.

Even in terms of U.S. origins, San Francisco's Afro-Americans were diverse, especially in the mid-nineteenth century. Relatively equal numbers came from northern and southern states in 1860. Among northern-born Blacks, New York had the greatest representation (177), followed by Massachusetts (115) and Pennsylvania (104). Maryland (119), Virginia (62), Louisiana (56), and the District of Columbia (54) supplied the largest contingent of residents from southern states. All foreign-born urbanites together (154) had as great a representation as every state but New York.[17] By 1900 a much smaller percentage originated in the north than in 1860, while the percentage of southern-born and foreign-born remained about the same. Significantly, nearly one-third of the adult Black San Franciscans (over sixteen years of age) came from California and other western states; the percentage is even greater when children, many of them born after westward migration, are included (see Table 5).[18] More than a regional metropolis, San Francisco was a world city; this accounted for the diversity in the origins of its Black citizens.

San Francisco's Negro citizens matched the accomplishments of most Americans insofar as they were frequently literate, although this is difficult to gauge precisely. The ability to start three newspapers and maintain two

*Table 5*
Origins of San Francisco's Black Residents, 1860 and 1900

| Place | 1860 | | 1900 | |
|---|---|---|---|---|
| | Percentage | Number | Percentage | Number |
| Northern states | 41 | 485 | 13 | 145 |
| Southern states | 37 | 432 | 41 | 476 |
| Western states | 8 | 90 | 30 | 343 |
| Foreign-born | 13 | 154 | 11 | 131 |
| U.S. (state unknown) | | 1 | 0.8 | 9 |
| Unknown | | 4 | 4 | 47 |
| TOTAL | | 1,166* | | 1,151† |

*Total includes all ages.
†Total includes only those over sixteen years old.
SOURCE: U.S. Census.
NOTE: Percentages have been rounded.

in the first fifteen years suggests an unusual degree of literacy at the very outset. The fact that the Blacks were so few underlines this achievement. Reliable quantitative data are scarce for the pioneer period, but later, there is considerable evidence of literacy as a salient characteristic. In fact, west coast Negroes had lower illiteracy rates than Afro-Americans in other parts of the nation. In 1910, western and Pacific-coast Negroes' illiteracy rates (7 percent and 6.3 percent, respectively) were comparable to that of all Americans (7.7 percent) and lower than that of all southerners (15.6 percent). While not as low as all New Englanders (5.3 percent) and all northerners (4.3 percent), the rates for Negro westerners were lower than for eastern Blacks. The 1910 census data show that literacy among Black San Franciscans and Oaklanders was comparable to that of U.S. Negroes and white Americans.[19]

Respect for literacy was expressed in efforts to establish, maintain, and attend schools before and after migration. In San Francisco and Oakland, Blacks formed public schools in the 1850s. Black newspapers and church and convention records indicate literacy was highly valued by a broad segment of the population. Trained professionals, erudite cosmopolitans knowledgeable of the European literary and legal tradition, and self-taught ex-slaves recalled their formal and informal schooling with pride. Literate residents had advantages in adjusting to the competitive urban milieu because of the habit of obtaining information from a variety of sources to form sound opinions. In this respect, the Black urbanites differed from the ghetto dwellers of the Great Migration era, who often depended largely on oral sources and folklore for their wisdom.[20]

The age distribution of the Black residents reflects another unique aspect of their adaptation for successful residency. Individuals in the prime of life were most capable of succeeding in the far western metropolis. In 1871, roughly four out of five Black San Franciscans were mature adults; there were few children. Probably the cost and difficulty of residency weighed heavily on Afro-Americans. Families with children suffered a considerable disadvantage in a world city where they had to survive on the service jobs that were commonly the lot of Blacks in the Bay Area.[21]

The proportion of adults declined significantly in the late nineteenth century, indicating the successful adjustment of families with children to the urban milieu, but then it rose again after 1900. Correspondingly, the percentage of Black children increased and then decreased. The earthquake and fire of 1906 caused an exodus of families, some undoubtedly to Oakland to stay. New migrants with few children also produced a larger proportion of adults in the modern metropolis. As late as 1930, the trend toward a high proportion of Black adults and few children (12 percent) distinguished San Francisco from both Oakland and Los Angeles, which had twice as large a percentage of Negro children. San Francisco's Black male population increased proportionally, while it decreased in Oakland and Los Angeles as the proportion of children increased.[22]

In this and several other respects, life in nineteenth-century San Francisco was like life in a frontier outpost. The high percentage of mature adults was ideal for pioneer activities involving risk, sacrifice, and labor. The large number of males influenced the quality of life, giving San Francisco an overwhelmingly masculine character. The need to travel long distances accounted in part for the excess of males, as men were in the best position to earn money for fares or to work on ships and trains. In San Francisco, single workers could remain residents more easily than heads of households who required job security and adequate income to support families. Accordingly, Black men outnumbered Negro women more than two to one in 1860, and this trend persisted for years.

After half a century of settlement, the city's isolation decreased, and the ratio of males to females was more nearly equal. Significantly, there was also a larger percentage of children than ever before. But as late as 1930, the Black San Franciscans were still largely young males, while Oakland and Los Angeles had excesses of women, just like northeastern cities (see Table 6).[23]

The large number of unmarried Blacks represented another singular aspect of their adaptation to the city. San Francisco hindered ordinary familial relations by separating male fortune hunters from their loved ones as well as by accommodating an excess of men. This situation existed for the average San Franciscan from the Gold Rush until 1915, and even longer for Blacks: It was not until 1930 that married couples predominated in Black San Francisco. Again Oakland and Los Angeles were different,

*Table 6*
*Ratio of Males to Females, for Total Population and for Black Residents,*
*San Francisco, 1860–1930*

| Year | Males/Females | |
|------|------|------|
| | Total | Black |
| 1860 | 187/100 | 261/100 |
| 1870 | 123/100 | 131/100 |
| 1890 | 150/100 | 123/100 |
| 1900 | 175/100 | 112/100 |
| 1910 | 131/100 | 166/100 |
| 1930 | 128/100 | 136/100 |

SOURCE: *City Directories* and U.S. Census.

having large numbers of married Afro-Americans at the outset. This probably resulted from the rapid economic growth of the new cities and the relative ease of travel at the time they developed.[24]

A plurality of San Francisco's Black citizens were married by 1930, but they still had unusually small families. Notably, San Francisco's percentage of Black couples with no young children exceeded those of Oakland, Los Angeles, Chicago, Seattle, and every major American urban center. Life was so competitive in the oldest western metropolis that married couples with children maintained residency with difficulty or simply did not like the city and left it. In all probability they went to Oakland, Los Angeles, or Seattle, if not to eastern cities.[25]

San Franciscans commonly had smaller families than other American city dwellers, but the Negro pioneers' families were smaller than those of every group of white San Franciscans in the federal census. The median family size in New York (3.36), Seattle (2.84), Oakland (2.84), and Los Angeles (2.57) was larger than in San Francisco (2.51). Similarly, Black families in New York (2.61), Seattle (2.13), Oakland (2.35), and Los Angeles (2.57) had more members than in San Francisco (1.98). The oldest western city was simply less supportive of Black family units than other cities.[26] Like other frontier communities, San Francisco supported a high proportion of workers, and children, the elderly, and sick folk were few.

The city's intense working character showed up in the percentage of Afro-Americans gainfully employed in 1930. Seventy-two percent of them (aged sixteen years or older) worked, compared to 57 percent of whites (over sixteen years old). Only foreign-born San Franciscans possessed a higher percentage of workers (89.6 percent). Significantly, Afro-San Franciscans were more likely to be employed than their counterparts in

Oakland and Los Angeles.[27] The high rate of employment was not confined to men. Black women were more likely to be employed than other women in the city. Among Negro females, 53 percent worked, a larger proportion than their white native and white immigrant counterparts. Black women in San Francisco were more likely to work than any female inhabitants of Oakland or Los Angeles.[28] Single working folk were in the best position to inhabit San Francisco. Black adventurers with families adapted to San Francisco by holding several jobs, by going to sea, and by working on the railroad. Some single men and heads of households returned to the east after trying their luck, while others located in western cities that provided more ready opportunities. Illiterate Blacks with large families and few marketable skills stayed in the north or in Dixie.

The Black scholar Charles S. Johnson noted that "cities have personalities" which determine the type of people they draw and hold.[29] This is clearly the case with San Francisco and its Black residents, who were successful city dwellers in a rural age and, later on, suburbanites in an urban age.

Versatile pioneers in an urban setting, the Black San Franciscans had characteristics and skills that are not usually regarded as typical of urban Afro-Americans. Unlike the southern migrants of World War I, the San Franciscans had a tradition of urban life. Their continued presence in a distant, expensive, union-dominated city suggests that they were thoroughly familiar with the urban environment and with the ways of its citizens. Despite the obstacles of racism, they managed to take advantage of San Francisco's economic, social, and cultural opportunities, as their complex roles as pioneers indicate.

San Francisco's Blacks were pioneers in a sense that is rarely associated with Negroes. As individualists who pitted their brawn against the rocky slopes of the Sierra Nevada, or the hills that presented on obstacle to building in San Francisco, the nineteenth-century Blacks were pioneers in the usual sense of the term. As trailblazers in race relations and in setting up institutions throughout the west for the benefit of Afro-Americans and, ultimately, for whites as well, they also merit respect. They constituted both the far western and the urban perimeter of a population which, in the nineteenth and early twentieth centuries, was basically southern and rural. Today, the average Afro-American is still a southerner, even though he is a city dweller. Differences in outlook and culture hindered communication between the western urbanites and the rural Negroes. The former moved from city to city in search of success, while the latter's attachment to the south was as tenacious as their belief that private property and agriculture were the basis for a good life.

Before their westward migration, many pioneers lived in such cities as

Boston, New York, Philadelphia, Washington, D.C., and New Orleans. The pioneers differed from those who stayed in those cities insofar as they were adventurous, versatile, and frequently without the encumbrances of marriage, dependents, illiteracy, and dire poverty. Nonetheless, Black residents of northeastern cities and, in the south, New Orleans probably had much in common with the San Franciscans. On the one hand, these other city dwellers included larger percentages of women and children. But on the other hand, insofar as they were successful and preferred the city, their outlook and ideals were probably comparable to those of the San Franciscans.

These different Black urban dwellers shared information they acquired from city residency and from travels. The Negro San Franciscans were fascinated by technological innovations, indicated by their interest in lectures on "animal electricity" and other scientific topics, or by their dependence on photography for creating ideal images of themselves.[30] They cultivated their knowledge of European history and culture, studied trends in politics and social thought, and adopted the latest fashions and fads in dress as well as in entertainment. They took pride in their urban condition, and their skills and knowledge produced a degree of self-esteem that insulated them somewhat from racism. Until the Great Migration brought masses of southerners, Black city ways and a rural Negro outlook remained distinct.

The pioneer urbanites also differed from the nation's whites. Rather than lagging behind other citizens—the condition usually attributed to Negroes—San Francisco's Blacks were in the vanguard. Until 1920, the nation was predominantly rural, and for a long time afterwards, Americans remained distrustful and suspicious of the urban life in which the pioneers were so much at home.

Blacks differed from other San Franciscans and city dwellers elsewhere in several respects, such as demographic characteristics. Blacks were more likely to be male, single, and gainfully employed. They lacked the percentage of children and women that made life in San Francisco more tolerable (and less unique) for other residents. Blacks were more likely to depend on their own individual or meager group resources, as they did not enjoy the aid of colonization societies, which helped other migrants, and labor unions, which secured white workers jobs, or the favor of a prejudiced community, which gave whites a feeling of superiority and sense of destiny as world leaders.

Closer comparison of the Black pioneers with other San Franciscans is a tempting but difficult task. Besides the Blacks, only Indians and Asians were unique enough to be analyzed as a group in the census. But even they were not treated consistently in the census from decade to decade. Analysis of white immigrant groups has been facilitated by the use of computers with Manuscript Census Data from 1850 to 1900. Few scholars have undertaken such an expensive project for ethnic groups in western cities, nor have they probed the quality of life of different immigrant groups on the Pacific coast. Further comparison is complicated by the fact that various ethnic and national groups settled San Francisco at different times and under different circumstances. Also, it seems unfair to compare native-born Afro-Americans to foreign-born Europeans or Asians, and unrealistic to liken them to groups which had not experienced recent generations of bondage. What is most remarkable about Afro-Americans as a group is the singular quality of their existence, and the degree to which it illuminates our understanding of American urban society and culture.

The Black pioneers remained in the vanguard of city life after the dramatic changes of the early twentieth century when Negroes moved to cities and the entire nation became urban. As early as the 1890s, groups of Black San Franciscans adopted a suburban life style by moving to the East Bay, where they enjoyed larger homes, more space for yards and children, and suffered less from noise and congestion. Also, rents were lower, so East Bay residents were more likely to have families with children. The earthquake and fire merely promoted a trend which had already begun. Nearly every informant's parents lived in the East Bay before 1906; later migrants of the post-World War I years inhabited the East Bay in the 1920s and 1930s; and in 1976 every informant but one resided in the East Bay instead of San Francisco, and had done so for several decades. As urban dwellers in a rural land, and as suburbanites when the nation had just become urban, these pioneers shed light on city life in the west as well as on their own group's experience in the region.

While some pioneer urbanites were born into citified households, many acquired urban ways through struggling to exist and prosper in a competitive economy, without the wisdom and aid of masses of Blacks. Native-born city dwellers and newcomers to the urban milieu developed skills and adapted in ways that other urbanites, because they had more options, did not. The reasons for their familiarity with the urban milieu will become clearer after analysis of their job patterns.

# 3

## Optimists

*'Tis but a few years since all this State was the abode of another race, who owned the soil and roamed at will, with none to molest or make them afraid. The white man came, and we came with him; and by the blessing of God we will stay with him side by side; wherever he goes will we go; and should another Sutter discover another El Dorado, be it where it may—north of the Caribbean or south of it—no sooner shall the white man's foot be firmly planted there than looking over his shoulder he will see the black man, like his shadow, by his side.*

*Darius Stokes, at the First State Convention of the Colored Citizens of California, 1855*

In 1944 Gunnar Myrdal, the Swedish sociologist, asked why Blacks avoided the American west. In San Francisco, the city that dominated the entire Pacific slope, racism and fierce economic competition operated to reserve the best opportunities for whites, often foreign-born, and to exclude Afro-Americans and Chinese from chances for good jobs or wealth.[1] But during the first two decades of settlement, Afro-Americans experienced successes along with other city dwellers. They boasted of their economic gains and foresaw a splendid future. Some owned a considerable amount of real estate in the nineteenth century, frequently bought with sums obtained during pioneer days. Resourcefulness and energy allowed some to overcome the disadvantages of race or a background of slavery. In 1862, Afro-San Franciscans owned a significant amount of real estate and personal property, and listed their total assets at $300,000, most of it in real estate. A *Pacific Appeal* correspondent reported the figure and concluded, "the evidence of thrift among our people is a source of much encouragement."[2]

The rarity of dire poverty was another index of the Black population's prosperity and comparatively better situation. An early Black settler, Jonas H. Townsend, noted that "the colored residents of California are in proportion to their numbers, the least recipients of public charity of any class in the State; and this, too, notwithstanding they are subject to great disabilities, and are entirely destitute of any protection in their persons or property from the laws of the land." Blacks regarded their prosperity "as clear proof of their capacity to take care of their families for the present, and to provide for the future." In 1874, the *Elevator* commented on the low incidence of pauperism and crime among Negro Californians, observing that pauperism was more than twice as frequent among whites.[3]

The achievements of individual Afro-San Franciscans were visible in the census data as well as in their own reports. Russell Davis, an illiterate wagoner, listed $25,000 in real estate in 1870. An uneducated janitor, Ezekiel Cooper, owned $10,000 in lots. A boarding-house keeper, Mary Ellen "Mammy" Pleasant, reported owning $30,000 worth of real estate in 1870. Richard Barber, the most prosperous Afro-San Franciscan in 1870, was a porter who commanded $71,800. All but $1,800 of this sum was invested in real estate.[4]

Afro-San Franciscans swelled with pride when others noted the accomplishments of one of their number, and they offered this as evidence of the existence of a new and freer society. These feelings were supported by such press notices as "Black and White," which marveled at "what a change has California wrought in the organization and feelings of society." The reporter expressed his surprise and amusement "at seeing a gentleman of the colored persuasion decked in a full suit of broadcloth and sporting a gold watch and chain, standing on the Square having his boots blacked by a good-looking white man."[5]

Their wealth supported the belief that San Francisco was one of the best places for an Afro-American in the mid-nineteenth century. In 1889 the San Francisco *Examiner* gave this credence. It discussed the affluent Afro-San Franciscans, summarized their achievements, and listed their actual wealth or estimates of their financial worth. In 1904, the San Francisco *Chronicle* maintained that Afro-American residents differed from those of other urban areas. Black San Franciscans succeeded in rising above the menial positions that typified the nation's Afro-Americans, according to the city daily. Unlike Blacks elsewhere, "the negroes of San Francisco, through the unusual conditions existing here, have turned to the trades and professions, and many have entered into business." They "have won success in many different lines far removed from the aims and capabilities of the race in general in its present stage of development."[6]

To some extent, this was true. But while many San Franciscans found meaningful economic opportunities when the city was young, from the 1880s their chances for wealth dwindled in the face of large-scale businesses, monopolistic corporations, and heavy industries. The situation was aggravated by the rule of the powerful, the growth of strong labor unions, the heritage of slavery and menial work, and the burden of race prejudice.

Ironically, the liberality of San Franciscans worked to the disadvantage of Afro-Americans. The pro-union sentiments of European-born workers and the city dwellers' sympathies for working men helped laborers and artisans exercise quite a bit of power, monopolize certain jobs, and remove the Blacks and Chinese who threatened their share of the city's wealth. Consequently, after pioneer days Blacks found they could hardly hold on to their jobs and residency.

In the heyday of the Gold Rush, the pioneers expected to overcome the disadvantages of a background of bondage. They believed that gold provided the key to the elevation of individuals as well as of the Black race in American society. "In proportion as men share his [gold's] bounties, in the same ratio will they hold places of power, combined with social and political privileges." Gold's power to change social relations bordered on the miraculous in a society where it had been "declared King in the dominions of the American heart."[7] Afro-Americans' faith that gold—or speculating, commerce, gambling, even honest toil—would change their status is remarkable. The law of the nation had failed them, as in the pro-south compromises of the 1850s and the Dred Scott decision. California statutes also discriminated. Nevertheless, they believed the American system was basically just and would reward them with social prerogatives if they made economic gains.

In the 1850s San Franciscans earned and lost fortunes with unprecedented ease. Reports circulated and rumors abounded to intensify the dramatic experiences of sudden enrichment and impoverishment. Because members of various social classes, nationalities, and races experienced elevation, the democratic character of the city was underlined, furthering the hope that anyone could get rich. The craving for money accounted for the city's rapid settlement. Lonely city dwellers were united by their migration, their desire for riches, and their very rootlessness. Few proposed to settle permanently, intending rather to make a bundle and return home. Meanwhile, they shared accommodations, drank, dined, and gambled with one another with a freedom that suggested equality for all, regardless of origins. This was, of course, particularly important to anonymous newcomers and especially to a group close to slavery and despised because of their color. When they became rich, San Franciscans found a new identity as refined city dwellers.[8]

Newcomers speculated in mining shares and merchandising to get rich quickly. Like speculating, merchandising was "full of large risks and sudden turns." San Franciscans regarded these means and even gambling as perfectly legitimate ways to get money. In the pursuit of wealth, they set aside the moral distinctions that separated legal and illegal activities. As a reporter for *Frederick Douglass' Paper* commented, "It is generally understood that the man who goes to 'California,' goes to get money *any* way he can."[9]

Speculation's potential rewards gave it widespread appeal. This field "had more frequent and greater fluctuations than those of any other stock market, making and marring many fortunes in a day," and offered "excitement more attractive than that of the gambling table." It was "the most prominent business in San Francisco" in the nineteenth century.[10]

The need for supplies also produced considerable speculation in commerce. A Black from Virginia, James R. Phillips, arrived in the west in the 1850s and, like many entrepreneurs, attempted to buy and sell "any commodity he could control the capital to speculate in and dispose of and make a reasonable profit."[11] A commodity's value dipped as soon as a ship laden with that item sailed into the bay. The highly speculative character of commerce diminished after telegraph, faster ships, and transcontinental trains lessened the chances for sudden shortages or surfeits. But there were still ample opportunities to grapple with chance.

Gambling appealed to San Franciscans not merely because it offered riches. In speculating, or faro, the anonymous resident pitted himself against fate and discovered how he ranked in the city's fluid society. For the resident seeking his fortune, gambling was a solemn occasion for deep meditation in preparation for profound revelations. Mifflin W. Gibbs described a typical gambling scenario in an "unprepossessing hotel kept by a colored man on Kearney street," where he found lodgings shortly after he arrived in the 1850s. "Seated at tables, well supplied with piles of gold and silver," pioneer San Franciscans were "getting something for nothing, or risking the smaller in hope of obtaining the greater."[12]

Gambling occurred in nearly every resort in the pioneer period. Black citizens frequently toiled as menials alongside gamblers in hotels, eating-houses, and "gambling hells." A traveler described one such place in the 1850s: "On one side is a bar attended by a *lady*, assisted by three young white men and two negroes." "All classes gambled in those days, from the starched white neck-clothed professors of religion to the veriest black rascal that earned a dollar for blackening massa's boots." Gambling was "another form of the everyday life which men of business consider natural and legitimate." The very solemn demeanor of participants underlined the seriousness of such occasions and among them "there appeared to exist a perfect understanding that the work in hand was pure matter of business."[13]

It is difficult to determine if a city dweller became affluent by dint of his labor or his perspicacity, by honest or dishonest means, or if luck played a role. The desire for respectability, of Blacks as well as others, prevented citizens from divulging every source of income. So the student of mid-century San Francisco cannot be certain that a prosperous hackman, janitor, or businessman made his bundle through employment in the job listed in the *City Directory* or federal census. The unique milieu of the 1850s and 1860s divests ordinary occupations of the meaning they had in cities with more stable economies.

Besides speculating, merchandizing, and gambling, Black San Franciscans earned high wages in a city that suffered from labor shortages. In the early 1850s, carpenters earned nine or ten dollars a day, depending on whether they were Black or white. Also, the generosity of fortunate citizens and miners on sprees made menial jobs lucrative for waiters, draymen, or porters. "All classes of labor were highly remunerative, blacking boots not excepted." It is no wonder Blacks waxed eloquent about the chances for improving their social station.[14]

During pioneer days, Black stewards on the river steamers earned wages of $150 per month, and "the perquisites were twice as much more." With the money they made on the ships, and through speculating in stock or real estate, William E. Carlisle, Peter H. Joseph, and Henry M. Collins acquired modest fortunes. Female employees profited, too. A steamer stewardess, Salina Williams, owned $12,000 property in 1870, ranking as one of the ten wealthiest Black residents and indicating the opportunities that existed among the traveling community. The prevalence (11 percent) of ship cooks, porters, and sea-going stewards among Negroes worth $100 or more in 1870 suggested the lucrative nature of such jobs. These pursuits appeared more frequently than any other single profession among San Francisco's most prosperous Blacks.[15]

Beginning in the 1860s, silver mining also supported the optimism of Black city dwellers, and triggered a spate of building. The palatial residences of the Bonanza Kings appeared atop Clay Street Hill in the 1870s, and the new name, Nob Hill, indicated the height to which a humble westerner could rise. Nevada silver also built the Palace Hotel; because its crew of more than four hundred employees included almost two hundred Blacks, Afro-San Franciscans could believe they shared in the prosperity and growth of the city.[16]

After the earthquake and fire of 1906, the immense need for laborers and artisans suggested Black newcomers could participate in rebuilding the city. In 1907 the Oakland *Sunshine* urged Negroes to stop complaining, to regain the hotel jobs they held twenty years before, to form businesses, and to grow with the cities. Also, Negro migrants now traveled long distances with greater ease, and the Afro-American population of other Pacific slope cities soared. While no large Black migration penetrated San Francisco, the optimism based on the pioneer experience persisted among Blacks as it did among other San Franciscans.[17]

The successes of Blacks dominated their newspapers, oral sources, and histories. One such success story was the career of George Washington Dennis. Dennis arrived in California before the adoption of the state constitution forbidding slavery. Blacks like him who came before statehood remained in bondage, and could be bought, sold, and even taken south when their masters left California. This state of affairs lasted until 1856, when the legislature forbade the recovery of bondsmen. The status of California's Afro-Americans was further complicated by southerners' habit of emancipating their slaves before migration (to insure their loyalty), and bringing them west as "servants" bound to toil for them for a period of time.[18]

Dennis reached an agreement with his owner, who incidentally was also his father: when he earned one thousand dollars as a porter in his master's resort, the Eldorado Hotel, he could purchase his freedom. Many of the resort's patrons tried their luck and lost, but Dennis was more fortunate. With his earnings and the sweepings from the gambling tables, he purchased his freedom in three months.[19]

In command of his labor, Dennis earned more money and was elevated in status, competing with city dwellers more nearly as an equal. But because freedmen by law could not testify in court or vote, he was hardly equal with most San Franciscans. Nevertheless, he saved his money and purchased his mother's freedom, and the two labored together in the resort on Portsmouth Square.[20]

Eventually the freedman became an independent businessman. He invested unsuccessfully in mining claims, returned to his original job, then opened the Custom House Livery Stable at Sansom and Washington Streets. He also married, settled in San Francisco, and reared several sons and daughters who themselves achieved success in various careers. The second generation's example provided further evidence of the opportunities of the city. In the late nineteenth century, Dennis transacted a number of real estate deals, increased his fortune, and displayed the speculative instinct of San Franciscans. In 1867 he opened the Cosmopolitan Coal and Wood Yard at 340 Broadway, selling fuel wholesale and retail. By 1889, he was one of the wealthiest Black San Franciscans, having amassed a fortune estimated at $50,000.[21]

The expectations and successes of Black San Franciscans are one

dimension of their economic life. As speculators, gamblers, and entrepreneurs, they achieved a degree of equality that was noteworthy for the
nineteenth century. But Negroes were more commonly service workers,
and in a city of anxious businessmen, plutocrats, and fortune hunters, they
endured an unusual and trying condition. They believed in the efficacy of
riches, in democracy, and in equality, but were denied chances to develop
the skills that brought wealth.

Compared to the eastern and newer far western cities, San Francisco
extended very limited economic opportunities to Blacks after the spectacular boom days of the mid-nineteenth century. The sparse Afro-San
Franciscan population, numbering approximately 1,600 until World War
I, suggests the stiff economic competition they then endured. In the
twentieth century, the combined Black population of the Bay Area still
remained comparatively small: While sixteen thousand Blacks lived
around the Bay by 1940, nearly four times as many (63,774) resided in Los
Angeles, indicating that the latter city offered Blacks far more. Eastern
cities, of course, also supported tens of thousands of Blacks before 1915
and hundreds of thousands following the Great Migration.[22]

An important basis for both residency and self-respect—a secure and
lucrative job—was often denied Blacks. Very possibly it was more difficult
for a Negro to obtain good employment in the Bay Area, especially in San
Francisco, than in just about any major American city until World War II.
Even in 1860, very few members of the Black working population held
attractive positions as artisans, proprietors of saloons, stores, and
businesses, or as professionals. Most toiled in the positions familiar to the
student of Afro-American history: 60 percent of the Black males occupied
the service sector of the city's economy, and 97 percent of Black women
over sixteen were servants and domestics in private homes, aboard ships,
and in their own households.[23]

The new El Dorado offered Afro-Americans the same kinds of jobs in
1910 and 1930 as in 1860. Employment in the service realm predominated.
In 1910, 48 percent of the men and 70 percent of the women labored in this
capacity.[24] And in 1930, after a large Black migration and several years of
prosperity, 51 percent of the Negro working men toiled in the service sector
of San Francisco's economy, as did 89 percent of the women.[25]

While the World War I years saw an increase in the number and
percentage of Negroes in manufacturing and industry, the next decade
brought a real decline in this category. Sixteen percent of the Black males
worked in this sector in 1910, increasing to 27 percent in 1920, but by 1930
the figure had declined to 18 percent.[26] Despite its reputation as a city of
fortunes and a good place for the working man, San Francisco did not offer
opportunities for many Blacks. Even when Oakland mushroomed around

1900, this still held true. Both cities extended the same kind of jobs as other American cities until World War II.

Pioneer urbanites suffered in the San Francisco job market at every step, beginning with recruitment. Capitalists and labor organizers sought European or Asian workers instead of freedmen, keeping the Bay Area's Black population small. The San Francisco *Elevator* commented on the competition for positions in the far west as early as 1865, and its discussion helps to answer Gunnar Myrdal's question of eight decades later.

Near the end of the Civil War, construction of the Central Pacific line provoked a debate on the desirability of recruiting freedmen. The suggestion that Chinese workers might build the transcontinental railroad raised the ire of a Black newspaper. In one of the most critical views Afro-San Franciscans expressed toward a foreign group, the *Elevator* argued, "we have enough, and more, of them here now, eating out our substance, polluting the atmosphere with their filth, and the mind with their licentiousness." The newspaper also held a low opinion of the European newcomers who caused the instant city's population to swell,[27] and asserted that the region should avoid the mistake of the eastern states, which erred by inviting "the discontented and vicious of all Europe to their shores." Bringing Asians to California would be a greater error, since Europeans at least professed to be Christians and shared similar customs. Freedmen, the *Elevator* held, should be recruited to build the railroad. But "the agencies at work to drive the colored man to the wall" preferred foreign-born recruits to native-born freedmen.[28] Such xenophobia indicated another side to Black San Francisco's ability to get along with other ethnic groups.

The recruitment of Chinese for railroad work and of Europeans for positions in San Francisco accounted for the small number of Afro-Americans on the Pacific slope. Like other groups, Blacks needed aid to make the expensive journey. Because that help instead went to foreign-born whites (and, until the 1880s, to Chinese), large numbers of aggressive, organized newcomers monopolized the attractive jobs. Afro-San Franciscans remained small in number, unorganized, and politically powerless, though they constituted the largest group of Blacks in the far west until 1900. They watched helplessly as foreigners displaced them beginning in the 1860s; they assumed the role of pawns in struggles between white labor unions and management.[29]

The *Elevator* discussed the subject in anguished tones, indicating the frustration of Black workers who lost jobs to Europeans and Chinese. White men were welcomed and invested with the vote, while even educated Afro-Americans were "expected to be thankful that they are . . . permitted to live."[30] The newspaper railed against every immigrant, even the native-born Californios, in one broadside.

The half idiotic and scrofulous peasant of the Swiss mountains, the lazzaroni of Italy, the bandit of Spain, the ignorant and unprincipled Greaser, the brutalized denizen of the English mines, the escaped convict from the penal settlements of Australia, all, all have been preferred to the man of color—native to the soil, and to the manner born.[31]

At every step, effective exclusion of Negro laborers indicated the degree of animosity or indifference toward them. It is unclear when or why capitalists decided to choose Chinese and European labor over native Black; perhaps economic ties with Chinese and European shippers, merchants, and labor recruiters facilitated the decision. At any rate, by 1865 Charles Crocker had chosen Chinese laborers to build the Central Pacific line, and their reputation for unceasing toil for low wages paved the way for more Chinese sojourners. The agencies that sought migrants in Europe and provided passage for Chinese neglected Blacks, and such unions as the typographical association excluded them. No one organized a Black migration or sought to bring Negroes to the Bay Area by the thousands until the 1940s. Again like the Chinese and later the Japanese and Mexicans, Afro-Americans who landed in the Bay Area discovered their job opportunities were circumscribed by white racial solidarity. This racism benefited other Americans and Europeans, excluded non-whites from good jobs, and was the basis for the organizations of workers, businessmen, and politicians in the late nineteenth century.[32]

The Afro-Americans' backgrounds and training served to present still other obstacles. Their absence from or presence in the skilled trades, on steamships or trains, and in the city's various hotels, restaurants, and resorts indicated the problem they faced. The lucrative construction and shipbuilding industries made the skilled trades attractive, but few Negroes found employment there until well into the twentieth century. While clearly some Blacks possessed these skills in antebellum days, the Manuscript Census of 1860 reported only six Black carpenters in San Francisco. Eleven were caulkers; the two occupations together constituted half the contingent of Afro-American skilled workers.[33] The *Elevator* noted, "We are compelled to acknowledge the humiliating fact that a majority of our people are better for that kind of [menial] labor than any other." "The fact is patent," the *Elevator* conceded, "and there is no use denying it."[34]

Leading Afro-Americans exhorted their youth and wage-earners to enter the trades, and pleaded with parents to train their children "to make them independent of the whitewash brush and slop bucket."[35] But racist white workers excluded Blacks who desired, and were trained for, skilled positions. As early as the 1850s, Mifflin Gibbs reported he was forced to abandon carpentry, because "white employees finding me at work on the same building would 'strike.'" A contractor told him, "I expect you will have to stop, for this house must be finished in the time specified; but if you can get six or eight equally good workmen, I will let these [white] fellows go. Not that I have any special liking for your people. I am giving these men all the wages they demand, and I am not willing to submit to the tyrany [sic] of their dictation if I can help it." Gibbs noted, "I could not find the men he wanted or subsequent employment of that kind." Similarly, when a resident tried to apprentice his daughter to learn sewing, he received twenty refusals until a French woman consented. But after one day, her customers abandoned her, so she let her apprentice go.[36]

The *Elevator* itself depended upon white printers for its presswork because of an organized effort to exclude non-whites. "At least half a dozen colored printers" were forced to work in other professions because of the policies of the powerful Typographical Union, which forbade hiring experienced Negroes or training colored apprentices. It "ostracizes all offices which employ negroes, either as apprentices or journeymen; and such is the power and influence of the oligarchy, that they can break up any establishment which opposes their mandates."[37] Three decades later the same opposition still prevented Blacks from working in these relatively attractive pursuits. The Reverend Obadiah Summers explained why Blacks had not constructed a building to advertise their skills at the Midwinter Fair in 1894. "If the mechanics' unions and other industrial organizations were open to us we might have had a building here which would be a credit to us and to the Fair."[38]

A few years later, W. E. B. Du Bois noted that only four Black carpenters belonged to San Francisco's union of 2,500. Such conditions prevailed throughout the state of California, where "on the whole a Negro mechanic is a rare thing." In 1913, *Crisis,* the NAACP publication edited by Du Bois, reported that the white trade unions "have held the Negro out and down" in San Francisco. "The opportunity of the San Francisco Negro to earn a living is very difficult."[39]

The lack of specific skills, and the inability of even skilled craftsmen to practice their trade, help account for the Bay Area's small Black population. Afro-Americans also suffered losses in the marine and steamboat service positions they had held since the 1850s. They occasionally found positions when white laborers went on strike, but the competition of Chinese workers capable of subsisting on lower wages undercut Black as well as white labor. The Reverend John J. Moore, of San Francisco's Zion A.M.E. Church, commented on this in 1868, when he discussed the significance of Chinese workers on board a ship. Twenty Asians labored on the vessel, earning $110 a year, substantially less than the salary paid whites and Blacks. Because Afro-Americans cannot survive on this income, "they will necessarily have to seek a living means from other sources." Eventually whites, not Chinese, posed the major problems, when an exclusively white coastal union opposed the employment of Chinese on ocean-going vessels and won.[40]

San Francisco's Black leaders observed that these service positions were viewed as demeaning by many city folk. "It is well known that white Americans will not be servants," the *Elevator* noted; only the Irish, Chinese, and Blacks accepted the unattractive jobs. When the Irish become "Americanized, or accumulate a little money, they seek other and more lucrative opportunities." Because Blacks frequently accept work that other city dwellers regard as demeaning and temporary, "the badge of inferiority adheres to our identity with a servile race."[41]

Particularly disconcerting was the contrast between the available jobs and the self-image that San Franciscans desired. In a city of men, Blacks labored at domestic tasks—cooking, cleaning, and waiting on tables. Proud Afro-Americans probably burned with indignation when they read in an early history of the city, "The Chinese and the free negroes . . . were 'the hewers of wood and the drawers of water' of the place; and performed washing and women's business, and such menial offices as American white males would scorn to do for any remuneration." As late as the 1880s, some of these jobs were in prestigious resorts and were highly valued by Afro-San Franciscans. But they also lost these positions to whites.[42]

The luxury hotel known simply as the Palace offered nearly two hundred coveted service positions to Blacks in 1875. The hotel's refined setting justified its name, the salaries were good, and patrons gave handsome tips. For Negroes, the chance to serve in the largest, most exclusive hotel west of the Mississippi was both a challenge and a magnificent chance to prove their merit. Success could bring the recruitment of more freedmen and would benefit all Blacks in the city. And the silver boom that produced the hotel would continue to provide more jobs for newcomers.

When the proprietor recruited Afro-Americans from eastern resort hotels, some observers were skeptical. The Palace's head waiter, William Orr, discussed the skepticism and the performance of the Afro-American staff at a banquet in 1878. When the hotel opened, "it had been predicted with fear by many, on their first arrival, that they could not successfully perform the duties required for them to do in the [finest] . . . hotel of the nation." They met the test, however; in fact, the banquet at which Orr spoke was given by the hotel proprietor in honor of their achievements. "This splendid banquet," Orr said, "was some emblem of their moral worth and integrity."[43]

The few glimpses we have of the crew at work indicate their contribution. The dark hues of their skin, their graciousness, and their experience at serving affluent urbanites imparted an atmosphere of gentility. A military-like efficiency was noted, and their very bearing suggested the dignified air of an elite cadre. Their behavior at a banquet for General Philip Sheridan in 1875 impressed the spectators. The Black workers were portrayed as an "army of waiters in swallow-tailed coats and white Lisle thread gloves, flitting noiselessly to and fro."[44]

The respect won by efficiency and poised bearing, while important, was not the most significant aspect of the work. From the Blacks' vantage point, they had valuable opportunities to meet famous travelers, wealthy San Franciscans, and influential politicians, allowing them to further their careers by developing their contacts. Through his Palace Hotel employment, Theophilus B. Morton, founder of the California branch of the Afro-American League, very likely made important acquaintances that served his political objectives. He eventually left the hotel to work in attractive positions as porter, then as messenger, and finally as librarian of the United States Circuit Court of Appeals.[45] Negroes also gained financially from attachment to the Palace. While waiting on patrons, the anonymous Black worker probably thought of the former Virginia slave, George W. Mitchell, a first floor bellman who parlayed wages and tips into a fortune said to range from $30,000 to $40,000 at the time of his death.

But after fourteen years of successful employment in the Palace, the dreams of the Black help faded as they found their very jobs threatened by white workers.[46] In 1878, a time of intense labor activity and anti-Chinese sentiment, San Francisco's white cooks and waiters organized the Cooks' and Waiters' Anti-Coolie Association. When they realized that the days of earning a fortune and becoming independent entrepreneurs were over, Europeans and Americans strengthened their organizations to improve working conditions. Most importantly, whites did not regard Chinese and Negroes as union brothers. In 1883 the white waiters and cooks organized a protective and benevolent union (possibly a spinoff of the Association) that spread along the Pacific slope, becoming second only to the seamen's union in membership in a few years' time.[47]

Like other San Francisco labor unions at the time, the cooks' and waiters' organization tested its power in a series of contests; the racist nature of society and of the union was reaffirmed repeatedly. In 1883 the working men claimed that working alongside Afro-Americans was not in the interests of white waiters. As the whites organized, they forced restaurants and eating-houses to hire union men or to seek workers at their headquarters. During a strike in June 1886, "some of the proprietors boasted that they would replace the lost help with negroes." But the striking white help "tranquilly asked them if they expected to have negro customers." This reply was based on a sense of racial solidarity shared by the dining public, which constituted a large segment of San Francisco's residents.[48]

The Cooks' and Waiters' Union increased its power by aiding other unions. In early 1888 it supported a strike of the Bay Area's bakers and confectioners. By this time, the expanding waiters' and cooks' organization had 1,100 members and branches in Sacramento, Stockton, and Los Angeles. The cooks' and waiters' walkout was successful except in French and Italian restaurants and in "the places where colored help is employed"; the recalcitrants were non-union. Efforts to induce the kitchen help at the large San Francisco hotels, including the Palace, to join in the walkout failed. Nevertheless the unions won this struggle.[49]

It is not certain that the white Cooks' and Waiters' Union replaced the Black Palace Hotel service workers in November 1889, but the union was at its strongest just a year before the change took place. Moreover, it was organized in 1888, and in the spring of 1889 conducted a boycott against restaurant-keepers who refused to hire certain white union men. This was the state of affairs in late June, just a few months before the change in the Palace staff.

Very likely the unions exploited the cleavage among the white and Black kitchen and dining room workers. Differences among the staff resulted from the simple fact that white help could keep their jobs by joining a union, regardless of their ambivalences toward such an organization, while Negroes were excluded even if they were sympathetic to the idea of unions.

No contemporary evidence proves direct union involvement in the Palace Hotel struggle, and newspaper accounts do not even indicate that unions played a role. But given the antipathy between white and Black restaurant and hotel help, and the white union's successes in preceding years, it is very likely that the union was active in the conflict. Whether it replaced Afro-Americans with its blacklisted men is unclear. It is possible, though not certain, that management placated the union by hiring non-union whites who would be both susceptible to the influences of the organization and eligible for membership. The fact that the Blacks were replaced by experienced whites in a few hours' time suggests that some kind of organization, union or otherwise, played a part. Delilah Beasley claimed that unions caused the Black workers to lose their jobs. Unfortunately, Beasley did not explain the circumstances or cite her sources, but presumably she obtained her information from participants or their descendants. To make their pressure felt, the unions needed a catalyst; a change in the hotel's management a few days before the Negroes' dismissal provided the opportunity.[50]

In early November of 1889, the new management, headed by Samuel

Thorn, released the Black cooks and waiters because of alleged thefts. This explanation, presented by the *Chronicle,* is hardly satisfactory. When white Palace waiters were accused of dishonesty in 1893, they were not removed; instead, new checking procedures were instituted. But because Negroes were said to be involved, Thorn insisted that they submit to searches when leaving the hotel, and he posted an ominous warning. The Blacks refused to serve dinner until he removed the notice and stopped the harassment. Thorn gave in to their demands, and the Black waiters and pantrymen returned to work. Meanwhile, management sent messengers on urgent errands. The next day, to the consternation of the Afro-San Franciscans and the hotel guests, white workers replaced the colored waiters and kitchen help.[51]

Before coming to the Palace on November 1, Thorn had managed the nearby Grand Hotel for several years. Otherwise, little is known of his past. His predecessor at the Palace, C. H. Livingston, headed the hotel for more than two years before resigning in October 1889 because of poor health. Unlike Thorn's, Livingston's relationship with his employees seemed cordial. They gave him a farewell gift to show their esteem. Livingston also managed the San Francisco *Daily Alta California,* and his account of the firing differs slightly from the *Chronicle*'s.[52]

Upon taking over, Thorn installed a new head steward who promptly dismissed thirty cooks, "simply to get new ideas in the culinary lines." Those dismissed might have been either whites who refused to join the union or undesirable union men. On November 9, 1889—one week after the initial change—the *Alta* said the colored waiters and pantrymen were also to be replaced by whites. "The object of this movement," the *Alta* explained, "is to do away with colored help altogether and have only white men in the kitchen and dining room." The few Black bellmen and porters were to be retained "for the time being."[53] Also, according to the *Chronicle,* Thorn had already released six Black chambermaids on assuming the management. These changes, all in nine days under a new head, indicated that racial antipathies and perhaps union pressures were more important than the alleged theft of food and utensils.

The statements of Thorn and the head steward after the installation of new workers showed that management–employee rivalry and a preference for white workers figured in the contest. Thorn told the *Chronicle* that the Black waiters, who had been on the scene since 1875, fourteen years before his accession, "had an idea that they owned the place, but I thought I would see whether I was boss or not."[54] The new steward, who was from Manhattan Beach in southern California, said: "I like the white help best, and they will stay as long as the present management continues."[55] Thorn also informed the public that the white waiters would remain as long as he did. The Palace never hired Blacks again, and racism and further charges of theft caused more Blacks to lose their positions at the Palace.

The firing of the waiters and chambermaids affected the remaining Black bellmen and porters. Racist white unions and management prompted the removal of the twenty-eight Afro-Americans who stayed on after 1889. In 1896, despite protests from the hotel's guests, the bellmen and porters lost their jobs to whites willing to work for lower wages. The prospect of paying whites less undoubtedly was further incentive for firing the Blacks. Again in 1896, as in 1889, allegations of thefts provided a smokescreen to cloud the controversy.[56]

The Afro-San Franciscans' powerlessness was reflected by the loss of their jobs and underscored by their uncertainty about the forces that acted upon them. Unfortunately, they depended solely on their ability to please customers and on their good standing with management. When whites desired their jobs, the unions exerted pressure and got the Blacks dismissed. Changes in management, hard times, and elections aided their efforts. The Blacks, who lacked influential unions and political organizations, were pawns of the powerful interests that contended for jobs and political spoils.

Although rumors of the replacement of the Black bellmen in 1896 were current days before the change, the Negroes could get no information until shortly before their dismissal. Thorn left the hotel in 1893, but still, conferences with management yielded no clues. And their removal was once again tainted by rumors that they were dishonest.[57]

Management had already reached an agreement with white workers. Very likely the upcoming November elections were involved, but their actual role is not clear. Moreover, while articles were reported missing from the Palace Hotel rooms, no one directly charged the Blacks with theft. One Afro-San Franciscan's statement indicates the tangled web of intrigue that rendered all Blacks powerless:

The guests are for us . . . but that don't make any difference. You see, there are a lot of skeleton keys in the possession of different people, and they go and come as they please. The laundryman has them; the housekeeper, of course, as that is to be expected, and is all right; the plumber, the locksmith, and others. Then there have been some little disagreements. So the result is that we all are to go. I don't know what we will do. None of us know. We expected we would go on November 1 [two days prior], but we were not notified, and now the general understanding is that we won't go till after the election. A notice has been put up that hereafter all employees are to be paid by the day, so we think it applies to our own case. It was settled today that the change is to take place soon. The uniforms of the white boys and men who are to succeed us have been finished and ready for them for several days.[58]

As the worker correctly surmised, when anyone's honesty was questioned, the Negro help, rather than the housekeeper, laundryman, or skilled worker, suffered. Similarly, in 1889, a white cook was detected carrying "several choice tenderloins" and other items, but Afro-Americans were blamed.[59]

Ironically, the grand experiment in Black help at the Palace Hotel failed because it succeeded. Negroes were given an opportunity to show their fitness for the task and they did so. They suffered because the unions refused to admit them and management always doubted their honesty. Afro-San Franciscans were too few in number and too weak in the political arena to object effectively. As Blacks lost out at the Palace Hotel, they lost their chance to find a secure place in San Francisco.

The trend in San Francisco paralleled the displacement of Blacks from traditional jobs throughout the nation. In San Diego, for example, Black help was replaced with white in the Nadeau Hotel in 1886, about the same time the Cooks' and Waiters' Union waxed strong. The change in service workers in southern California indicates that events at the Palace Hotel reflected a larger pattern which kept Afro-Americans from finding a suitable place in the far west. The region attracted those Negroes who were resourceful, and retained those who could engage in a variety of different pursuits. Many found that if they could not develop contacts or adapt to a new job, they could not contend with either the racism or the big businesses that figured in the economic development of the Pacific slope.[60]

San Francisco, like other developing American cities, promised considerable economic opportunities during the Gilded Age. Exploitation of the far west's rich mineral ore and fertile valleys earned fortunes for businessmen who owned mining companies, factories, land, and railroads. (Notably, recent scholarship has raised doubts as to whether many white entrepreneurs actually benefited from the city's potential.) The economic situation could have enriched Afro-Americans, who because of their background yearned for economic advances. Yet during the World War I years, when northern cities as well as Los Angeles and Seattle experienced large increments in their Black populations, San Francisco's remained comparatively small.[61]

The summer of 1916 was particularly eventful for labor, as unions attempted to increase their power and improve working conditions. As the First World War raged and American industry strove to meet the Allies' needs, unions sought to benefit from a situation that allowed large profits for business. In San Francisco, restaurant and kitchen workers were in the midst of bargaining when the city's restaurant and cafe proprietors united to force union members out of their establishments. The lockout occurred after lengthy negotiations had failed to produce shorter hours and better pay. Inevitably, a sanctioned strike ensued, pickets were set up, and injunctions were issued against picketing. The restaurant and cafe managers, meanwhile, declared an open shop policy and brought in new help, some of it Afro-American.[62]

Black Pullman workers were rushed by taxi to an O'Farrell Street establishment, where fifty of them waited on tables. A few days later, the Restaurant Men's Association, formed by the various managers, opened an employment bureau to fill the remaining openings caused by the lockout. In one day more than one hundred applicants appeared, fifty of them Afro-Americans, to fill the positions. They were rushed wherever needed. Within the next week some four hundred non-union men were placed in jobs.[63] The new workers' situation was precarious. That of the Negroes was even more so, because they were not eligible to join unions, and because of the tradition of enmity between white and Black culinary workers from the 1880s. The Blacks' custom of strikebreaking when racist unions struck or were locked out only exacerbated the hostile competition. Events of the summer of 1916 exemplified the degree of discord between white and Black workers.

In mid-July two non-union Blacks who filled the positions of striking longshoremen were assaulted by union men along the waterfront. On another occasion, one of the few Black stevedores who belonged to the local union was also beaten. The assailant was a union brother who automatically assumed the Negro to be an enemy of the white working men. Such incidents highlighted the serious predicament of the Black waiters who found themselves besieged by white pickets outside the restaurants.[64] Because of the potential for violence, the Black help at one cafe lived in the basement rather than run the gauntlet of pickets. The establishment's proprietor was "prepared to withstand a long siege." The dilemma Afro-San Franciscans faced on securing employment was expressed by a waiter: "Law'd, man, this is la'k a dining car. You cain't get off and you cain't get out."[65]

Blacks hoped the ready employment of 1916 in first-class hotels, restaurants, and other places was permanent. But it "lasted just long enough to make the Negro happy and hopeful that the pioneer days of good work and good pay were returning to the city and the Negroes could again earn a good livelihood." Writing shortly after the outcome, Delilah Beasley explained how Blacks' hopes were shattered by the realities of their employment. "Before winter returned they were all out on the cold bricks hunting for a job, with good references from the men who had recently employed them, but were forced to manage their business at the dictation of the labor unions."[66]

In some ways Black San Franciscans suffered from their increased numbers on the Pacific slope. The pool of footloose colored workers who roamed the far west, going from longshore work to the factories, or from

Pullman cars to cafes, increased competition for the few jobs reserved for resident Afro-Americans. While the new migrants meant more Black customers, they also caused greater competition among Negroes and aroused the ire of white working men who lost positions to colored strikebreakers.

The situation summarized by the waiter's statement and illustrated by the labor struggles dramatized both the obstacles and the opportunities San Francisco presented. Events repeated themselves; paradoxically, opportunities made Blacks targets for white workers, and exclusion from labor organizations meant marginal jobs and positions as tokens in labor conflicts. Similar scenes occurred during the longshoremen's strikes of 1901, 1916, and 1919. After strikes were settled, Blacks invariably found themselves jobless.[67]

The power of the labor unions temporarily ended during the 1920s. Anti-labor sentiment during the Red Scare and after a number of bombings hurt the workers' struggles, and an open shop policy prevailed in San Francisco. Negroes gained employment, and the Black population increased 57 percent, to nearly 4,000. The growth reflected job opportunities, the end of foreign immigration, and mass internal migration of Blacks. For the first time since pioneer days, the national census showed a large increment to Afro-San Franciscans' numbers, beginning in 1910 and peaking in the next decade. But employment was still in the menial positions Blacks had occupied since the 1850s. Gains in industry, a notable departure for Afro-San Franciscans, lasted only through the 1920s.

In San Francisco, as in every other major American city until World War I, employers refrained from hiring Afro-Americans, preferring foreign-born Europeans and, until white workers organized against them, Chinese laborers. This prevented many Blacks from inhabiting the far west or the north until the Great Migration. In other words, the urbanization of Afro-Americans lagged behind that of whites because of the preference for white workers and because most Blacks inhabited the most rural sector of the nation. During World War I, when industry expanded and European immigration dwindled, labor recruiters sought help from southern Blacks.

Of course, the labor unions also played a role in preventing the urbanization of Afro-Americans. This is particularly apparent in San Francisco, which had one of the strongest labor movements in the nation. When an open shop policy prevailed in the 1920s, San Francisco's Black population (like Los Angeles's, where unions were particularly weak) increased enormously. The northern metropolis did not experience the massive Black penetration characteristic of Los Angeles, New York, or Chicago until similar conditions occurred again in the 1940s: a world war, a labor shortage, and active recruitment by the war-related industries.

Moreover, new federal regulations made it more difficult for management and labor to exclude Afro-Americans from jobs in the war plants.

The comparatively late urbanization of Afro-Americans was not merely the result of their slavery heritage, their lack of skills, or their lack of preparation for urban living. Eastern and southern Europeans were not particularly equipped to deal with the industrial city either. Besides the late arrival of Black masses to the urban scene, the preferences of management and the policies of unions must be considered. Indeed, these latter factors may have been the decisive ones, for they furthered the urbanization of Europeans who were both more distant from and less familiar with American culture than Afro-Americans. The drastic economic changes accompanying industrialization and urbanization did not significantly improve Blacks' quality of life, even as they improved the situation of the new immigrants. In fact, the changes made matters worse for Afro-Americans, because by the time they arrived the opportunities of the cities had been monopolized by older immigrant groups and by new arrivals. Moreover, pioneer urbanites, small in number and weak in influence, were not in a good position to aid the masses who comprised the Great Migration.

The few gains early Black urbanites experienced, as at the Palace Hotel, only served to underline their precarious situation. The positions there looked so good only because San Francisco, like other cities, offered so little. When hotels were modernized and businesses made more efficient, Blacks realized the weakness of their position as they were sacrificed to meet the demands of progress and of labor unions. This happened in San Francisco in the 1880s, in the World War I years, and in the Depression. Those who remained relied on a variety of stratagems to keep good jobs, to travel in search of a better life, and to improve the quality of their existence.

# 4

# Survivors

*Boy, I was hustling.*

Edward J. *"Buster" Johnson*

The Black San Franciscans' responses to narrow job opportunities permit appreciation of them as actors instead of as passive subjects, and of their skills and the enormity of the problems they faced. They schemed, diversified, hustled, politicked, and passed as white to get secure jobs and extra money; their triumphs were testimony of their worth, and enabled them to remain in the city. They held American ideals and desires for advancement, and believed that business enterprises would benefit both individuals and the race. It was better to be an employer than an employee. The *Pacific Appeal* noted, the Black Americans "are moved by the same impulses, guided by the same motives, and have the same Yankee-like go-aheadativeness of the white Americans."[1] Those consigned to menial jobs valued chances to be individual entrepreneurs even more than other Americans, who could advance without the hindrances of racism.

In the late 1920s Matt Crawford, a Bay Area resident, experienced a sentiment felt by pioneers. "The main thing that motivated me . . . was the idea of being a professional man, and I wanted to be my own boss." As a youngster, Crawford and his brothers helped their father clean offices after school, a task the boys detested. As a young man, Crawford worked with several other Blacks as a file clerk in the basement of an underwriters' insurance company. There was no chance for advancement, and his desire for independence increased, so he attended chiropractic college. "This business of . . . not having to take orders and wanting to have a certain kind of dignity had a lot to do with . . . [my] settling for that."[2]

A handful of Black professionals and businessmen acquired a degree of independence as early as the 1850s. They owned a few manufacturing concerns, reflecting both their success as entrepreneurs and the somewhat less competitive conditions of the mid-nineteenth century. Shadrack Howard ran a hydraulic hose factory; John P. Dyer maintained a soap-making establishment and a tallow factory until his death in 1869. But these businesses were exceptions to the prevailing economic patterns,[3] for through the nineteenth century no more than 5 percent of the colored city folk were businessmen. Moreover, Black entrepreneurs were usually confined to particular areas of the economy, running second-hand or repair shops, house-cleaning businesses, barbershops, restaurants, saloons, and boarding houses. The capital required could be raised in a short period of time by thrift, speculation, or gambling, and such businesses supplied goods and services needed by footloose adventurers. In 1860 Peter Anderson, the future proprietor of the *Pacific Appeal,* operated a clothing store, James E. Brown kept a livery stable, Henry Smith ran a lodging house, and Henry C. Cornish dealt in second-hand furniture.[4]

Like all enterprising San Franciscans, they sold whatever promised a sure, swift profit. But while opportunities were available to ambitious Black San Franciscans, some successes were short lived, even if hopes persisted. Significantly, none of the entrepreneurs of the late 1850s, with the exception of George W. Dennis, appeared in the ranks of the prosperous in 1889. Furthermore, with one exception, no descendants of the Black businessmen of the 1850s were among the successful in the 1880s. And enterprises were less numerous in the 1860s than in the 1850s—even though the population had increased.[5]

Many pioneer entrepreneurs left San Francisco by 1869. The exodus occurred either before the right to testify in court was given and voting restrictions were dropped, or despite these improvements. Opportunities in British Columbia and the Comstock boom spurred pioneers to leave San Francisco. The Supreme Court's 1857 Dred Scott decision, which stripped Negroes of their citizenship and presaged future injustices, caused some to leave for Canada. The California legislature attempted to limit the immigration of Negroes on several occasions in the 1850s. And after the Civil War, new opportunities in the south drew westerners.[6]

The nature of the growth of California's economy also frustrated Black businessmen's attempts to share in the west's economic opportunities. The formation of large industrial monopolies, which marked the east's economy in the mid- and late nineteenth century, also characterized California's economy. Hardrock and hydraulic mining, which required considerable capital and machinery, replaced the simpler methods of the Gold Rush days. Individual miners could no longer compete, so they labored for the corporations. Similar developments occurred in the city's economy, as large corporations forced smaller concerns to fold. Communication with the east coast via telegraph (1861) and railroad (1869) stabilized the economy in the 1860s, and opportunities for the average San Francisco-based entrepreneur narrowed. Westerners forced to compete with eastern manufacturers found it increasingly difficult to succeed or to remain successful.

Exceptional energy, unusual foresight and organizational talents, a measure of ruthlessness, and some good luck were required to successfully maintain a business. The Bonanza Kings were skilled, shrewd, and extremely knowledgeable in their respective fields. They commanded large sums of capital, counted wealthy men among their friends, and were either associates of local politicians or were elected officials themselves. The most successful frequently owned every vital phase of their operations—mining, lumber, water rights, railroads, shipping, and banking as well. By the 1870s a gulf yawned between the rich and the working folk.[7]

Although the competition afforded Blacks few business opportunities, the importance of their enterprises cannot be overlooked. They gave Afro-Americans the independence and status that every American desired, and provided employment for their Black citizens. San Francisco's successful Negro enterpreneurs were models for all energetic and ambitious Afro-Americans, and their businesses were emblems of pride. One example was a husband-and-wife team, the Phillipses. The husband ran a bath and barbershop, and the wife managed a hairdressing salon. Located at 218 Post Street, Madame Phillips's firm was "very elaborately fitted up" in 1902, featuring all the modern conveniences—electric lighting, electric hair dryers, and private booths, five for hairdressing and two for manicuring. The stock owned by the pioneer couple totaled more than $3,000. During World War I and in subsequent years the undertaking establishment of John Howard Butler and Luther M. Hudson was also a source of both pride and employment.[8]

Sometimes businesses were seen as evidence that Blacks prospered in and had a fair share of the city's economy. In 1902, the *Pacific Coast Appeal* boasted that "the principal barber shops in the city are owned by young Negro businessmen." In the 1920s barbershops ranked as the largest single group of Black-owned enterprises—five out of seventeen counted by a University of California researcher. By owning barber shops, pool halls, express wagon businesses, rooming houses, and cafes, San Francisco Negroes could make a living and occasionally become quite affluent.[9] Like other fortunate Americans, these successes tended to regard others as less disciplined, lazy, or unenterprising.

But failure was perhaps more typical of Black businesses. Even with the expertise needed to raise capital and manage an establishment, competition could cause grave difficulties for even large businesses and (as Peter Decker observed) for the white-collar class. The vicissitudes of California's economy were so formidable to the establishment and survival of enterprises that, beginning in the 1870s, white workers formed a powerful labor movement in order to have some share of the wealth monopolized by large businesses. The *Elevator,* usually optimistic, reported: "The prospect for extensive colored business enterprise in California, for this generation at least, would be anything but promising." In 1902, the largest employer of colored San Franciscans, Brittain Oxendine of the Silver Dollar Trading Company, counted a force of ten men. If this was the largest Black business, the average must have involved a few partners and a few more employees at best.[10]

Despite the growth of San Francisco's Black population in the 1920s, a number of obstacles still prevented the formation of extensive business enterprise. A study of Black businesses mentions a "dearth of knowledge of the methods of and reasons for their success." The lack of business knowledge and techniques also characterized the operations of the more successful Black entrepreneurs. Afro-San Franciscans customarily ran small or one-man enterprises. Many were not certain how many customers they served and did not follow the practices of larger concerns that constantly emphasized marketing analyses, modern management practices, and close study of various phases of operation.[11]

The physical dispersal of colored folk throughout San Francisco and the East Bay made it difficult for small shops to monopolize the Negro trade. This was a special problem in both San Francisco and Oakland, where in the early twentieth century a larger Negro population supported more Black businesses. Concentrated in one area like Harlem or Chicago's South Side, the Bay Area's meager Black population might have sustained more businesses than were enumerated in Robert Coleman Francis's University of California study. Also, colored folk often chose to spend their money in non-Black establishments. The bias of brown-skinned Negroes against darker-skinned Blacks hurt Afro-American enterprise. Also, "doubtful social activities" in barber shops discouraged residents from patronizing those places. Fearing they would not get support, many Blacks did not risk business ventures or moved to Los Angeles.[12] After 1900, the few Afro-American businesses in San Francisco were dwarfed by those in the new Pacific coast cities. Oakland and Los Angeles drew the ambitious and restless whose movement marked the beginning of the Great Migration. Los Angeles Blacks were characterized as "pushing and energetic,"[13] while Oakland was described as a "beehive of industry."[14]

The East Bay establishment of William L. Vance and Simon A. Dedrick, two Texans who had worked on trains, illustrates the opportunity that existed in Oakland. When it opened at the turn of the century, the restaurant employed as many workers as The Silver Dollar Trading Company of Brittain Oxendine, but the East Bay establishment eclipsed in size and scope the San Francisco concern in a few years' time. Significantly, more than half of the restaurant's patrons were white. After the earthquake and fire of 1906, the former Texans remodeled and enlarged, making improvements totaling $4,000. The increased seating capacity included a dining room that accommodated sixty and twelve private rooms that seated fifty-four. Electric chandeliers and fans and high ceilings provided attractive and comfortable surroundings. The restaurant served one thousand meals daily.

The organization of the work force indicates that some Oaklanders possessed the skills, the concern with efficiency, and the degree of specialization required for success in the urban age. Vance supervised some of the kitchen activities, where three men, working eight-hour shifts, prepared the meats; the range also needed three workers, the steam table required two, the pantry included three more, and night duty required six others. The waiters totaled twenty, including a night crew of eight; the two lady cashiers divided their task into two shifts. The organized work force, the "excellent discipline" of the crew, the gleaming brass and steel utensils, and the well-scrubbed floors and woodwork attested to the business acumen of Vance and Dedrick.[15]

Because ambitious urbanites settled in Oakland rather than San Francisco, Black businesses in the older city languished still more. Businessmen who relocated after the earthquake and fire found such congenial conditions that they stayed after the rebuilding of San Francisco. By 1915 San Francisco's Negro enterprises were said to be at a virtual standstill, and in the next fifteen years of migration and growth, most colored businesses in the city retained their service character and small size.[16]

In addition to business enterprises, the Black pioneers tried to improve their situation through political action, but they lacked the numbers of other ethnic groups. Racism precluded the recruitment of thousands of Black workers for industry until World War II, and prejudiced white workers took the best jobs. Chinese and Italians—followed by Japanese and Filipinos—commonly occupied the lowest-paying positions, while Afro-Americans worked in those that remained. Conditions worsened for Afro-San Franciscans, many of them descendants of pioneers, in the early decades of the twentieth century, as Los Angeles and Oakland attracted thousands of energetic migrants. Faced with these conditions, Negroes developed special ways to deal with working longer hours for less pay. These methods succeeded to a degree while political efforts failed to produce tangible benefits until the 1930s and 1940s. But before examining these techniques, we must review the political failure.

Before and after emancipation, the American political system insured that Black folk remained oppressed. Because law and custom prevented a bondsman from earning money without his master's consent, a slave in San Francisco during pioneer days could not even claim his own labor. A state of virtual freedom was therefore necessary to acquire the money for emancipation and economic progress. But freedmen also suffered from statutes that left them easy prey for any ruthless white in the 1850s and 1860s. A white thief shot and killed George W. Gordon, a prosperous Black businessman, in front of his San Francisco barbershop shortly after the Gold Rush. The bold murderer was confident that no white man would testify against him, and he knew that no Afro-American could testify against him in a California court. He was, however, apprehended and convicted of second-degree manslaughter by the evidence of a white resident who was sympathetic to Gordon. In a similar incident, Mifflin Gibbs watched helplessly as a white customer caned his business partner, Peter Lester. Such injustices were not uncommon during pioneer days, and led to the formation of the Franchise League and the Right of Testimony petition campaign, which ultimately won Blacks the right to testify in court.[17]

The Dred Scott decision seriously disadvantaged Blacks, and attempts by the California legislature to forbid free Negroes from entering the state threatened future growth. A burgeoning Negro population served Negro interests much as a fast-growing native and foreign-born population furthered the objectives of other Californians. The Civil War and Reconstruction amendments increased the likelihood that Afro-Americans could compete as equals and enjoy the successes that made humble Americans wealthy and respected captains of industry and financiers.[18]

During the 1860s one color bar after another fell, and San Francisco's Negroes waxed optimistic as they shared the enthusiasm of slaves in the south and freedmen throughout the nation. A long civil rights campaign made it possible to protect their lives and property in California's courts. Emancipation sustained their hopes. It meant prospective migrants and customers to increase their numbers and strengthen their entrepreneurial efforts. The triumph of the Radical Republicans in Congress also augured well, and new amendments to the U.S. Constitution promised full citizenship rights. Thus Black city folk could demand equal protection and, also important, serve their own interests more easily and effectively. But the lower salaries paid to Black soldiers in the Civil War indicated that white Americans would never view Afro-Americans as equals.

American politics reflected this bias. U.S. citizens formed innumerable associations, parties, and businesses to improve their condition. The agitation of abolitionists and the legislation of Radical Republicans figured in the emancipation and enfranchisement of slaves and freedmen, who lacked the political rights and power to help themselves. In California, civil rights activities of Afro-Americans resulted in some victories. During Reconstruction, as a result of their own efforts, and with the aid of their white friends, Black San Franciscans won the right to attend unsegregated public schools. Some Blacks who realized that this was just the beginning of race elevation formed clubs and organizations to increase their political power. Among these organizations were the California Colored Conventions, the Executive Committee of San Francisco (which launched the *Elevator*), the California Colored Citizens' State Union, the Afro-American League, and the NAACP. Black pioneers also belonged to the major political parties, through which they made their desires known to candidates and politicians. Court battles, petitions, legislation, and voting were means utilized by Afro-Americans to end race discrimination. They were also concerned with receiving jobs as political spoils in the tradition of urban politics. Such jobs promised good salaries and constituted recognition of merit, but constitutional amendments and civil rights statutes were more readily obtained than attractive and steady jobs. Such civil rights activities undoubtedly drained finances and energies that might have been devoted to forming businesses and improving working conditions; but first the political and civil rights that whites took for granted had to be won.

After the enactment of the Fifteenth Amendment, colored city dwellers registered to vote, usually supporting the Republican party. But their dealings with the major parties, especially regarding patronage jobs, were inevitably frustrating. Republicans promised positions in exchange for votes, but rarely followed through. Some Black pioneers switched to the Democratic party in the early 1880s, with similar results.

A "Fourth Warder" (an inhabitant from near Broadway and Powell) complained of the politics of San Francisco's Republicans in 1873. He recalled the last municipal election, in which Black voters heard the Republicans "descant . . . with oiled tongues . . . on equal rights, equal privileges, and equal spoils." The party promised a number of "subordinate offices" and, eventually, colored representation on the Republican ticket. "Children in politics, as we [Black folk] were, our faith was great. We went the whole ticket blind. We swallowed several bitter pills. . . ." Nothing happened. Excuses were given, but jobs were withheld. With new elections coming up, leading Blacks thought they could count on a position as policeman for their group. But the "Fourth Warder" wryly commented, "the Ethiop could not change his skin, nor the white fox his cunning."[19]

Black support of the Democratic party in October 1882 produced no good jobs, let alone recognition. William H. Blake's letters to Governor George B. Stoneman indicate the disappointment of Afro-San Franciscans. Beginning in January 1883, and on at least three other occasions that year, Blake wrote Governor Stoneman concerning Blake's appointment as a notary public. As vice-president of the California Colored Citizens' State Union and as chairman of its Executive Committee, a steering organ, Blake had successfully convinced the California Colored Convention of 1882 to support Stoneman's candidacy. The politician promised positions as notaries public in return for colored votes. "I am satisfied you will do *what* you said," Blake wrote in his first inquiry about the proposed appointment.[20] The governor's answers, if they ever existed, are not available.

Blake's correspondence includes a petition signed by his supporters, some of whom were supreme court judges. It expresses both his hopes and his keen sense of disappointment over the delay. It remains in the state archives as testimony to the disappointment of a Black San Franciscan who desired an appointment as honorific as notary public. It also reminds us of the political disenchantment of Afro-Americans throughout the nation.

Blake's inquiries show that California's few thousand Afro-American voters carried little weight, and that the several hundred in San Francisco mattered still less; the political arena was dominated by corporations, urban bosses, and white labor unions. Blacks' political organizations could not improve their condition after the gains of Reconstruction. They failed to win attractive or well-paying jobs, while whites reaped the benefits of the American political system. Twenty years passed before William Blake was appointed notary public. The petition requesting the position was as brief as it was formal. It represented one of the few positions accorded Blacks by the local government or either political party.[21]

At the end of the nineteenth century, San Francisco's Afro-American League listed the positions Negroes had obtained from the federal and local governments. Three held relatively attractive positions as clerks for the city government and in a railroad office. In addition, there was a mail carrier, three messengers, a painter, a gardener, an attendant at the Children's Play Ground in Golden Gate Park, thirteen porters, and sixty deputy U.S. Marshalls who acted as election officers.[22]

Negroes in Los Angeles were more successful at getting jobs. They numbered more than all northern California Blacks by 1910, which undoubtedly increased their political influence. At an annual meeting of the Afro-American Councils of California at Riverside in 1906, the successes in Los Angeles were noted: The Democratic mayor had rewarded political support with positions in the fire and police departments, on the street works, and in city offices. The number of positions was not given, but they represented prestigious and lucrative jobs. Ironically, Los Angeles's reputation for giving government jobs to Negroes probably reinforced Black San Francisco's faith in the political system.[23]

Because of civil service examinations and the tendency of newcomers to participate actively in politics, Bay Area Blacks made some significant gains in the early twentieth century. Leon F. Marsh became Berkeley's first Black mail carrier; in the 1920s Blacks joined Oakland's fire department, although they were segregated in their own fire house. In the 1940s Ruth Acty became a teacher in the Berkeley school district, and a Black man earned a position in that city's fire department. The writer and actress Maya Angelou became the first Black conductor on a San Francisco cable car in the 1940s.[24] These breakthroughs were more likely in the East Bay than in San Francisco. According to Royal E. Towns, one of the first Black firemen in Oakland, the difference was that "Oakland was more progressive."

They had the balance of the political power here [in Oakland]. That's how they got a fire department down there. A man was running for commissioner and he said, "If you folks down here vote for me I'll get some Blacks in the fire department." He won and we got the Blacks in the fire department.[25]

These changes, when they occurred, were due to "political pressure. . . . Power of the Black man's votes." A number of residents sustained this opinion.[26]

The failure of Black businesses and politics reveals as much about the Bay's society as it does about Afro-Americans. Prejudice, the competitiveness of the city, and narrowing economic opportunities accompanying industrialization prevented Afro-Americans from making the substantive economic gains they desired. The disadvantages of a group close to slavery, lacking skills and knowledge suitable for big business, and the size of the Negro population thwarted enterprise in both business and politics. Efforts to aid Afro-Americans in the south and to combat discrimination in San Francisco diverted funds and energies that other ethnic groups used to improve their employment situation. When conditions changed for Blacks in the Bay Area, it was due to labor needs in war-related industries, increased activism among the growing Black population, and federal regulations limiting discriminatory hiring.

Yet the small contingent of pioneers found means to acquire jobs and supplement their incomes to reside in San Francisco or the East Bay. They were invariably persistent, resourceful individuals who often had little aid from group efforts, though sometimes cooperation figured in their successes. Their methods were important because labor unions, party politics, and businesses failed to aid most Bay Area Afro-Americans until the 1940s. To obtain employment, Blacks depended on life-long associations and friendships with white city dwellers, on cooperation with other Afro-Americans, and at times on their ability to pass as white.

Growing up in predominantly white neighborhoods, the pioneers relied on contacts with influential residents to obtain jobs that otherwise would have been denied them. When they took civil service examinations, Afro-Americans frequently required the aid of well-placed friends to obtain jobs despite a passing score. Edward "Buster" Johnson, an Oakland native and third-generation Californian, explained:

I took every kind of [civil service] examination you can name. Every time I would go in the post office, I'd see "Custom House Inspector," "Immigration Inspector"— oh, anything like that, and I'd go take them examinations. And I'd pass them. They never called for me.[27]

He experienced these troubles during the Depression, while working as a doorman at an exclusive San Francisco apartment building. Johnson's difficulties were common for Afro-Americans.

Eleanor Carroll Watkins graduated from the library school of the University of California, Berkeley; despite success on at least two examinations, she ultimately had to depend on her mother's contacts to get the job she merited. In the early 1930s she took the exam for library assistant and got the second-highest score, but said that "fifteen people at least below me were hired." When she made inquiries, she discovered they had been working on a temporary basis waiting for the examination, and were therefore given preference. She accepted this explanation. Then she took the examination for junior librarian, with the same results. "Here I was passed over because in Oakland civil service, the appointing officer has a choice of one out of three. So you can—the same person could be passed over indefinitely because the three names are submitted and he has to take only one of those three." Fortunately, her mother was a businesswoman with a client on the library board. The young applicant allowed her mother to intervene, because "finally I was convinced I wasn't getting a fair deal." Some words were exchanged with the customer about the matter and, shortly after, Carroll was hired.[28]

Royal Towns had similar problems with the civil service in the 1920s. When an employer asked Towns why he had not obtained a better position, the Oakland native responded: "Well, I would like to be either a policeman or a fireman, but every time we go down there to take an examination, they find something wrong with you." His employer advised him to consult a mutual friend for advice. This worked, because when Towns went in for the medical examination, the doctor asked, "You have a lot of friends in this city?" Towns answered, "Yes, I have a lot of friends. (Well, hell, I ought to have, I was born and raised here.)" After the examination he asked if he had passed; the doctor candidly replied, "Well, how are you going to fail with friends like you got?" Towns began working for the fire department, but noted, "there wasn't another Black hired until fifteen years later."[29]

Many Black workers depended upon their contacts with influential whites. Alfred Butler's father, a Pullman worker, was a favorite among the railroad executives. "He was so well-liked, . . . [that]. . . whenever they wanted to make a trip to New York, they would call up . . . and find out when John Butler was going out." Walter G. Maddox won a position as timetable expert for the Southern Pacific Railroad because he befriended the elderly white man who held the job. Aurelious P. Alberga obtained life-long employment as a kind of valet to a friend's brother. Samuel E. Young, a railroad man, secured a good position "for all time" from Claus Spreckels, the sugar magnate.[30]

Blacks won jobs by manipulating their narrow circumstances and by relying on old friendships or an ability to cultivate new ones. Like industrialists and other fortune hunters, they created opportunities to ensure themselves of secure tenure, large tips, and chances for advancement. Leading Blacks and various organizations also secured jobs for Afro-Americans, but it is impossible to determine how many benefited. Certainly relatives and friends helped one another, as might be expected, but the collective efforts of newspapermen, information agencies, and women's clubs are noteworthy. This is particularly significant for a people traditionally characterized as lazy and incapable of self-help.

Specific Black organizations aided both newcomers and long-time residents. The newspapers served this purpose. The *Elevator* office operated as a clearing-house; whites in need of servants contacted Philip Bell, who spoke with individuals or publicized the positions in his newspaper's columns. In 1866 the journal announced, "We have daily applications for colored servants, and we could find situations for a hundred in half as many hours." Following the tradition of such establishments, the Pioneer Seamen's Boarding and Lodging House, at the foot of Broadway, procured jobs for waiters, cooks, and stewards "at the shortest notice."[31] An information bureau managed by two Black residents was set up to help Blacks find jobs. Its proprietors claimed thorough acquaintance with the city and contacts with local and traveling people. They also gave advice on housing and lodgings, bought and sold goods for out-of-towners, offered aid to those in need of legal information, and promised to help their clients save money. During World War I, the San Francisco Colored Women's Club started an employment bureau for

Afro-Americans. And in Oakland, the Negro Business League promised positions and "information given freely to strangers on any subject."[32]

Negroes acquired jobs otherwise reserved for other city dwellers by passing for white. The testimony of the respondents indicates that this tactic was fairly common. Some penetrated the color barrier and remained on the other side, isolating themselves from Afro-America and rarely visiting their Black kin. Others passed while they worked during the daytime, and then returned to their families in the evening. To permanently pass as white smacked of disloyalty for some, but those who could do so temporarily held few qualms about the ruse. Photographs in family albums show how difficult it must have been to distinguish some light-complexioned Afro-Americans from Caucasians—particularly for employers who did not even expect a Black to appear as an applicant.[33] Yet this recourse was probably not as important as the practices of diversifying, of working extra jobs, and of hustling to obtain money to make up for low-paying work.

The lack of skills among Black urbanites is usually emphasized. Admittedly some twentieth-century ghetto dwellers do not possess the training needed to manage bureaucracies or to deal with the sophisticated machines and computer technology of the present age. But this regrettable situation does not warrant viewing Blacks as untrainable, as idlers who are unfit for urban life and who are ultimately responsible for their lack of knowledge. The possession of skills reflects both opportunities and abilities; the Black population has often used its intelligence and developed its abilities. Because Blacks have had few chances to prosper in post-industrial society, it is unfair to describe them as unskilled and untrainable.

Furthermore, the condition of Afro-Americans must be regarded in the appropriate social context. The same individuals who are "unskilled" in middle-class eyes often have considerable talents. For example, an urbanite who might have difficulty communicating in standard English during an interview can, among his peers, reveal the talents and imagination of a poet. Recently Black ghetto dwellers have won some recognition for their "street smarts," or ability to manipulate individuals through persuasion and cunning, to obtain money, goods, or services, doing so with a flair that is not exhibited in more forbidding circumstances. They develop these skills not only to deal with their environment, but also because opportunities for advancement are lacking outside the ghetto. The skills of the pioneers gain clarity in light of these conditions.[34]

Because of circumscribed job opportunities, Afro-Americans developed talents for which others had little need. As service workers, they sought to befriend tourists and strangers to obtain tips and secure better jobs. Those who wished to stay in San Francisco diversified, worked at extra jobs, hustled for tips, saved, invested, and speculated in real estate, businesses, and a variety of other schemes. Bay Area Negroes possessed an array of talents even if we allow for their exaggerations. Sometimes city dwellers diversified by pursuing lines similar to their chosen professions. Cooks, waiters, and bartenders catered or opened their own restaurants and saloons. Successful barbers went into business for themselves. Dining car waiters and cooks were especially prone to follow this path. William Vance and Simon Dedrick, Oakland restauranteurs, were both former train men. Edward Johnson's father, who worked on the road for years, also managed an Oakland restaurant. Johnson's uncle cooked in their establishment, in a resort area south of San Francisco, and finally opened his own restaurant, Stephens, in Oakland on East Fourteenth Street.[35]

Diversification, either into a spin-off of a present job or into a new situation, was fairly common. Newspapermen used their columns to advertise their talents and businesses. Peter Anderson, proprietor of the *Pacific Appeal,* maintained a clothing shop before and after he went into the newspaper business. The *Appeal* also took orders for printing and issued cards, billheads, and circulars. Philip Bell, editor of the *Appeal* and later the *Elevator,* advertised his services as a real estate agent.[36] James B. Wilson, a long-time resident and editor of the *Pacific Coast Appeal* at the turn of the century, was a porter in the pioneer era, manufactured shoe polish, and, after learning shorthand and typing, taught these skills to other residents later in the century. Charles R. Persons was an electrician, a locksmith, and a journalist; also an accomplished musician, he played piano and organ in the Third Baptist Church. Another leading citizen, William H. Blake, was a barber by training. Not content with this single outlet for his talents, intelligence, and ambitions, he gave guitar lessons, directed concerts and musical events, sold his own formula hair prepara-tions, participated actively in political affairs, and, with James Wilson, edited the *Pacific Coast Appeal.*[37]

Some realized that languages afforded special positions and extra money. In 1872, a Black hairdresser gave up his trade to avoid Sunday work. While seeking a job as porter or messenger, he advertised that he spoke English, Spanish, French, and Swedish, and was acquainted with business methods. Margaret Dennis, daughter of the pioneer livery stable proprietor, won a position as court interpreter because of her knowledge of Chinese and Spanish. Oscar Hudson, a lawyer and consul for Liberia, served the Spanish-speaking community (as well as Afro-Americans) because of his expertise in that language.[38]

The average Black San Franciscan probably lacked such language skills. Southern and northern migrants and other residents whose sole language was English responded to job discrimination by holding extra jobs and by hustling—working extra hard and relying on their ingenuity to see a job and to fill it. Because whites disdained barbering, it was common for Afro-American youth in the nineteenth century to learn that trade. A number of Afro-San Franciscans who went on to other professions, often to gain a degree of affluence, learned haircutting in their youth. Such Black pioneers as James R. Starkey, William H. Blake, George Gordon, and Jeremiah B. Sanderson were barbers. In the twentieth century, barbering at night or on weekends was a means of supplementing income.[39]

The hustling spirit is perhaps best exemplified by Edward J. Johnson, who, like many Negroes, had to develop contacts to supplement his income. As a doorman and maintenance man working nights, he came into contact with a number of affluent residents.

People would come in there with their cars, and if their car was covered with dust, I swept the car out, cleaned the glasses off, and I had my special way to wipe 'em all off. And if the car looked kind of bad, I tell 'em to leave their car and I would simonize it. It'd be $5.00 for simonizing the car and by keeping it clean every day, when he'd go downtown his car would be nice and clean, you see.

He also drove the women downtown in the morning and returned their cars to their husbands. "Boy, I was hustling." His employer wanted to know how much extra money he was making, but Johnson refused to divulge the information, quit, found another apartment house up the street, and continued hustling. He viewed the affluent apartment dwellers as his clientele, reversing the usual relationship—being *their* doorman. He ticked them off as if they worked for him: "I had old man Sandler [of] Sandler's jewelry place. . . . I had English and the Sloan family. . . . I had people that . . . had come from . . . Yosemite, had a gold mine down there. The district attorney, everybody, high class doctors and everything." The widow of the owner of Dutch Boy Paints "had so many million dollars she didn't know what to do." "Anything I had on my mind that I wanted to do, there was one of those people who could take care of it for me."[40]

Of course, hustling was not the only means of surviving. Other Afro-Americans depended on the aid of various members of their households. From pioneer days, Black San Francisco women added to the household income by taking in boarders. In 1930, 28 percent of Afro-San Franciscans had households with boarders, a figure that exceeded other groups several times over. This was one of the "few ways open to a gentlewoman to earn money." They also sewed in their own homes, did needlework, and dressed hair.[41]

Only those with few or no children were in a good position to live in San Francisco. According to the Fifteenth Census, the Black San Franciscan family was smaller than any other urban family unit. This enabled Afro-

Americans to use their incomes for necessities, entertainment, dues in social organizations, and perhaps for a few luxuries.[42] Blacks fought race prejudice and weak political influence, because the only alternative was to leave the Bay Area. Their numbers indicate that the survival techniques worked for only a handful of pioneers in the late nineteenth and early twentieth centuries, and were no substitute for union organization, owning big businesses, and political influence. Their successes knit them into a group that was extraordinarily proud of its accomplishments. The means used to get and keep jobs shed light on their adjustments to San Francisco. The factors that prompted them to travel to the distant city, to leave it for a season, and often to return, are still another aspect of their urban condition. We will investigate another essential skill—the ability to migrate long distances, to aid other travelers, and to befriend influential citizens—in the next chapter.

# 5

## Scouts

*I fancied myself Mungo Park, faint and weary among strangers.*
*Abner H. Francis, while crossing the isth-*
*mus of Panama en route to California—*
Frederick Douglass' Paper, *October 16,*
*1851*

Many Black pioneers migrated to, then temporarily left, San
Francisco, to wander in search of fortune. Their movement resulted from
the specific urban setting and from the obstacles facing all Afro-
Americans; initially caused by political weakness, the propensity to travel
became a source of strength. Rudolph M. Lapp has analyzed the motives
and routes of Black migrants during the Gold Rush. I will focus on the
pioneers' travel abilities—what made them capable of acquiring and
sorting out information, selecting the best option, and journeying
distances that were remarkable in the nineteenth century, especially for a
group which had recently been enslaved. Their ability to travel to San
Francisco, to cross and recross the continent, and to roam the Pacific slope
highlights their determination and pluck, their resourcefulness, and their
adventurousness, all traits rarely attributed to Blacks.

I use the term *travelcraft* to designate the outlook and complex of skills
that facilitated both long-distance travel and residency in the Bay Area.
Travelcraft distinguished Pacific slope Black urbanites from the mass of
Negroes tied to the land in the south, and set them apart from Black city
folk in the east who chose to stay close to the Atlantic shore. Before
analyzing travelcraft, we must delineate the habits which underlay it and
the frequency with which Black pioneers undertook lengthy trips.

Letters in San Francisco's Black newspapers of the 1860s and 1870s
indicated that Afro-Americans valued information on the geography of

distant places, on travel routes, on the likelihood of economic advancement after migration, on the presence of race discrimination, and on the
successes of other Negroes. To help collect and disseminate such
information, pioneers sent foreign and domestic newspapers to the offices
of the San Francisco *Pacific Appeal* and the San Francisco *Elevator* for
interested citizens to read. William H. Hall was thanked by the *Pacific
Appeal* in 1863 for furnishing issues of a Panamanian and several Jamaican
newspapers. Another pioneer, A. G. Dennis, returned from China in 1873
with copies of the Hong Kong Daily *Press,* the Calcutta *Englishman,* and
the Japanese *Gazette,* for which he was publicly thanked by the *Elevator.*
Seamen delivered copies of San Francisco's Black papers to Afro-
Americans in distant lands.[1]

Before leaving San Francisco, travelers were asked to give information
based on their personal experiences and observations; others supplied
intelligence because of a felt need for such information. Correspondents
prefaced their letters with such statements as, "I promised you, when
leaving the Bay City, to write you a few lines on reaching my destination."
One correspondent, having made four trips "across the continent," wished
to "give . . . readers a synopsis of my recent trip to the east and back,
hoping to be able to furnish some information of the many curiosities to be
found along the line of the great Central Pacific's road." Daniel Seales, a
prosperous businessman, sought to "drop . . . a few lines of information
which may be of interest to the traveling community."[2]

As well as general information, the letters included those tidbits that
habitual travelers readily appreciate. Daniel Seales wrote from Cleveland,
Ohio, about an oversight that occasioned some hardship: "I very headlessly
[sic] neglected putting on extra flannel when leaving San Francisco, and I
must suffer for my carelessness." "Il Roberto" in New York wrote his
California friends: "People of California, when you come to New York and
want dry goods, don't be afraid to go to Stewart's great Dry Goods Palace,
for you will not be cheated or sold. My landlady says she has dealt there for
ten years, and from experience has found she could invest her money more
profitably there than at any other store in the city."[3]

Black pioneers' letters indicate a coordinated effort to aid one another
by sharing information and insights derived from actual experiences. Their
letters and newspaper columns trace the movements of Negro westerners
and suggest the extent to which some continued to travel after migrating
west. Pioneers' obituaries also indicate that nineteenth-century Pacific
slope Negroes moved distances with a frequency that jars our notion that
Black folk were demoralized and dehumanized first by slavery, and then by
industrialization and urbanization.[4]

Besides those we might expect to follow a nomadic course—miners and adventurers—Afro-American travelers included businessmen who, in the eyes of their contemporaries, were self-made men and successful entrepreneurs. Henry M. Collins came west shortly after the Gold Rush, returned to the Atlantic coast to collect his wife and family, then moved to San Francisco, from where he made frequent trips to the mining country. John Upshur, who in 1889 lived comfortably as one of the affluent "self-made colored men of San Francisco," migrated west as a valet for William M. Gwin, a leading California politician, in 1854. He soon left that position to live in British Columbia, in Washington state, and in Sacramento, California, before finally settling in San Francisco.[5]

Some pioneers were lifelong travelers. Inclination, habit, and job opportunities at sea or on the road made long-distance journeys an integral part of their life and work. Alexander Dove, born in the West Indies in 1798, emigrated to Boston as a youngster. He went to sea, visiting "every quarter of the globe" before settling in San Francisco in 1849. After making the city his permanent home, the "successful mariner" pursued his calling until his death in 1869.[6]

Mifflin W. Gibbs, an Arkansas judge during Reconstruction and U.S. consul to Madagascar in the 1890s, lived in California in the 1850s and made lengthy trips all his life. As a young man he sailed from the Atlantic states to San Francisco shortly after the Gold Rush. In 1858 he migrated to British Columbia with a number of other Black Californians. The next year he returned to the east coast to marry and to visit friends in Rochester, New York, and Philadelphia before undertaking the 4,000 mile trip by steamship to Victoria, Vancouver Island, with his bride. Besides traveling to Madagascar years later, Gibbs stopped in San Francisco in 1895 and reflected on his life there in the 1850s. For Gibbs, as for a number of pioneers, travel remained a lifetime habit.[7]

Heads of Black institutions also ranged over the Pacific slope. Reverend T. M. D. Ward probably traveled more than any other Black San Franciscan in 1868, covering 14,000 miles in seven months. After going from San Francisco to the east coast on church business, he returned to the city by the bay. A week later he headed for Virginia City, Nevada. The next month he steamed to Portland, Oregon, and British Columbia to attend to church matters before returning east.[8]

Such long-distance travel was characteristic of various classes. Permanent residents regarded the city as home, but frequently visited friends and relatives in the east. They included in their ranks men like George C. Smith, a cook and barber, who, "allured by the reports of mineral discoveries, and led by a spirit of enterprise, . . . followed the tide of adventure in the pursuit of wealth." Some pioneers sojourned in the West Indies, Latin America, and Asia, keeping contact with their home

city through personal letters and by reading Black newspapers brought by
friends and other travelers.[9] The frequent long-distance movement, and
the travelcraft on which it was based, is striking in the historical context of
a homeless people searching for a place to develop its potential and achieve
wealth and status without the injustices of American racism.

Afro-Americans differed from other Americans because of the
circumstances surrounding their migration, settlement, and status in the
New World. Black slaves were unwilling migrants and unwilling workers.
As freedmen they did not enjoy the same political privileges and economic
and social opportunities as whites. Under slavery, Blacks were subject to
relocation at their master's whim, despite their own desires. Rejecting their
place in the south, some bondsmen fled, seeking refuge in the northern
states or in Canada. They nonetheless encountered segregated facilities,
disfranchisement, and violence in northern cities of the United States.[10]

Some freedmen searched for a home on the African continent. After the
American Revolution, a number of Blacks settled in Sierra Leone, West
Africa. With the aid of the American Colonization Society, Afro-
Americans of the early nineteenth century, convinced that racism was
invincible in the United States, founded Liberia to further their vision of a
Christianized Africa. Before the Civil War, American Blacks discussed the
pros and cons of colonization in their newspapers, in antislavery meetings,
and in the convention movements.[11]

Black support for colonization declined in the 1840s, but was revived
again when Negroes suffered a number of setbacks in national politics in
the crisis-ridden 1850s. In addition to Canada and Africa, Afro-Americans
regarded the West Indies and Central America as possible havens for an
oppressed populace who felt they would never win full citizenship, equal
rights, and economic opportunities in the United States.

The discovery of gold near Sacramento offered the ambitious a new
chance to realize their desires for fortune and status. Colored easterners
expressed a madness known as the "California excitement" and began
making preparations for departure. Bachelors wed their sweethearts before
departure, and married men left their wives and families. Some left
profitable pursuits and "a certainty for an uncertainty"; "discretion and
reasonable considerations seemed to have been abandoned," noted
*Frederick Douglass' Paper* in 1852.[12]

Those who migrated in the 1850s in the wake of the Gold Rush
appreciated the importance of wealth in American society and the effects it
might have on their condition. One pioneer noted, "The American mind is
one temple of avarice, and gold is the lever that levels all distinctions."
William H. Hall highlighted the magical qualities all Americans attributed
to money and to gold. "Wealth, and the knowledge how to apply it, is to the

colored American, the alchemy that turns everything it touches into gold, changes their dark repulsive features to a tolerating hue, penetrates and exhibits qualities before unseen, transforms him from a thing uncared for to the sublimety of manhood, a citizen, a neighbor and a brother in all that tends to conduce to prosperity and happiness."[13] Black pioneers expected to prosper from mining and from the high wages unique to pioneer California. But when the legislature passed laws severely limiting the rights of Afro-Americans, many reluctantly concluded that California was not the place they sought. Articles and letters in the newspapers reveal that in the 1860s, particularly before Emancipation, Black San Franciscans still searched for a place where they could realize their ambitions. The debate concerning prospects and conditions of life overseas sheds light on travelcraft and, specifically, on the manner in which the Black pioneers collected evidence, disseminated it through their journals, and used it to make decisions.

In the early 1860s the *Pacific Appeal* featured specific articles and letters reflecting Afro-Americans' interest in finding a suitable place to live. In late 1862 a westerner could peruse "The Future of the Colored Race in America," "Thoughts on Colonization," and "On Colonizing"—all of which ran for at least two issues. "The Liberian Republic" was reprinted from an eastern source along with "Eight Reasons for Objecting to the Haytian Scheme." In April 1863, the *Pacific Appeal* published the "Forty-Sixth Annual Report of the American Colonization Society" for interested readers.[14]

Both well-known and ordinary Afro-Americans advocated overseas migration in the early 1860s. The speeches and activities of the Reverends Alexander Crummell and Edward W. Blyden, the foremost advocates of African settlement at the time, appeared in the *Pacific Appeal*. Others felt that because of Haiti's unique history as the first and only Black New World nation, and the earlier Emancipation in the British West Indies, those island communities should figure in the debate concerning migration and colonization.[15] Haiti, in particular, laid claim to migration-prone Negroes. There they could escape race prejudice and join with other Afro-Americans in building a better society. The call that appeared in the *Pacific Appeal* in 1862 must have been especially appealing:

Listen, then, all ye negroes and mulattoes who in the vast Continent of America, suffer from the prejudice of caste. The Republic calls you, she invites you to bring to her your arms and minds. The regenerating work that she undertakes interests all colored people and their descendants, no matter what their origins or where their place of birth.[16]

To help its readers decide how to respond to such a call, the *Pacific Appeal* printed letters and speeches of prospective and actual migrants to Haiti. "Notes of Travel in Hayti," "Emigration to Hayti—The Port-de-Paix Brigade," and "Mr. J. P. Williams to his California Friends" appeared in 1862. Williams found Haiti unappealing; the problems of acclimating, the lack of water for cultivation, and objectionable customs among Haitians posed formidable obstacles. Haiti was "not the place for colored Americans to emigrate to."[17]

Advocates of overseas migration remained a minority among Afro-Americans, including San Franciscans, and interest in remaining in the United States increased after the Civil War. The Reconstruction amendments seemed a guarantee that the United States was serious about equal rights and opportunities for Blacks. By the late 1860s Blacks stopped discussing colonization in San Francisco newspapers. Interest in new settlements and a better life persisted, however, and so scouts sought news of new places. Before and after these national developments, Black San Franciscans ranged over the entire Pacific slope in search of opportunity and wealth. Racism in California and mineral discoveries in the Sierras spurred pioneers to travel to Canada, to the northwest territories of the United States, and to the mining communities and towns of Nevada and California. Their letters in the *Pacific Appeal* and the *Elevator* informed readers of the conditions of life and travel in these places.

In the mid-nineteenth century, Reverend John J. Moore went to the mining country and encountered "many personal friends and acquaintances" from California among the one hundred Afro-Americans in Cariboo, Canada. He believed they had "fine prospects ahead," referring to this particular mining bonanza as "the Ophir of modern times" and "a blessing to many of our colored Californians." As for race prejudice, it was reported, initially at least, that the situation was "of course more encouraging than in California, for the reason that the laws know no distinction."[18]

"Jamaica," a correspondent for the *Pacific Appeal,* believed splendid opportunities were to be found in the new community of Victoria, on Vancouver Island, British Columbia. He boasted that "the growth of our city challenges your California enterprise" and reported that some former colored Californians owned $30,000 to $40,000 in Canadian real estate. In 1864 a correspondent maintained that "the colored inhabitants of Vancouver Island are in advance of the colored people of this city in point of wealth," suggesting where Blacks should move to prosper. Still, the new settlement was marred by the age-old problem of racism. While "in some cases, the social and political position of the colored people is more favorable than here [California], . . . the Americans and Jews from

California who have settled there, have formed a public opinion unfavorable to us."[19]

Black scouts visited and commented on the mountain communities in the Sierras and settlements in the valleys and along the coast. A pioneer in Wadsworth, along the Central Pacific railroad above Sacramento, claimed that wages were magnificent. Using the slang of the times, he advised his San Francisco readers, "Boys, copper the bay and play the mountains straight up, for at least one season, and give *Lunch* a chance." Nor was this the only favorable report on the mountain towns. In 1867, a correspondent wrote that "the condition of the up country colored people, for prosperity, is of marked character. They are, as a general thing, building themselves up in an independent mode of living."[20]

Travelers noted the material progress of the colored families in towns a few miles from the bay, south along the coast, and in the inland cities of Sacramento and Stockton. Napa City, north of the bay, received praise; one correspondent emphasized the successes of wheat growers in the region. Others reported on the few Black pioneers in San Jose, Petaluma, Vallejo, and Benicia—all within a few hours' train or steamer ride of San Francisco. Sacramento earned favorable reports, and in Stockton, the colored inhabitants "appear[ed] to be in very comfortable circumstances." It was thought that Stockton "has been underrated. We believe the colored people are doing as well there as elsewhere, and there appears to be a spirit of encouragement among the whites."[21]

Despite its reputation as a place of opportunity, the American west withheld some benefits from Black citizens while it extended others. Years of experience with discrimination in the west taught Blacks to view the rest of the nation differently after the end of slavery. Travelers in eastern cities reported favorable conditions for Afro-Americans, causing some westerners to return. The author of a "Letter from Chicago" compared the midwestern city to New York, Sacramento, and San Francisco. He found little prejudice, as "all the churches . . . receive colored persons kindly and respectfully." The theatres, opera house, and concert rooms also admitted Negroes as equals. Unlike San Francisco, Blacks could ride the horse or streetcars "without insult or molestation." "In short," he concluded, Chicago "is a very pleasant and agreeable city . . . far in advance of San Francisco."[22]

Black San Franciscans constituted the largest urban Negro contingent in the far west until 1900, but with new mining discoveries and improved conditions in the south and east, they wondered how long this would last. In 1863 the *Pacific Appeal* expressed concern about the exodus from the Pacific coast metropolis. "We are certainly getting jealous of Victoria and British Columbia, for attracting so many of our most valuable men to their domain." About the same time, the *Elevator* noted: "Several of our warm personal friends have lately left this State to return east as under the new conditions of affairs the southern and western states offer a better field for enterprising colored men than California."[23]

By 1868 Black San Franciscans candidly expressed their fears that, because of its distance from the east and the segregated schools and public facilities, easterners would avoid the west and pursue opportunities elsewhere. Upon encountering discrimination on a California steamer in 1868, Reverend T. M. D. Ward wrote, "Our people in other states, hearing of this treatment will hesitate in immigrating to the Pacific coast." A traveling correspondent, visiting eastern cities, including Washington, D.C., reported on the conditions of Blacks resident there and of his unsuccessful attempts to interest them in California. The colored residents of the capitol "maintained and enjoyed a good position," so when he "preached immigration to California—they would not listen." He persistently "praised our climate and its claims, but to no avail."[24]

The optimism attending Reconstruction drew some Blacks to the south in the 1860s. This region maintained their interest through the end of Reconstruction and until the northward migration of the early twentieth century. Partly because of racial loyalties, San Francisco's (and California's) Black population remained at a few thousand until the growth of Negro Los Angeles around 1900. Nevertheless, the remaining pioneers believed the Bay Area was the best place for Negroes even if they could not convince many others, and even though they themselves left the city from time to time.

Train or steamer fare often presented a greater obstacle to Blacks than to whites. In the 1870s, sea passage from New York cost about $50, and a railroad ticket cost from $65 to $140. These prices must have been prohibitive for most country dwellers, and were quite a sum of money for workers in eastern cities. Salary earners in the competitive economy had the money—but few of them were Black. Prosperous Afro-Americans used money that could have gone for passage to support their families, to free relatives and others from bondage, and to promote abolition. Potential migrants earning good wages probably preferred to stay with employers and near relatives and friends rather than hazard migration to a new land.[25]

The rigors of sea travel also discouraged many prospective Black migrants. Unless they wished to make the difficult journey overland, the pioneers traveled by sea until the completion of the transcontinental railroad in 1869. They sailed either around the Horn or to Central America, where they crossed the isthmus. The sea voyager could expect to encounter a cold wind, then "moderate to extreme heat," and perhaps disease and pirates, too. The isthmus route from San Francisco to New York City took twenty-five days.[26]

In the West there were hardships that Blacks shared with others. Enroute to Cariboo, a shipboard passenger said the journey to Canada was "no slight affair under the most favorable circumstances." "In the first place, the preparations necessary for starting, and then the villainous accommodations, on the filthy crowded steamers, inviting sea, and all other kinds of sickness, render the journey anything but a pleasure trip, until you reach the end of that kind of conveyance." Then "a different order of troubles" was encountered—several hundred miles over mountains "equal to the fortitudes of the stoutest heart."[27]

In addition to the usual hardships, Black travelers faced special difficulties. Aboard the *Pocahontas* in 1852, Negro passengers with tickets for cabin passage were denied admission to the cabin and forced to occupy the sailors' berths while the crew took their places in the cabins. More humiliations followed. Black travelers were prevented from eating until both white passengers and crew had dined. When the ship stopped in Puerto Rico, one distinguished Black passenger was evicted from the "first table" of a restaurant on shore. Similar problems were encountered in California; Reverend Jeremiah B. Sanderson and Philip Bell reported an incident on a river steamer which marred a journey to Sacramento, and hotels and restaurants also discriminated against Blacks.[28]

If these obstacles did not discourage Black travelers, there were other difficulties unique to their ethnic group. The comparative advantages of white and Chinese travelers were reflected in their larger representation in San Francisco. For Black pioneers, the large foreign-born presence in San Francisco indicated they received aid more readily than native Afro-Americans, even though the foreign-born had to cross an ocean to reach the New World. In 1880, more than 100,000 San Franciscans (44 percent) originated overseas. Most came from Europe, but the figure also included 21,213 Chinese. In an editorial, "Immigration and Employment," the *Elevator* noted the large influx of foreigners with some concern, and discussed the factors that facilitated European and Chinese migration and hindered Negroes. Despite the demand for domestic workers and westerners' reported preference for Black servants over Chinese or white, no one promoted large-scale Afro-American migration. In fact, Californians preferred Asian and foreign white laborers over native Black citizens. Furthermore, whites were often aided by "Immigration Societies whose agencies are spread over the Eastern States and in Europe," while Blacks did "not possess like facilities." The fares of Chinese migrants were paid by capitalists who needed cheap labor, because merchants and businessmen profited from Chinese migration as they had from the migration of other foreigners.[29]

The unique situation of American Blacks was highlighted by the fact that whites asked compatriots in their native land to join them in the New

World. Chinese told their brethren of the opportunities awaiting them in California. Black Americans, on the other hand, were more likely to scour the African continent for opportunities rather than recruit African workers for the New World. Afro-Americans traveled entirely on their own, or depended upon personal ties as servants, or migrated as a result of their work on ships and trains.

Based on individual efforts, travelcraft served Afro-Americans just as immigration societies, capitalists, and Chinese companies aided foreign-born and brought them to San Francisco. It involved a particular outlook in which the determination to succeed, reflectiveness and rationality, and racial consciousness assumed important roles.

Because the best jobs were closed to them, Negroes had to be especially alert for opportunities, actively pursuing chances for money instead of waiting for them to arrive, and traveling to dismal, forlorn places. In a letter to his wife, Jeremiah B. Sanderson explained why he left Sacramento for Shasta county, hundreds of miles to the north. Snow had fallen for two weeks after his arrival when he wrote, "I have made another change; discouraged, sick at heart, and doing little in Sacramento, I was ready to do anything, accept any chance, that seemed to offer a reasonable prospect of saving something." When offered the chance to earn $2.50 a day in winter and more in the spring, he left for the distant mountainous region in northern California. The isolation he endured was typical of that suffered by many Black pioneers.[30]

Hardships were compounded by separation from relations. As noted, some left families in the east, while others housed them in San Francisco before heading for the interior. Sanderson described the travails of the Blacks, and the reasons they endured prolonged separations and hardships. "My thoughts are continually of home, of you and the children—at times I have felt anxiously and wretchedly enough to get up and start at once for home poor as I am—Heaven help me to be patient for a few months longer. I am now making one more effort to get together a few dollars, at least enough to come home to my family." He planned to stay until the end of the summer, but confided, "I know not if I shall be able to stay, but I will try." As if his wife would question the sacrifice, he asked rhetorically: "Is it for myself? No, it is because I have always hoped, and do hope to do something better for my family here than I can at home this summer."[31]

The determination and spirit necessary for lengthy and repeated trips was expressed by a Black miner in a letter to the *Elevator*. Chances for sudden riches disappeared in Silver City, Idaho Territory; everyone packed to find another bonanza. While preparing to leave, the correspondent stopped to report to his San Francisco readers. "I know not whether I will better my condition by going, but I am determined never to surrender to adversity, until the last hope has withered." He viewed hardship as a personal enemy: "I have fought him [adversity] long and hard—often he has had the best of the conflicts. I have never declined yet to give him battle when attacked by him."[32]

In addition to such determination to succeed, Black travelers had the penchant for rational analysis needed to obtain and sift useful information, to select a job or place to live, and to overcome unexpected difficulties. The necessity for deliberate reasoning was discussed in a letter from Alexander Ferguson in 1872. During a hazardous wagon trip in unsettled, forbidding country, one of his wagon's axles nearly broke in two. Keeping a cool head on discovering the danger, and not wishing to abandon his load, Ferguson considered his alternatives before sending his passengers ahead by stage. He drove very slowly over the mountain road to Santa Barbara, contemplating what he would do if his problem worsened. Shortly after his safe arrival in southern California, he wrote to the *Elevator,* "I make it a point through life to speculate as to what course I would pursue should such and such contingencies arise."[33] In a region where every undertaking was a gamble, this bent was crucial.

Black pioneers valued factual evidence to offset rumors and speculation about conditions and opportunities in distant places. Reporting from Victoria, Vancouver Island, Philip A. Bell, editor of the *Elevator,* reminded readers of the value of accurate information. "From carefully compiled statistics we learn that the yield of agricultural products . . . exceeded by four fold that of any preceeding year." Thinking probably of the original California excitement and various rumors of riches, he observed that "facts like these are of infinite advantage in forming an opinion, and are more to be valued for permanent results than the advent of thousands lured thither by an excitement which is but temporary."[34]

Discrimination in employment and travel produced a racial dimension to travelcraft. To avoid embarrassment and inconvenience, Negroes traditionally looked after their own, using an "intricate and involved system of reciprocal entertaining" to "soften the impact of prejudice on the Negro traveler." By lodging and entertaining visitors and then enjoying similar privileges while on the road, Black folk found "a method of avoiding insults in restaurants, refusals in hotels, and discrimination in places of public entertainment."[35] Debate in ethnic associations, conventions, and newspapers heightened the racial consciousness caused by oppression and developed racial awareness and pride by knitting Afro-Americans together and providing intelligence. Miners in isolated mountain communities, solitary individuals and families in distant locations, and residents of the metropolis all eagerly awaited the arrival of the San Francisco newspapers. A correspondent in Idaho Territory wrote the *Pacific Appeal:* "Your paper is the only comfort we have, to pass away the sad evening moments. . . . It is to us, in this far-off Territory, like the *Union* and *Bulletin* to the whites."[36]

Racism isolated Blacks, encouraging them to form their own newspapers and institutions, which in turn contributed to racial consciousness as much as or more than prejudice itself. What is impressive is that their outlook found expression in compiling travel intelligence and in devising methods of overcoming the difficulties. The methods of Black pioneers were predicated on their rationality and their racial outlook. Race-conscious correspondents and agents for the newspapers collected subscriptions and obtained information. The newspaper offices were clearing houses, and the editors were intelligence officers who solicited information, then decided what to publish, and perhaps even suggested what correspondents should note and communicate.

The names of a newspaper's agents and correspondents were frequently printed on the front. The October 4, 1862, *Pacific Appeal* listed thirty-three intelligence officers, including a "traveling agent," Reverend T. M. D. Ward. The town or site of each was listed; agents reported from such nearby cities as San Jose, Stockton, and Sacramento, from the interior towns of Marysville, Grass Valley, and Placerville, and from Nevada, Los Angeles, Portland, Oregon, and Canada. One agent was to be found as far away as Panama, and Peter K. Cole sent information from Japan.[37] Some of these men, for example Reverends Ward and John J. Moore, were leading citizens. In addition to the regular agents and correspondents, others occasionally provided information or services. Daniel Seales, a businessman, wrote of his travels in the east, and performed important tasks for pioneers who needed a representative to conduct their business affairs on the Atlantic coast.[38] Thanks to the agents, Black pioneers could stay abreast of business and personal affairs in distant cities and states.

Pioneers also sought the wisdom of prominent Blacks on the lecture circuit. The Bay Area churches frequently featured well-known and well-traveled Afro-Americans who spoke on a variety of topics of the day, including conditions in foreign lands or in the eastern states. Peter K. Cole addressed Black city dwellers on the economic possibilities resulting from trade with Asia. Reverend E. T. Anderson, "who spent four years in Great Britain, visited Rome and many other continental cities," lectured at the A.M.E. Church in 1890. He described "the grandeures [sic] of Europe as he saw them" and inspired San Franciscans to see these sights for themselves. The well-traveled divine also informed the audience that one did not have to stop and ask a European porter if prejudice forbade Black guests in a hotel.[39] Another visitor was Ida B. Wells, a leading Afro-American at the turn of the century. After lecturing in the United States and Europe, this courageous journalist visited the west coast and addressed San Francisco's citizens in 1895. Other speakers were the Reverend Adam Clayton Powell, Sr., father of the late congressman; James Weldon Johnson, the lawyer, scholar, and songwriter; and Booker T. Washington, head of Tuskegee Institute. Through both speaking engagements and less formal occasions, well-traveled Black citizens increased residents' understanding of their larger situation and the opportunities it held.[40]

Other important disseminators of travel information have been neglected by scholars. Workers on trains and ships aided Negro travelers, providing information, amenities, and some protection from prejudice. Because many Black San Franciscans worked on ships and trains, it is necessary to consider their importance for travelers.

"Clio," a correspondent for the *Elevator,* wrote of the important roles played by porters on the Central Pacific Railroad. While it is not clear that all porters were Black, some were, including such leading pioneers as James R. Phillips. Clio noted that train crews included "intelligent, polite and experienced employees . . . who, while attending to their duties, give the traveller every information necessary to business or pleasure." Afro-Americans listened to these respected workers "because they knowd [sic] the porters [has] been everywhere" and was "able to let people know what was happening."[41] Whenever the pioneer urbanites landed in a strange place, without friends or knowledge of the city, the service workers, who also suffered from prejudice, were invaluable. A Black sociologist noted this phenomenon. Horace Cayton was "reared in the isolation of the Pacific Northwest" and possessed "few friends" in the east or middle west, so he was not a part of the complex family–friendship system that softened the impact of prejudice for other travelers. "Not having such connections, I soon learned to size up a city with a quick look-see and a few questions directed toward persons who had specialized knowledge of the area." This twentieth-century scholar and race leader had the same consciousness of techniques and outlook that traveling Afro-Americans, similarly situated, had developed in the nineteenth century.[42]

Afro-American strangers in different cities became adept at sizing up a locale or situation and acquiring the advice they needed. Sometimes workers offered free passage or other vital help to leading Afro-Americans, friends, or relatives. Philip Bell graciously accepted when a steamer steward offered free passage to Vancouver Island from San Francisco. When Henry Collins's son Joseph became ill in the east, John Jones, a Pullman worker from San Francisco, informed the railroad's vice president of Joseph's desire to return to California. A sleeping car was added to the train for the ailing youth. Sometimes porters and ship workers acquired inexpensive or free food in the course of their travels to feed their own or other families.[43]

By the late nineteenth century, travel to the Bay Area was easier and information was more readily obtained. Cheaper fares, new railroad lines to southern California, and the dissemination of travel intelligence by Black newspapers, societies, and Pullman porters brought drastic changes. These factors, combined with increased hostility and oppression in the south, prompted mass migration. When they emerged at the end of the nineteenth century, Black migration societies might have provided settlers to enlarge San Francisco's Afro-American population. But most migrants settled in northern or eastern cities, and as early as 1886 migrants to the west chose southern California over the Bay Area. A group of Black southerners migrated to work in the vineyards and hop fields of Elias J. "Lucky" Baldwin near Los Angeles. In addition to ticket money, Baldwin provided salaries, board, and housing. Both white and Black westerners urged newcomers to locate in a region to which Afro-Americans, particularly southerners, seemed "naturally fitted."[44]

In 1910 Los Angeles contained 7,599 Blacks, and the number continued to grow while the Bay Area's contingent remained comparatively small. Elsewhere along the Pacific slope, new Black communities grew in such booming cities as Seattle, whose Black population increased from a handful in the nineteenth century to 2,296 by 1910, when it surpassed San Francisco's. By 1920 these increasing populations indicated that the new cities offered more chances for success than the old metropolis, which could not match their growth.[45]

The difficulties that the nineteenth-century pioneers overcame made them unique. They viewed adversity as a challenge, and valued courage and self-reliance. They were individualists who journeyed by themselves, or with family and a few friends, but never in large organized groups. When Afro-Americans finally traveled en masse with the help of colonization societies or recruiters, it was another era and they settled in another place. The hardy character of the pioneers was exemplified by John G. Wilson, an adventurer and former student at Oberlin College. Wilson traveled overland on the Pacific slope, searching for his fortune, even though a local doctor did "not know what keeps me alive— . . . both lungs are almost gone . . . I . . . cannot hope to get well." Similarly, Philip Bell, at the age of fifty, did not let his age prevent him from migrating from New York. On his sixtieth birthday, he boasted that he could eat "three hearty meals a day, and supper at night, and . . . drink a bottle of wine without flinching. . . . Walk four miles an hour, and tread a stately measure with a sprightly dame." It was no wonder he readily traveled to Canada via steamer and along the coast by ship and rail in the 1860s.[46]

Other characteristics acquired in their travels aided the pioneers. They developed the habit of befriending influential whites and the traveling public to obtain the things that whites won by right or because of union, family, or business associations. Black urbanites cultivated their knowledge of human character because their fortunes rose and fell according to the whims of white Americans. Especially among San Francisco's Negroes, years of traveling, working as porters or servants, and meeting with different people constituted a valuable education. Occasionally the pioneers drew praise for their faithful toil, and for pleasing employers or the public. The ubiquitous Negro handyman was described as "a right hand-y help, . . . from the driving of a nail to the driving of a bargain. . . . There is no weightier article in demand at the dinner table, than himself as a table waiter. He knows all your wants sooner than you know them yourself." The commentary concluded with an observation that is remarkable considering the nation's frequent denigration of Afro-Americans and the emphasis on their historical and social insignificance: "He is one in a community that would not be perfect without him."[47]

Their jobs and the travel experience constituted an education which could never be obtained from formal institutions of learning. A Pullman worker, Nat Love, explained what he eventually learned on the job about the public. He maintained that "porters must necessarily be good judges of human nature to be able to please the majority of people who travel under our care." Mary Ellen "Mammy" Pleasant, who rose to power, wealth, and influence to become a legend in her own time, explained that she needed no "book education," for she succeeded by studying people. "You will find such knowledge much more advantageous than all the book-learning you ever knew." After all, those "that have studied books till they knew nearly all the books in the library" become "lost out in the world" when they meet people because their knowledge remains "locked in the library."[48] The Bay Area Afro-Americans' knowledge of humanity was a singular characteristic that underlined their acute sensitivity to human needs and problems. Ironically, this characteristic was rarely recognized in Blacks in the nineteenth century, and is not attributed to them today.

Black travelers enriched the Afro-American world in the city by the bay. In 1870 Peter K. Cole noted that critics might wonder whether Negroes overseas were only returning to reap the rewards of freedom, and question why they were not around during the lean years. The Japan-based correspondent answered: "In being where we have been and being where we are in this wide world, we can bring to you a knowledge of how mankind is ruled in other spheres, from this knowledge, we will help you to deduce facts for important legislation—facts to be gathered from our demonstrations of the great peculiarities of the Eastern world."[49] The intelligence that underlay such a statement filled the newspaper columns and provided a sorely-needed perspective. It allowed readers to see their problems in a way not ordinarily permitted the descendants of slaves.

Travelcraft highlighted devotion to race, because Afro-Americans needed one another to find a place to realize their potential, to assess the degree of prejudice in various lands, and to soften the effects of racism. Jeremiah Sanderson's devotion as a provider, father, schoolteacher, and minister exemplified this love of Black folk who, according to some modern sources, are filled with self-hatred. The sentiments and actions of John G. Wilson, wandering along the Pacific coast, are an example of the race consciousness of a people often separated from family and from the mass of Afro-Americans. About to undertake an overland trip and resigned to a short life expectancy, he told *Pacific Appeal* readers, "If I fall by the way, remember, I depart with an ardent love for the rising progress of the great Africo-American people, the only love I know, next to my God, and that of my brother, . . . who I hold as dear to me as my own existence."[50]

Besides reminding us of their devotion to their cause, travelcraft was significant as an essential element in the life of the Black citizens of the Bay Area. It accounted for their presence and continued residency, for new arrivals could succeed in the urban center if they watched for the right opportunity, consulted informed citizens, and cultivated their relationships with the influential. Collecting and sifting data on routes and places was a skill that could be used in real estate or mining schemes, or in figuring where a Black person could quickly find a job. This talent was also useful for keeping an old job or acquiring a new one, so that the Pacific slope residents survived the onslaughts of white labor unions, competition with the foreign-born, and the increasingly large-scale, specialized nature of industry and commerce. Just as prejudice made the pioneers acquire travel information and adopt a mobile existence, San Francisco's specific setting promoted their adoption of a cosmopolitan way of life.

# 6

## Neighbors

*The day I was born . . . I heard all these different women, different names—like in those days you weren't born in the hospital, you were born at home, and I heard them speak about Mrs. Moriah, Mrs. Tracy, Mrs. O'Brian, Mrs. Silva, Mrs. Riposa, and Mrs. Filotta, all those different names, I said, "Doctor, hey, doc, what kind of a place is there where all these people of different nationalities come to help this old Black woman with her baby?"*
*And he said, "This is West Oakland."*
*And I said, "Well, jeez, West Oakland really must be a heaven on earth. It must be a really fine place."*
Royal E. Towns

The pioneers were neighbors of many national, ethnic, and racial groups; scattered throughout the city, they knew nothing of a ghetto. In fact, ghettos were nonexistent in all Pacific slope cities until World War I, and, in San Francisco, Oakland, and Berkeley, even beyond that date. This was also true in southern cities, as well as in Boston, New York, Chicago, Minneapolis–St. Paul, Cleveland, and Cincinnati. Thus we must revise the popular notion that the ghetto is the usual physical setting of Black urbanites.[1] In San Francisco, the different neighborhoods mirrored the social and cultural complexities of the pioneers. As the city grew, and specific sections like the waterfront and the entertainment district appeared, complex residential locations became the pattern for Afro-Americans. These areas were located in different neighborhoods and, later, in East Bay municipalities as well. Their distribution indicates that Blacks were thoroughly familiar with the entire Bay Area.

Early San Franciscans lived near their workplaces, within walking distance of the original settlement, Yerba Buena, in the midst of the business blocks. As the population rapidly increased, the city spread south of Pine Street, beyond Market Street, west to Nob Hill, and across the bay to Berkeley, Oakland, and Alameda. Real estate developers filled the swampy terrain at the bay's edge, leveled hills, extended streets, and erected buildings.

Initially, San Franciscans found accommodations along the waterfront that stretched from south of Market Street around the tip of the peninsula and west almost to Fort Mason. If not on the urban perimeter, near the foot of Broadway, they dwelled in central business blocks along Montgomery, Kearney, and Dupont (later known as Grant). Some resided on Market Street, the city's widest boulevard, which ran diagonally southwest from the northeast tip of the peninsula. They dwelled on east-west streets like Pacific, Washington, and Clay, and later on the routes south of Pine, and on secluded back lanes like Hinkley, Pinkney, Scott, and Stone, in houses and flats, above shops, and in rooms for boarders.[2]

Throughout its history, the city's many hills have been "barometers of wealth and position." Beginning in the seventies, silver kings and railroad barons built palaces atop Nob Hill. Below the summit dwelled the moderately well-to-do. Still lower, businessmen, tourists, transients, and various citizens found situations in the downtown hotels, in lodging houses, and in ethnic enclaves. After 1906, affluent San Franciscans occupied the expensive hotels and apartments on Nob and Russian Hills, and the less fortunate inhabited the slopes.

Even with the development of the flatlands south of Market and Pine in the 1860s, and the advent of cable cars in the following decade, San Franciscans remained neighbors within walking distance of each other. They preferred living in a tightly packed cluster in the midst of businesses, shops, and offices, remaining between Van Ness and the waterfront until the earthquake and fire.

Blacks also inhabited the walking district of nineteenth-century San Francisco. Some lived near the waterfront, especially in the 1850s. Others resided in the entertainment districts, such as the Barbary Coast and along lower Broadway. A few lived in Spanish-speaking enclaves near Kearney Street and Broadway. Most stayed around the residential area at Broadway and Powell (Fourth Ward) and, after 1870, in the artisans' and workingmen's districts south of Market near Third Street. Table 7 gives their residential patterns and distribution in 1870. The difficulties of enumeration in a large city were particularly apparent in Ward Four, where residences, businesses, churches, government offices, and Chinatown were all jammed together.[3] Unlike the Blacks, the Chinese, considered by contemporaries to be the most foreign of foreigners, lived in a few square

Table 7

U.S. and San Francisco Enumerations, by Color and by Ward, 1870

| Ward | White | | Black | |
|---|---|---|---|---|
| | U.S. | S.F. | U.S. | S.F. |
| 1 | 10,385 | 10,426 | 77 | 77 |
| 2 | 11,359 | 11,368 | 145 | 137 |
| 3 | 2,400 | 2,509 | 13 | 6 |
| 4 | 10,282 | 10,672 | 621 | 389 |
| 5 | 2,758 | 2,790 | 3 | 3 |
| 6 | 6,139 | 6,250 | 216 | 220 |
| 7 | 10,228 | 10,189 | 16 | 12 |
| 8 | 16,006 | 16,188 | 88 | 89 |
| 9 | 10,420 | 10,564 | 49 | 49 |
| 10 | 21,985 | 22,099 | 48 | 46 |
| 11 | 21,825 | 22,003 | 43 | 45 |
| 12 | 12,270 | 12,343 | 22 | 21 |
| TOTAL | 136,057* | 137,401 | 1,341 | 1,094 |

*Total is incorrectly given as 136,059 in the *Directory.*
SOURCE: Henry G. Langley, comp., *The San Francisco Directory, 1872,* p. 13.

blocks in the eastern part of Ward Four. But as late as 1940, the Black San Franciscans maintained their dispersal, spreading out with the city's population to new areas of the metropolis.

The changing waterfront reflected San Francisco's development in shipping and transportation; its growth marked the formation of a metropolitan area. More and larger piers and wharves penetrated its waters as the city expanded, and its waterfront was lined by a variety of ocean-going vessels, river steamers, ferries, and smaller craft, crowded with a hodgepodge of wheeled vehicles on shore, and populated by tourists, adventurers, hackmen, and seamen. The piers, which extended the city into the bay, and the variety of people highlighted San Francisco's inter-dependence with the far west and the world. In the twentieth century, the waterfront functioned even more as a zone of transition for the metropolitan area. Oakland possessed a substantial waterfront of its own, where oceanic vessels docked and local ferries landed. It was a familiar sight for East Bay-bound urbanites, commuting workers, and East Bay residents out for a night in San Francisco.[4]

Black sailors inhabited this, one of the roughest, most notorious waterfronts in the United States, from pioneer days. In 1860, 16 percent of San Francisco's Afro-Americans lived there, often because of connections with sea travel, along with newcomers and other residents. Boarding-house keepers maintained accommodations, and also provided banking and employment services. Colored sea rovers, cooks, and waiters resided in these establishments, some of which were run by Afro-Americans.

The Golden Gate Boarding House, probably at Broadway near Sansom, accommodated thirty Blacks, mostly mariners and cooks, in 1860. At the foot of Broadway, Abraham Cox, a seaborne waiter, ran the Pioneer Seamen's Boarding and Lodging House. In 1866, John Callender, another former seamen, assumed control of the establishment. Callender, his family, two Black sailors, and thirteen lodgers from Europe and the United States lived there in 1880. As the seasons changed, so did his customers. When the whaling fleet arrived in one autumn, a newspaper reported: "Colored gentlemen of every shade frequent his hostelry, and there remain until their hard-earned dollars have finished."[5] This milieu was as harsh and violent for the ordinary seaman as his conditions of work, particularly in the nineteenth century. Mariners, who had few rights until the twentieth century, probably suffered more if they were Afro-American, as that group could not rise through the ranks and become officers until well into the twentieth century. They remained ordinary seamen, just as Negroes on shore were destined to occupy menial positions all their lives.[6]

When they came ashore, the Black seamen were prey for avaricious boarding-house keepers and were likely to be shanghaied. In 1873 Edward J. Scott, a ship's steward, was drugged and robbed after one beer in a resort appropriately named Hell's Kitchen. Aurelious Alberga recalled a saloon, The Last Chance, where a trap door was used to kidnap unwary sailors. Hoodlums or "footpads" waited outside the "blind tigers" (illegal saloons without liquor licenses), dance halls, dives, and underground melodeons.[7]

These conditions changed somewhat as seamen's unions emerged and after reforms in working conditions, beginning in the late nineteenth century. Equally important, the waterfront's role changed. An urban transportation revolution led to more warehouses, wharves, and factories, and fewer accommodations on the waterfront. Thousands of rush-hour commuters passed through these sites every morning and late afternoon.[8]

In the twentieth century, fewer Blacks inhabited the waterfront, but transients and seamen still spent time there. When trains supplanted passenger ships, Blacks worked as redcaps, cooks, waiters, and porters, while others became newspaper vendors, bootblacks, and lodging-house operators. They congregated near the transbay terminal, at the railroad depot on Third and Townsend, and across the bay on Seventh Street and near the Oakland Mole, where the trains crossed the bay to San Francisco.[9] At such active spots, Afro-Americans learned of distant places and gauged the variety of citizens of the metropolis. When William E. Towns, an early settler who worked on the trains at the turn of the century, took his youngest son, Royal, to the Ferry Building, he explained the workings of the metropolis, pointed out a clamshell dredge, and, as Royal recalled, informed him that the vessels had names for identification.[10] Like William Towns, the Black inhabitants and workers of this zone served as bridgeheads to the distant world for isolated Afro-Americans on the Pacific slope. They taught Negro urbanites of the faraway places whose vessels, products, and citizenry made San Francisco a worldly spot.

The famous entertainment districts were another dimension of city life. The Barbary Coast and the Tenderloin housed both permanent inhabitants and tourists and transients. The oldest entertainment area, the Barbary Coast, matched in notoriety New Orleans's Storyville. It was linked with the waterfront by resorts on Pacific and Broadway streets and was bounded by Stockton, Kearney, Broadway, and Washington. In its heyday the Coast possessed "a few dives . . . patronized by negroes and drunken sailors, and where white and colored women of the lowest class [were] employed as waitresses." Similar places lined the streets near the bay south of Market.[11]

As the Coast declined in importance in the nineteenth century, spin-offs appeared on Morton Street (now Maiden Lane) near Union Square and along Dupont between Bush and Pine. On Berry, Morton, and Dupont streets, "the windows are left open, [and] half-naked and brazenfaced, painted prostitutes are seated at pianos playing and singing lewd songs, while others are standing at the doors in tights inviting every passerby to enter." Men of all ages, messenger boys, and policemen collecting graft entered the resorts that came to form the Tenderloin.[12] In the 1870s a new entertainment district emerged along Market Street near Third and Fourth, amidst hucksters, charlatans, patent medicine dealers, and actors and actresses from the theatres near Union Square. In the twentieth century, East Bay cities, seaside resorts, and new neighborhoods possessed night clubs and vice centers. Regardless of their location, the nineteenth century resorts were crowded and noisy at all hours.

From pioneer days, Black San Franciscans participated in the life of the entertainment districts. Their involvement ranged from jobs as entertainers to the usual positions as cooks, waiter girls, and porters, to roles as rounders or "sports"—swaggering urbanites out for a night of good times. Some Black workers and members of the sporting crowd won a measure of fame, success, and independence, while others earned little money and less recognition. They engaged in legal and illegal activities in a milieu where respectable and underworld citizens met and commingled in search of good times and profits. As in the ordinary business and workaday world, racism and discrimination limited Afro-Americans' opportunities and dimmed their successes.[13]

Some Afro-American prostitutes lived on side streets with co-workers of every nationality. In 1880, a few Black prostitutes occupied a Morton Street address with thirty-five other prostitutes; a few more resided several blocks west of the Coast, on Morse Place, and one lone Black prostitute dwelled with six white women, a housekeeper, and a boarder, at 502½ Broadway.[14]

Blacks who won a degree of fame in the districts inspired the anonymous urbanites who toiled as porters or as waiter girls. Deacon Jones gained recognition and respect as the vigilant bodyguard of the operator of the Bella Union, a famous resort on Portsmouth Square, in the 1870s and 1880s. Another Negro served Calico Jim, a Chilean, in the same capacity. John Tuers, a Black minstrel and pistol marksman, became famous among the sporting crowd after his pistol discharged in Snug's during a brawl, killing a well-known theatre manager. He was acquitted at the second trial. The "large attendance of theatrical and sporting men," and the favorable testimony of witnesses, showed the respect and support a Black person could get in a milieu whose members showed considerable loyalty to one another.[15]

Black-owned saloons and night clubs drew Afro-Americans along with other city dwellers to the entertainment districts. Gamblers were to be found in the resorts on Broadway and Pacific streets, and in 1865 the *Elevator* complained, "We can scarcely go into a place of entertainment of any kind but we hear the falling of cards, the rattle of the dice-box, and the oaths and imprecations which usually accompany such 'amusement.'" "Match games" around the billiard table were the rage in the 1870s. Some church members were said to spend "half their time and all their money in the Chinese Lotteries."[16]

Scattered throughout the city, the Black resorts were never numerous or close enough to form a distinct Afro-American district. A traveler of the 1860s and 1870s might visit The Iron Clad at 420 Pacific, near Sansom Street; at the Lincoln Exchange, at 823 Washington near Stockton; in William H. Hall's billiard saloon on Mason near Vallejo; or at Snug's, at Powell and John streets.[17] Later in the century, Black saloons and clubs moved with the expanding city and the newly emerging entertainment areas that, in the San Francisco tradition, were adjacent to residences. The Arcadia Club rooms, at 11 Stockton (near Market), offered drinks, cigars, and billiards. South of Market Street, Black clubs of the 1890s included the Acme at 668 Mission Street, the Unique Saloon and Club Rooms at 189 Jessie, and The Lotus, featuring gentlemen's private club rooms, at 24 Third Street.[18]

In the twentieth century, Blacks desiring drink, companionship, or diversion went to Purcell's on the Barbary Coast, the Bancroft Cafe at 236

Townsend Street, or the Cafe Dixie at 750 Pacific Street. In West Oakland, Blacks met at several places along Seventh Street near the railroad tracks. Some of these places were important centers for Afro-American song and dance. Purcell's, for example, drew slummers and celebrities out for a night on the town, including the famous Russian ballerina, Anna Pavlova, and her escort, Arnold Genthe, the San Francisco photographer, one night around World War I.[19]

Night club men, entertainers, boxers, bodyguards, and waiter girls lived the bohemian life of the entertainment districts. Knowledgeable of the various ranks and customs of this complex milieu, skilled raconteurs and entertainers, known and respected among the denizens, they experienced the freedom and variety of acquaintances their sensitive natures required. They moved on from one resort to the next in an evening on the town in the same way that they shifted from one city to another, experiencing the freedom, sense of adventure, and allure of glamor that characterized these urban locales.[20]

Like the waterfront, the entertainment districts provided a freedom and gaiety that lightened the burdens of Black workers and that gave San Francisco drawing power. The glamor and bright lights both enticed sinners and slummers and provided opportunities for the occupants of Morton, Pacific, Broadway, and Market Streets. The districts drew entertainers from as far as the Atlantic states and Europe and audiences from the entire Pacific slope; they also provided graft for policemen and civic officials. Political ties made it possible for the districts to exist in open defiance of conventional standards until Prohibition.

After the entertainment and waterfront areas, ethnic enclaves were a third element in San Francisco life. Because of cultural ties, and to escape white racism, a handful of Blacks resided in the Mexican, Italian, and Chinese enclaves of the city center. There were a number of national, ethnic, and linguistic neighborhoods or enclaves, including Chinatown, unique among U.S. cities, which struck visitors as "a small section of an actual Chinese city." Parts of the downtown reflected Spanish-Mexican, Irish, Italian, and later Japanese influences. The ethnic districts date from the 1850s and still exist today. Some were distinctive in architecture, while others blended with the drab buildings typical of the urban settlement. Frequently overlapping one another and dispersed above stores and behind businesses, the clusters of foreign-born imparted a cosmopolitan quality to San Francisco's architecture, streets, cuisine, and tenor of life.[21] Chinatown, the Mexican quarter, and the Italian settlements in North Beach and on Telegraph Hill stemmed from rapid and recent settlement by foreigners who wished to cling to their cultures. The desire to recreate past settings expressed itself in the clustering of foreign-born, in architecture reminiscent of distant homelands, and in the languages heard in those areas.

The contrasts between the ethnic neighborhoods resulted from the fact that, aside from a desire for money and residence in the same city, San Franciscans lacked a common cause or background. The communities distributed through the downtown blocks represented both the residents' diverse interests and their heterogeneous backgrounds. The singularity of the metropolis, particularly before the earthquake and fire, lay in its polyglot character, established several decades before the "new" immigration to and the rise of foreign-born ghettos in eastern cities.[22] Living in these enclaves shaped the lives of some Blacks and attracted others. Some pioneers lived among ethnic groups with common cultural and linguistic ties. Blacks with Spanish surnames and Central and Latin American origins occasionally lived with Mexicans, Panamanians, Peruvians, and Portuguese.

Infinite combinations of heritage and culture resulted in a region newly colonized by varied ethnic and national groups, where individuals associated with one another according to their inclinations. Fifteen Afro-San Franciscans resided with Mexican and Spanish-surnamed urbanites near Kearney and Broadway in 1880. A foreign-born Black was apt to be of African descent and Central American background, or a dark-skinned Iberian, or not Black at all, but a Hispanicized Indian, whose dark complexion confused the census taker. Determining a resident's background and racial heritage is difficult, if not impossible, for the contemporary scholar, just as it was for the federal census enumerator.[23]

The area around the 500 block of Broadway reflected the mix of nationalities and the way their neighborhoods overlapped. Although part of the Barbary Coast, and situated on the edge of Chinatown, the area housed a number of Central Americans, Latin Americans, and Italians on Kearney, Hinkley, and Pinkney streets. It also had a governmental character, as the county jail was located in the 500 block. The dwelling at 522 Broadway represented in microcosm San Francisco's mix of nationalities, races, and linguistic groups. A Black cook from Peru named José Seminario, his Panamanian wife, their four children (all but one born in Panama), and a Mexican boarder (designated "mulatto") lived at this address. A Black Panamanian with the family name of Cajar and two Mexican Black women with Spanish surnames shared the site. In the various apartments Chileans, European-born Irish, Italians, and Germans, and United States citizens mingled. The same pattern was found offshore. The U.S.S. *Pensacola*, which was anchored in the bay, was home for several foreign-born Blacks, principally from the West Indies and the Canary Islands.

*William E. Towns exhibits the refined manner typical of Black pioneers. He had ample reason to pose proudly; head of a large family, he knew some Spanish and Chinese, was an agent for the San Francisco* Elevator, *and was treasurer of the Brannan Guards, a Black military society. In the five decades he lived in the Bay Area, Towns worked as a cook for the transcontinental railroad line under construction in the Sierras, as a porter on the steamer* Princess, *and on various Pullman trains. He also preserved photographs of his family and travels, some of which are now in the collection of his son, Royal. Royal E. Towns Collection.*

*A stereotypical portrayal of an Afro-American from the early twentieth century. The white men have individual characteristics—moustaches, different kinds of hats, eyeglasses, and facial wrinkles. The Black man's face is more of a mask, a mark of his inferiority, and his white coat and brushes also signify his low status. Such cartoons appeared regularly in newspapers and magazines. San Francisco* Chronicle, *August 5, 1914.*

*This unidentified woman left a striking image of a successful late nineteenth-century Black. Consider the amount of time and work that went into preparing her hair and clothing, accumulating money for the jewelry and the richly-tiered dress, and cleaning and maintaining the apparel. Note the material at the collar and cuffs—there are pleats, lace, and possibly ruffles. The front of the bodice and bottom of the skirt are also decorated and bordered in different fabrics. Certainly the photographer at the Elite studio on Market Street was technically accomplished, but the serene confidence and beauty of his subject made possible an image that is still arresting after a hundred years. Courtesy of Bancroft Library.*

*Captain William T. Shorey, from Barbadoes, went to sea, ended up in San Francisco, and commanded whaling vessels. At the turn of the century he and his wife, Julia Ann, and children, Zenobia Pearl (left) and Victoria Grace, spent many months at sea. The richness of this studio portrait suggests the prosperity some residents attained. California Historical Society.*

*Photograph albums were often a standard size. A pocket-sized one such as this is rare. Walter L. Gibson Collection.*

*Royal E. Towns, in one of several children's photographs in his family collection. These photos reflect Black parents' love and adoration of their children. Royal Towns preserved family records and became an avid photographer, passing these documents and interests on to his descendants. Royal E. Towns Collection.*

*California-born children of William E. and Alice Rochford Towns, who came to the Bay Area in the 1850s. From left to right: Wallace, Henry, Nellie, and William. Royal E. Towns Collection.*

*An unidentified cosmopolite. Royal E. Towns Collection.*

*Charles H. Tinsley displays the bearing suitable for a Palace Hotel bellman. He was one of the employees who was fired in 1896 and replaced by white men. He later worked as a butler, waiter, and insurance salesman. This gentlemen also liked to perform in Shakespearean productions. Lora Toombs Scott Collection.*

*This Butler family portrait of the father and his sons shows the pride, sense of poise, and formal bearing of pioneer urbanites. Standing (left to right): Abraham Lincoln, John Hanson, Jr., Floyd, William Wesley. Seated (left to right): Charles Sumner, John Hanson, Sr., Walter Archibald, and Benjamin Franklin Butler. Circa 1905. Courtesy of Bancroft Library.*

*Kate Grasses enjoyed some financial and job security as a postal employee. Born in California, she was the granddaughter of Reverend Jeremiah B. Sanderson, who migrated west in the 1850s. Courtesy of Bancroft Library.*

*A well-dressed urbanite from the collection of Mary ("Mayme") Netherlands.*
*East Bay Negro Historical Society.*

*Ethel Terrell, from New Jersey, came to San Francisco in the 1920s as a pianist and leader of the Syncopated Seven, on the Keith and Orpheum vaudeville circuit. She settled down, continued to play, married, moved to Oakland, and participated in Bay Area civic and social life. Ethel Terrell.*

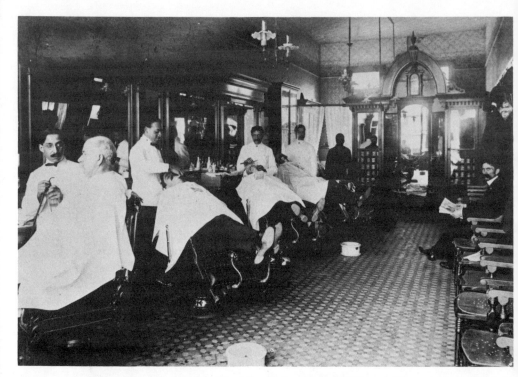

*Many prominent pioneers were barbers. The Mint Barbershop of William A. Towns (standing far left) at Tenth and Broadway in Oakland accommodated four patrons at a time. In such a setting, barbers and customers discussed politics, sports, and the affairs of men. Royal E. Towns Collection.*

Black residents had a number of options on where to live in the city, one of which was to stay with the Chinese. Described as a "coal black" Spaniard, Ong Fung Yu lived with the Chinese for nearly three decades. Born in Spain and named Montoya, he went to sea, was shipwrecked off the Chinese mainland, and spent twenty-seven years in servitude in China. When his master emigrated to San Francisco in 1881, Ong Fung Yu accompanied him and then gained his freedom. Interviewed in the mining country, he explained in Spanish that he preferred to associate with his adopted countrymen, to wear their clothes, and to speak what had become as much his language as theirs. In the twentieth century, as well, Blacks lived with Chinese for various reasons.[24] Jean Ng, "a well-known character of San Francisco's demi-monde," resided at 520 Pacific (formerly Lester Mapp's Olympia and before that Purcell's), where the Coast and Chinatown met. Born in Kansas of Afro-American parents, she seems to have abandoned her ties to marry a Chinese rooming-house operator and underworld figure. When she died shortly after her husband, her adopted people claimed the body, prepared it for the funeral, and interred it in their cemetery in 1934.[25]

Few Afro-Americans went that far, but some associated with or, if necessary, claimed to be foreigners. Occasionally traveling musicians roomed with Chinese to avoid white discrimination. "There used to be a hotel next to the Orpheum on O'Farrell Street," Ethel Terrell, a bandleader and pianist, recalled. "That's where I stayed. And then as now people would come in San Francisco and didn't know where to stay, you stayed in Chinatown because they would always receive you. The Chinese would always let you stay anyplace where other people would not accept you." At least one informant, drawing upon her Panamanian background, assumed a Spanish identity to find accommodations for her large family in San Francisco.[26]

More typical were the Black individuals and families living on secondary streets or back lanes near Broadway and Powell and behind the Palace Hotel on Market Street. Prosperous Blacks resided on Sacramento and Washington Streets in the Fourth and Sixth Wards. In the 1870s newcomers inhabited the long narrow streets of Minna, Tehama, and Natoma, a few Black families to a city block. A total of four Afro-American families lived in the 1100 and 1200 blocks of Clay Street among German- and American-born residents in 1880. Similarly, the 100 block of Tehama housed ninety-seven whites, eight Chinese, and eight Afro-Americans.[27]

The largest contingent of Black pioneers (nearly 33 percent) inhabited the Fourth Ward (between Chinatown and Russian Hill) in 1880, but they were nonetheless widely dispersed. On Auburn Street fourteen Afro-

Americans lived among 103 urbanites, including Irish, West Indians, Germans, Mexicans, and Italians. Even on Stone Street, off Washington and Powell, the high percentage of Negroes (thirty-four of fifty-three citizens) resulted from two Black boarding houses located in this narrow lane. More commonly, Blacks lived in frame buildings next door to whites, sometimes sharing homes with them.[28]

A number of Afro-American gathering places, including the three Black churches, sat on the east slope of Russian Hill west of Chinatown. The two Methodist churches were on Stockton near Sacramento and on Powell near Jackson. The Baptist Church was also on Powell, between Bush and Sutter. Young Men's Hall, Prince Hall Masonic rooms, and billiard parlors were found on Broadway or on Pacific near Powell. The traditionally Black-operated boarding houses, one at 28 Stone Street and another at 1109 Stockton Street, were nearby. While the twentieth century brought important new developments in Black residential patterns, the Afro-American pioneers remained scattered over the metropolitan area.[29]

Across the Bay in West Oakland, Berkeley, and Alameda, Negroes similarly lived among native and foreign-born whites. John T. Callender, Ezekiel Cooper, and Jeremiah B. Sanderson lived in the East Bay in the late nineteenth century. Other Black pioneers soon followed, most of them living near the railroad terminals and the harbor west of downtown Oakland. The West Indian sea captain, William Shorey, and his family resided at 1774 Division Street. Their neighbors included an actor, a marine engineer, and their families (at 1778); a Swedish-born boilermaker (at 1770); an English railroad car repairman and three lodgers (at 1768); and an English railroad foreman and his family. All were white.

Near Brush Street, just south of the railroad tracks that ran down Seventh Street (where the elevated Bay Area Rapid Transit runs today), lived a number of Afro-Americans. A cook from British Guiana and his family inhabited a one-story frame house at 804 Brush. Across the street at 805 lived a carpenter, his wife, and their in-laws. A little way up, in two attached flats, were another Black couple and three boarders and lodgers (one white). A white Irish domestic probably owned these dwellings at 812. Further along lived a day laborer, his wife, grown children, and their spouses (860). Two Black families shared a two-story dwelling around the corner on Fifth Street (721), and on Sixth Street Afro-American families occupied one, one-and-a half, and two-story frame structures (713, 721, 758, 760, 765).[30]

These Black living trends call for an explanation, particularly in the older urban area. In a city famed for its ethnic neighborhoods and heterogeneous population, no "Negro quarter" existed. The *Chronicle* observed this in 1904, pointing out that San Francisco's Blacks were the prosperous descendants of pioneer servants and businessmen. According to J. S. Francis, the editor of the *Western Outlook,* the reasons for this were simple. Colored citizens were "allowed to rent in most parts of the city" as "no strong color line [was] drawn in this city." Their singular status, he claimed, resulted from the fact that "influential members of the race" actually discouraged "the undesirable element" from coming to the city and aided only those "negroes of education and general eligibility." The article is the only mention of a Black district, or the absence of one, in San Francisco until 1944.[31]

In a study of Bay Area Negroes during World War II, Charles S. Johnson, the noted Black sociologist, observed that until the 1940s "no rigidly segregated Negro community existed in the city." Unlike eastern cities, "Negro inhabitants were to some degree lost in the city's population complex." Even as, in the 1930s, they congregated along Fillmore Street, one site of today's ghetto, they lived among Japanese, Chinese, Filipinos, and "sizeable groups of whites."[32]

Because before the 1940s Blacks migrated as individuals and over a long period of time, they scattered over a wide area. They found accommodations as single family units and as individuals, not as a large contingent of newcomers. On the other hand, we know that when thousands of Blacks suddenly entered a city, as in the east during World War I and in the Bay Area during World War II, the familiar ghetto resulted. (The same institution emerged when masses of foreign-born whites occupied American cities.) Discrimination, profit-seeking real estate agents, and housing shortages promoted ghettos more than did any desire of Blacks to live together. Varying occupations and specific preferences among Negro San Franciscans also accounted for their scattered locations.

The presence of dark-skinned inhabitants from southern Europe, Latin America, Oceania, and Asia, and traditions of cosmopolitanism enabled Blacks to enjoy uncommonly numerous options in terms of neighborhood locations. Black culture also assumed an important role in permitting their distribution in the city. American customs, institutions, and language were the heritage of the vast majority of pioneer urbanites, and, when merit and ability were the sole criteria, they found easy access to different sections of society. But merit and ability were not the only standards, and discrimination barred entry to some places. Yet to an extent their color also worked in their favor, permitting entrance to certain circles as servants and menials, jobs which would have been denied them if they were considered equals.

With their knowledge of the language and customs of the United States and San Francisco, the pioneers acquired job skills, a degree of literacy, and a variety of social contacts out of the reach of recently arrived European and Asian immigrants. Such foreign-born residents needed years, if not generations, to acquire vital language and job skills and to adjust to the American urban scene, unless they possessed wealth, high social station, or professional training when they came to the U.S.

San Francisco and Oakland Blacks learned the accents, intonations, jokes, and vocabularies of their foreign neighbors. Royal E. Towns maintained that his association with a variety of urban dwellers allowed him to learn many distinctive speech patterns and idioms. He said that a uniquely cosmopolitan atmosphere existed in West Oakland (and the Bay Area) because so many national and ethnic groups shared a tradition of neighborliness, cooperation, and goodwill. To illustrate what a Black child might learn, he recited incidents and jokes in first an Irish and then a Jewish accent.

Towns told of visiting his son on a ship in Brooklyn Harbor in New York in the 1940s. Stopped by an Irish policeman, Towns explained that his son was in the merchant marine, but the Irishman, "with all the flannel on his tongue that he could possibly have, he said, 'No yuz don't,' he says, 'nobody goes down to the ship, and arders is arders.'" Towns then showed him his identification, indicating he was a lieutenant in the Oakland Fire Department and had a port pass for San Francisco. "'I don't give a damn who you are, you just don't go down to the ship,' he says, and 'arders is arders.'" Towns replied, "'You know something, you are the first Irishman that ever believed me. When was you born—in the year of the black potatoes or the year of the big wind?' And he said, 'Where did you get the blarney?' I said, 'Out where I live.' He said, 'Many Irishmen out there?' I said, 'Ha! I was born in old man O'Brian's house right next to Mr. Tracy's,' and I said, 'There's O'Boyle, O'Hallihan, McAllister, . . . ' and jeez, I started naming a whole gang of micks, you know, and he said 'Wait a minute, wait a minute!' He said, 'Hey, Pat, come here and take this Irishman down to the boat.' (Laughter.) It's all in knowing the language or the vernacular of the particular ethnic group that you live with. . . . This has happened in many instances in my life where I have utilized some of the things I learned from those kids down there [in West Oakland]."[33]

By contrast, Asian and European migrants sometimes balked at learning English, and often retained an accent or manner of speaking that evinced their origins. The accents and dialects, not to mention the languages, that characterized San Francisco were evidence of the recent arrival and distant origins of many of its inhabitants. While foreign newcomers attempted to preserve their traditions, Afro-American culture was not only American, but had been American for several generations. If it served their ends, Blacks learned the languages of the newcomers, thus acquiring a European and Asian veneer.

Asian and European immigrants, in fact, preserved their original cultures while learning American ways in San Francisco, re-creating their homelands in their ethnic enclaves. Newcomers imported countrymen, foods, and goods to surround themselves with familiar remnants of home. Afro-Americans, on the contrary, felt little desire to bring anything but a bit of New Orleans, Philadelphia, or New York City to the far western metropolis. They were at home any place in the American city where prejudice did not make conditions intolerable; the variety of their neighborhood locations, and their eventual shift from the city center highlighted their familiarity with the urban scene much as their speech evidenced a native acquaintance with American culture. The dispersal of pioneer urbanites, and their shifting locations accompanying the city's expansion, contradict those who desire to see all Black urban life in the ghetto environment.[34]

In 1906, the earthquake and fire all but destroyed downtown San Francisco. Residents moved temporarily to the lightly settled Western Addition beyond Van Ness Avenue and to the growing East Bay, Oakland in particular. The city was quickly rebuilt, but large business blocks and expensive hotels rose where businesses and residences had been mixed. The well-to-do and the Chinese built stores and accommodations in the downtown districts. The growing metropolis penetrated the residential Western Addition and enveloped suburbs which were sometimes cities in their own right. The typical Black San Franciscan located in these expanding regions, inhabiting the rowhouses and flats along Bush, Pine, Sutter, and Post Streets, rooms above stores on Divisadero and Fillmore, or the larger homes of Oakland. East Bay residents, who depended on trolleys, trains, and ferries to travel to the city center, had overcome their inclination to dwell more than walking distance from downtown.[35]

By World War I the Bay Area's residential patterns had crystallized. This was partly due to the growth of industry in the East Bay, but transportation changes were also crucial to both the city's expansion and the new living patterns of Blacks. The introduction of cable cars in the 1870s accelerated the city's growth and settlement of the steep hills. Eventually electric trolleys and rapid trains enabled San Franciscans to live some distance from their workplaces in the city center, while an efficient ferry system hastened the growth of Oakland and Berkeley. The ferries traveled at regular intervals, and in 1912 carried 15,000 transbay commuters during each rush hour. The advent of the automobile and consolidation of the city's transportation system around World War I spurred suburban development. Construction of the Bay and Golden Gate bridges in the 1930s facilitated the movement of trains, trucks, automobiles, and commuters. As distinct commercial and residential neighborhoods appeared, the new mobility of commuters complicated matters.

Swiftly moving motorized transportation (public and private) obliterated distinctions between the city proper and its surrounding regions, whether suburbs, countryside, or seaside resorts.[36]

Bay Area Blacks took advantage of the residential shift and adopted the new life style, embracing suburban ways more readily than other urbanites. After 1906 a few relocated on Russian Hill, in the city center, and in the Western Addition, but by 1910 most Bay Area Afro-Americans lived in Oakland. In the 1920s, when San Francisco's total population out-numbered Oakland's by more than two to one, almost twice as many Blacks lived in Oakland as in San Francisco. Usually viewed as members of American society's rear guard, Blacks had adopted a life style that would not become the norm until the mid-twentieth century.[37]

In the nineteenth century, Blacks who lived in the city center for convenience's sake often used the pastoral East Bay for excursions and picnics. As early as 1880 nearly six hundred Afro-Americans lived in Oakland, constituting the second-largest group of Black city dwellers in the state. Oakland's rustic character disappeared during the economic boom of the 1890s, but the city retained a decidedly suburban atmosphere and, characteristically, a lower population density than San Francisco. The East Bay's proximity, suburban character, expanding economy, cheaper rents, and larger homes accounted for the more than 8,000 Afro-Americans in Oakland and more than 3,000 in Berkeley by World War II.[38] The Black migration to the East Bay in the 1890s also followed the rise of the white labor unions that excluded Blacks from their traditional positions (see Chapter 3). Afro-Americans found jobs quite readily on the trains which terminated in Oakland; as these positions were reserved for Blacks, discrimination forced them to adapt to new trends while whites stayed in San Francisco.[39]

The East Bay's cheap and available housing also caused many pioneer families to relocate. Though as a rule racism was not as rigidly imposed on Afro-Americans as it was on Chinese in California, it eventually affected Negroes' housing choices. There are no complaints about housing discrimination in the remaining copies of the nineteenth-century Black newspapers; probably San Francisco life was initially so rich that when discrimination occurred, it hardly mattered. Perhaps city folk were too busy seeking wealth to exclude Blacks from neighborhoods or even from households. At any rate the problem of discrimination in housing was first mentioned in a white newspaper in 1889.[40] Richard C. O. Benjamin, author, newspaperman, and political organizer, argued that San Francisco was as prejudiced as the south. "Right here in San Francisco," he exclaimed, "it is impossible for respectable negro families to rent homes except in certain communities." Eighteen years later, the Oakland *Sunshine* echoed this sentiment. "To live in either of the [Bay] cities, it is almost necessary for you to own your own home; rents are high and real estate agents do not care to rent to Negroes." One advantage of suburban living was that homes could be purchased "at the price of a monthly rental." In the 1920s, an informant said, discrimination made it all but impossible to obtain anything but "rundown" accommodations in San Francisco.[41] In 1930 Black householders in San Francisco paid an average of five dollars per month more than their counterparts in Oakland, usually for less space. The East Bay's lots were wider than San Francisco's, making possible commodious houses, yards, and gardens, and room for children.[42]

A conscious choice of alternatives was evident in the move to Oakland. Rather than flee the metropolis because of job discrimination, expensive housing, and increasing racism, devotees of the Bay Area moved to new residential sections. Faced with limited opportunities, the Black urban dwellers devoted their time and energy to improving their immediate home environment, buying spacious houses in the East Bay or comfortable Victorian dwellings in San Francisco's Western Addition. The less expensive East Bay homes freed portions of householders' budgets to buy furnishings, plant flowers, and devote space to their children's play activities. The new suburban residential districts provided a quieter setting that contrasted with the expensive, crowded, noisy, downtown districts.

It is impossible to ascertain how many Blacks moved to the East Bay at the turn of the century. What is significant is that adoption of the suburban life style, based on motor transport, entailing residency in a neighborhood far from downtown, and implying an affinity for trees, flower gardens, and more space, distinguished the pioneers from the average American and from many San Franciscans. The pioneers embraced the new pattern more quickly than most Americans, white or Black, because they were flexible and willing to seek new opportunities to better their lives. They chose to enrich their home lives because other forms of advancement were not readily available. In the late nineteenth century, as working conditions worsened due to labor competition and chances for wealth dwindled, home and family became the new means of expressing ideals.

For newcomers to the Bay Area, the East Bay offered both jobs and an attractive physical locale that especially appealed to migrants from southern small towns and crowded, dirty eastern cities. Noisy, expensive, and exclusive, San Francisco repelled all but the most cosmopolitan and skilled newcomers; the high cost of living there also discouraged migrants with families. When single Black San Franciscans married, they moved to the East Bay for the welfare of their families. Most of the informants' parents left San Francisco to live in Oakland or Berkeley by 1900, and the informants themselves often purchased homes in the East Bay for good prices during the Depression.

The pioneers and their unique urban ways went relatively unnoticed by contemporary observers and, perhaps as a consequence, have been neglected by scholars. They merit attention because they contrast with both the contemporary ghetto dweller and the average white urbanite of the late nineteenth and early twentieth centuries; analysis of these pioneer suburbanites might shed light on the problems of metropolitan life in the late twentieth century. At the very least, study of their conversion to suburban living furthers our understanding of the historical origins of that way of life and its implications for whites as well as for Blacks.

Emphasis on the "problems" of Black and white urban life results not so much from careful analysis of the history of different ethnic groups, but from scholars' concern with social policy, crime, and health. The experiences of pioneer urbanites in the Bay Area show that the availability of different neighborhood locations can improve those aspects of urban life—given the right setting. While contemporary residents enjoy emphasizing the Bay Area's liberal, multi-racial, and multi-ethnic heritage, the region's history indicates a more complicated picture. Perhaps the city did accommodate versatile and literate Afro-Americans in the nineteenth century, but it was not so generous with Chinese of that era or with the Japanese in the twentieth century. And when large numbers of Black southerners arrived during World II, the Bay Area cities finally faced the problems that had plagued eastern cities since World War I. Black ghettos formed at Hunters Point, along Fillmore Street, and around Seventh Street in Oakland. The "Negro problem" emerged full-blown, and the area's singularity and belief in its non-racial ways disappeared. All the characteristics of ghetto life—high mortality rates, inadequate housing, and crime—heralded a new phase for San Franciscans. Comparison of the two different urban patterns—those of pioneers and those of ghetto dwellers—should illuminate our understanding of each.[43]

The pioneer experience forces us to modify the usual portrait of Negro urban life and to take into account differences between cities and between regions. Analyzing Black San Franciscans' neighborhood locations shows the complexity of city life. Negro urbanites learned of the city's complicated functions and of the larger world outside it by living in or working on the waterfront. The entertainment and ethnic districts lent a bohemian, if not a licentious, quality and a degree of ethnic sophistication to Black life. From their neighbors, the pioneer Blacks learned to be sophisticated urbanites who valued lasting friendships based on childhood experiences and individual preferences, rather than on ethnic background. In many ways this freed them from some of the effects of racial oppression.

Such living conditions may have been the prevailing pattern on the Pacific slope, although much research needs to be done on this subject. Edward J. "Buster" Johnson, who worked on the trains along the Pacific coast, said that there was little variation in Black life from city to city. "Up and down the coast, . . . Seattle, Portland, San Francisco, Los Angeles— it was all the same . . . Negroes lived the same as they did here all the way up and down the coast." There was also considerable freedom. On public transportation, for example, "you paid your fare and sat down and rode and you didn't have to ride at the back of the bus or somewhere else, just wherever you could find a seat. We didn't have none of that funny stuff like they had in the south."[44] Despite Jim Crow restrictions, Blacks seem to have been well dispersed in many nineteenth-century U.S. cities. The relationship between this living pattern and racial prejudice needs to be explored in order to compare the quality of Black urban life from region to region.

The Bay Area pioneers shared another characteristic with Negro urbanites outside the far west. While Black urbanites are frequently viewed as laggards behind the nation, they were in the vanguard in San Francisco and Boston. Starting in the late nineteenth century, Black Bostonians moved to the "streetcar suburbs" because of lower rents, lower home purchase prices, more pleasant physical surroundings, and less antipathy for their group. Boston and San Francisco Blacks moved to the suburbs at comparable rates, if only at the outset: "So far as increasing residence in the more open and healthful outlying districts is concerned, the Negroes have in the main fared better than the rest of the population."[45]

The benefits of urban life seem to have counterbalanced discrimination in employment, or so many Black San Franciscans believed—and their opinions must be weighed when we assess the effects of racism and the quality of their lives. If their childhood memories minimized racial strife and were a bit nostalgic for the cosmopolitan pre-ghetto era, their segregated social life reminds us of the restrictions they faced.

# 7

# Leaders

*We have men among us who would shine in any sphere, and
shed lustre on any position, however high. We have orators who
with words of fire can enchant and electrify an audience; divines,
eminent for their virtues, piety, eloquence, and theological and
scholastic lore; poets, who breathe their thoughts in harmonious
numbers; writers, whose productions would grace the library of the
most learned and refined; mechanics, inventors, merchants, men
of scientific attainments, men of wealth, professional men, and in
fact, representatives of every station, and every avocation and
grade in life. . . .*

*Some of these men were born under the influence of slavery;
some may have been slaves themselves, all have felt the baneful
effects of that prejudice which American slavery engenders; all!
all!! have suffered that martyrdom of the soul which the colored
American has to bear when he aspires to a higher status than that of
a serf.*

San Francisco Pacific Appeal, *May 23, 1863*

Despite the color barriers that hemmed it in, Black San Francisco's
organized social life was rich. Sensitive, race-conscious Afro-Americans,
roused by the social, economic, and political injustices leveled at their race,
formed institutions, held offices, and worked with other Blacks to improve
conditions; this stripped Blacks of their anonymity and gave them a sense of
control over their lives. Meeting regularly at the state and local levels, the
organizations interpreted the injustices from which Blacks suffered,
recalled historical traditions, and provided values and the means to realize
them. At the same time, the leaders developed valuable organizational

skills. The setting that produced the ethnic institutions was made up of many parts, each complex in itself. Among them were prejudice, the opportunities available to ordinary Black San Franciscans, and the backgrounds of those who founded and led the institutions.

For many Afro-Americans, the lack of a family was compensated for by membership in churches, fraternal lodges, benevolent societies, and literary and social clubs. These organizations provided valuable connections on the Pacific slope and in cities along the Atlantic coast. For five decades, San Franciscans dominated the Black world from British Columbia to southern California and east as far as Utah. Their influence, which belied their numbers, went unchallenged until the rise of Black Los Angeles shortly before World War I.

Before 1848, racial prejudice seemed virtually non-existent in California. In Hispanic California, cultural, class, and national differences were significant, but race was not foremost in the minds of settlers until large numbers of United States citizens arrived. Historian Eugene Berwanger claims: "White Californians and Indians accepted Negroes as equal individuals before 1848 and even intermarriage among the three groups was not frowned upon."[1]

The English-speaking newcomers who made California a state behaved according to the practices prevailing in the United States in the mid-nineteenth century; those practices included slavery and Jim Crow laws. Entrance to the union brought an end to the peculiar institution in California, although a few Blacks remained enslaved as long as their masters were temporary residents. California statutes excluded non-whites from voting, from serving in the militia, from testifying in court when whites were involved, and from marrying whites. Like several midwestern states, California also tried to exclude Negroes from settlement in the 1850s.[2] In addition to bondage and discriminatory legislation, American customs limited the work world of Black Californians. Afro-Americans were unpopular in the gold fields because of the belief that they were too lucky. In San Francisco they suffered various kinds of economic discrimination (see Chapter 3).[3]

Social restrictions also humiliated Afro-Americans. Discrimination in public places aroused protests and resulted in some court cases. At the turn of the century, the proprietor of the Baldwin Hotel, a leading San Francisco establishment, explained that the race issue was treated delicately by both the hotel management and Black customers. Although "it would be impolitic to discuss it in the press," he observed that "the colored people who travel are, as a rule, as intelligent as white folk and, being as sensitive, do not often place themselves or us in embarrassing positions." As a consequence, "happily the color line does not enter into our calculation."⁴ But a hotel clerk spoke more candidly: "It is a law in all first-class hotels throughout the country . . . never to give accommodation to negroes. Of course, the line is drawn in a delicate way, so as not to give offense or to render the manager liable to the law." The subtlety shown here makes it difficult to accurately assess racism in San Francisco's social life.⁵

Yet it is fairly clear that even the "better element" of Black pioneers suffered from discrimination. Peter Jackson, the prize fighter, figured in an incident at the Baldwin Hotel. He registered, went out, then returned to find that his registration and baggage had been switched to a room in the hotel annex. Jackson told reporters he had never encountered anything like this in his lifetime. A local bootblack also expressed the disbelief that Jackson and other Blacks must have felt. " 'It's a shame,' said a colored bootblack at one of the hotels, 'to refuse to give a room to such a gentleman as Peter Jackson. Didn't he walk arm in arm with the Marquis of Queensberry in Picadilly? Didn't he shake the hand of the Prince of Wales? Ain't he the best fighter in the world?' And the bootblack expectorated in disgust. 'Some of these hotel men make me tired [!]' " By including prominent as well as anonymous Blacks, discrimination outraged and united Americans who otherwise shared very little.⁶

Clearly California was not as oppressive as the deep south. Southerners openly expressed their racist views—unlike the Baldwin Hotel proprietor. Before westerners viewed Black Americans as a threat, they victimized Asians, discriminating against the Chinese in the nineteenth century and the Japanese in the twentieth.⁷ But there is not sufficient evidence to support James Weldon Johnson's comparison of San Francisco with the Jim Crow south and some northern cities. Traveling with a song and dance team a few years before the earthquake, Johnson found "no bar against me in hotels, restaurants, theaters, or other places of public accommodation and entertainment." He delighted in the freedom of the city, moving about "with a sense of confidence and security, and entirely from under the cloud of doubt and apprehension that constantly hangs over an intelligent Negro in every Southern city and in a great many cities of the North."⁸

Despite Johnson's opinion and the difficulty of assessing California's racial climate, it is certain that prejudice did humiliate and degrade Afro-Americans, even if only occasionally. Prejudice was mild compared to anti-Chinese sentiments or Negrophobia in the south, but it was still disturbing, partly because it was not as iron-clad as elsewhere. Blacks could never be sure if they would be evicted from a streetcar, assigned to the rear in civic parades, refused service in public accommodations, or, as in the 1940s, restricted to certain rows on the commuter train from San Francisco to Los Angeles. Informants who lived in the Bay Area before 1930 invariably minimized the extent of race prejudice in public places before the 1920s, but they admitted its enormous effect on employment patterns.[9]

The leadership roles and organized activities of the Black San Franciscans stemmed as much from the city's unique opportunities as from race oppression. The booming economy of pioneer days provided funds for a vast array of social and cultural institutions, some of which survived more than a century. Although the economy's spectacular growth abated in the late nineteenth century, San Francisco and Oakland continued to sustain religious, cultural, and civic organizations. The social benefits of life in a remote worldly city appealed to the Black residents, as it did to other northern Californians. Chances for status, recognition, association, and elevation met important social needs and gave individuals an identity and self-esteem. It was only natural that being a church leader, newspaper columnist, Masonic officer, or guest at refined social affairs would be meaningful to former slaves and descendants of slaves. The Black cultural heritage also accounted for the desire to become involved in social activities. Like others, Blacks came to the Bay Area to improve their material condition, and American social institutions provided the means. As they had belonged to ethnic associations before migration, it was natural for Blacks to form independent or branch organizations in San Francisco.[10]

The Black newspapers wrote about Black needs. In 1862, the *Pacific Appeal* reminded its readers that, "notwithstanding the flippant doctrine of inferiority, . . . we are just like other men, in inclination, instinct and capacity, and can do whatever it is right and proper that other men should do, similarly circumstanced." Because of these basic similarities, "every project for his social well-being that attracts the attention of the white American should also attract the attention of the colored American."[11] But because of oppression, Blacks had "special duties to perform, a special work to accomplish, different and distinct from any other class in the community." In an editorial, "Special Work for Colored Men," the paper urged its readers to form political, religious, and moral organizations, because that was the American method of social improvement. Moreover, Blacks must organize to attain their legal rights. Clubs and societies should be formed "wherever there are half a dozen Colored people." Although they could accept aid from friendly whites, the principles of self-help were stressed: "As we are the parties most concerned, we should petition [for our rights] ourselves."[12] Winning the right to testify in court and to receive equal educational benefits required organization "in every town or precinct where there are Colored." The journal also emphasized the necessity of supporting a newspaper for the race, then concluded: "These things are a portion of the special work which Colored men have to perform, and they are derelict to themselves, their country and their race, if they neglect them."[13]

Because oppressive conditions persisted, some Black pioneers held to this point of view for several decades, maintaining and enlarging their numerous institutions (with the exception of the Black schools, which were absorbed in the 1870s). But after the Civil War a different opinion emerged as one barrier after another fell before new legislation, constitutional amendments, and a growing optimism that Blacks would eventually become assimilated. Four California State Conventions of Colored Citizens (or Colored California Conventions) were held between 1855 and 1865; an attempt to convene a fifth failed during Reconstruction, indicating that many Afro-Americans no longer felt a need for such conventions.[14]

Meanwhile the *Elevator* reminded its readers that "in all our communities there are separate and distinct social relations which no law can rule or govern, nor is it desirable they should." This is "one of the attributes of our present high state of civilization, and it marks the progress of the human race." If Blacks abandon their separate institutions, "where will we go?" Black churches, newspapers, and associations reflect the fact that, despite common public and political interests, American "social interests are distinct, and on these grounds require separate organizations."[15] As long as Blacks are seen as members of a specific race, they should maintain their own institutions. "Until we can separate ourselves from the race with which we are identified, and each one can unite with the class with which we affiliate by education, fortune, and other adventitious circumstances, we must maintain our separate organizations; and to keep up a unity of thought, feeling, and interest, frequent deliberation is necessary." Many Afro-American leaders shared these views; the alternative was exclusion from influential positions in Bay Area society.[16]

Against the backdrop of urban growth, war and reconciliation, the pursuit of wealth, and continental and overseas expansion, a small core of dedicated Afro-Americans labored daily, though virtually unnoticed, for the cause of human rights. They lacked the advantages of birth and education, but felt as talented and as deserving of recognition as most citizens. These humanists formed institutions and supported causes with remarkable zeal and perseverance. The skills of the leading Black urbanites contrast sharply with our preconceptions of Afro-Americans. While many contemporaries held them in low regard, Blacks appreciated their own attainments, as reflected by their leaders. In a series of articles on California's "representative [Black] men," the *Pacific Appeal* observed: "We have men among us who would shine in any sphere, and shed lustre on any position, however high."

Many of these exemplars resided in San Francisco, and all were without the benefits of high birth or extensive formal education. Two San Franciscans, William H. Newby of the *Mirror of the Times* and William H. Hall, president of the 1857 Convention, were typical of the Californians described by the *Appeal* as "mostly self-made and self-educated men, . . . [without] the advantages of an early liberal education." A closer look at other leading Afro-Americans sheds light on their unusual qualities and their social contributions.[17]

Actual bondage and an antislavery tradition motivated William H. Yates to reform American society. A steamboat steward in the 1860s, Yates was president of the Colored Convention in 1855, indicating the high esteem in which he was held by Black Californians.[18] Born a slave in Alexandria, Virginia in 1816, Yates chafed from the cruelties inflicted by alcoholic relatives of his master. He eventually gained his freedom, but rather than leave the slave south he stayed to help runaways escape, and also worked to purchase his family from bondage. When local officials became suspicious, Yates moved to New York City. He migrated with his family to California shortly after the Gold Rush.[19]

In the east, Yates had learned leadership and organization while active in a benevolent and a moral reform society, forming a military band, and speaking out against the colonization of Blacks. As a porter of the U.S. Supreme Court from 1837–42, the former slave was said to have become "better versed in the political history of the country and the science of our government than many professional politicians." But prejudice forced him to earn a living as a porter, a steward, a keeper of a hackney stable, and later as a restaurant owner in New York City. His "knowledge of Congressional affairs, his legal acquirements and his personal influence made him the most fitting person to preside" at the First Colored California Convention.[20] Besides continuing to participate in the conventions, Yates served on the San Francisco Executive Committee, a steering organ which assumed political leadership when the conventions were not in session. Under the pen name "Amigo," he wrote letters to the *Pacific Appeal* and was responsible for starting the *Elevator* in 1865. Yates, a Mason, supported the religious activities of Black San Franciscans.[21]

The ex-slave shared these social responsibilities with other former bondsmen, including Reverend John J. Moore, James R. Starkey, and David Ruggles. T. B. Morton, founder of the Afro-American League in California, and J. C. Rivers were other former slaves active in various civil rights and social organizations at the end of the century. Despite their origins and the menial positions society reserved for them, these men held numerous prestigious offices in Black San Francisco. Their experiences as slaves naturally lent a strong abolitionist strain to their humanitarian endeavors, and their personal fortunes often suffered because of this reformist impulse.[22]

Another leading pioneer, Henry M. Collins, a steamboat steward, exemplified the talented and organization-minded free-born individuals who served San Francisco. Born in Pittsburgh, Pennsylvania, about 1820, he worked on the steamers plying the Ohio River and earned a reputation as a shrewd real estate speculator before he was twenty-one. In 1847 he established a newspaper, the *Mystery,* with Martin R. Delany, the colonizationist, Black nationalist, and military officer, and Alexander Ferguson, a barber who also migrated to San Francisco. Collins, moreover, was credited with discovering how to erect "an improved style of building." In 1852 Delany observed that Collins stood "among the men of note" in Pittsburgh.[23]

Besides migrating with his family to California and speculating in Cariboo, Canada, Collins actively promoted Black causes. When a savings fund and land association was formed in San Francisco in 1859, Collins was its president; he also played a leading role in the convention movement, helped launch the *Mirror of the Times,* worked in the petition drive to win the right to testify in court, and served on the Executive Committee. In 1864 he effected the A.M.E. Zion Church's purchase of the First Unitarian Church building on Stockton Street. His leading part in a variety of endeavors was typical of a number of race-conscious Blacks, particularly in pioneer days. In the twentieth century, the activities of such distinguished and prosperous lawyers as Oscar Hudson and Walter A. Butler were reminiscent of Henry Collins in an earlier age.[24]

Significantly, these Afro-San Franciscans might have abandoned their ethnic identity in the tradition of those white Americans who left the slums to become assimilated. Their dedication to improving Afro-American life shows that humanitarian strains and racial loyalties were frequently stimulated by personal experiences. Because middle-class Blacks are often thought to merely pursue creature comforts and engage in conspicuous consumption, it is impressive to see relatively affluent Afro-Americans with strong racial loyalties—especially when their status shielded them from some of racism's effects. The existence of pride in the heritage of a people close to slavery is also noteworthy.[25]

A few Black San Franciscans, the heads of churches and newspapers, known as "race men" in the early twentieth century, made institutional activities a life-long pursuit. Reverend T. M. D. Ward and Philip A. Bell exemplified those who remain unknown and unheralded. Ward's abilities as a minister and orator led to his selection as a "representative Californian" in 1863. As missionary elder for the Pacific coast in 1854, he took over the San Francisco A.M.E. Church, also known as Bethel or

Union Bethel. Other ministers helped in the services, but Ward was "the first regularly ordained [A.M.E.] minister" in the region. His successes in purchasing and remodeling a new building in San Francisco and in starting new churches along the Pacific coast resulted in his reappointment, "with additional powers," in 1861. In 1868 he became episcopal superintendent for the region before leaving to work in the south during Reconstruction.[26]

An eloquent orator, Ward was touted as "golden-mouthed," "the greatest preacher the [A.M.E.] church ever produced." Similarly, the *Pacific Appeal* described his voice as so "full-toned and sonorous, [that] at times its intonations [were] almost musical." A contemporary noted that Ward's speeches, always brief, were the "best short sermons (from twelve to fifteen minutes) of any one he ever heard." A white passenger on a steamship who heard Ward speak extemporaneously in 1868 left his impressions: "For beauty of conception, elegance of diction, and thorough comprehension of the task his Master had allotted him, [he] could not be surpassed by the most gifted prelates of the day." Afterwards, "all who could get near the modest Bishop did so, pressed his hand and offered congratulations."[27] A distant relation of Samuel Ringgold Ward, the distinguished abolitionist orator and Congregational minister, Thomas Ward was born in Hanover, Pennsylvania in 1823. His formal education was limited. Converted in 1838, licensed to preach at the age of twenty, and ordained an elder in 1848, Ward was associated with New England churches until his migration to California in 1854.[28]

Several other ordained ministers were prominent leaders. Reverend John J. Moore was born into slavery after his free-born mother was kidnapped by slavers; eventually they escaped. One of the founders of San Francisco's A.M.E. Zion Church, Moore also started the city's Black public school. He published a short-lived periodical, the *Lunar Visitor,* worked in the Colored Conventions, and wrote newspaper articles on Black politics. Interest in politics and freedmen eventually led both Moore and Ward to travel south during Reconstruction.[29]

A sojourn on the west coast was not uncommon for Black ministers and race leaders of the nineteenth and early twentieth centuries. Talented and often eloquent, they met Blacks' spiritual and social needs at a time of severe discrimination. The leaders' anonymity stems from their race and their cause, rather than from their deficiencies. Neglect of the Pacific coast's role in Afro-American history compounds the problems. For example, the story of Bishop Alexander Walters's life is fairly well known, except for the Pacific slope phase. A bishop in the A.M.E. Zion Church, Walters presided over the first Pan-African Conference in London in 1900. His early years were spent as a minister on the Pacific slope; in the 1880s he was appointed to the San Francisco Zion Methodist Church.[30]

Other Afro-Americans, once well known on the east coast, dropped out of sight on the Pacific slope. For example, Philip A. Bell virtually disappears from eastern-oriented histories after his move west, and he has not been treated by contemporary historians, despite his journalistic and political accomplishments. At the time of his death in 1889, Black newspapers heralded Bell as "the Napoleon of the colored press." With his passing, they wrote, "the Negro race loses the oldest and one of the ablest" of American editors. For years the *Elevator* had been "the oldest secular Negro newspaper" in the United States, having outlived *Frederick Douglass' Paper* and other journals. It was not Bell's only attempt in the field of journalism.[31]

Born in 1808 and educated in the African Free School in New York City, Bell attended the first American Negro Convention in 1830, was secretary of the second, and was active in others. He organized a protest against the formation of a New York branch of the American Colonization Society, and helped draft a report on the social conditions of free Negroes. Moving into journalism, Bell was among the first New York agents for the *Liberator,* the abolitionist journal of William Lloyd Garrison. In 1837 he launched and sustained the New York *Weekly Advocate,* later the *Colored American,* "the chief organ of the colored people" until 1841. He was also head of an intelligence office in New York and in San Francisco. As a labor recruiter, Bell earned a reputation for his humanitarianism in the U.S. and in England.[32]

Bell developed a number of life-long associations with well-known and less famous Afro-Americans. In New York, he associated with such prominent Blacks as Frederick Douglass, James McCune Smith, Henry Highland Garnet, and other abolitionists and temperance leaders. Bell maintained these contacts after he migrated to California on the eve of the Civil War. His newspapers, first the *Pacific Appeal* and later the *Elevator,* were instrumental for maintaining contact with leading Blacks in the east coast cities. Thanks to Bell, Pacific coast Blacks were informed of major developments and new publications on the Atlantic shore.[33] Bell also aided the Black quest for equal rights and justice. Shortly after migration, he read selections from Shakespeare to help pay the court costs of the California fugitive slave, Archy Lee. He also served as recording secretary of the San Francisco Literary Institute and president of the San Francisco Executive Committee; he had a reputation for keeping "the colored voters in unbroken harmony, in state, municipal and national elections" for the Republican party. His political service won him the honorific but noteworthy office of assistant sergeant-at-arms of the California Senate in 1879.[34]

A life's devotion to the cause of his race brought Bell few material rewards. His newspaper and political activities drew most of his energies and meager finances; simply keeping the *Elevator* solvent would have sorely tried a younger man. Its circulation was "about 800"—large for the population, but small in business terms. By the end of his career, Bell lived on meals donated by the Palace Hotel kitchen help and on funds raised by volunteers. Typically for a nineteenth-century Black who dedicated himself so fully to human rights, he died in relative obscurity—and in Bell's case, in the local almshouse.[35]

We might for a moment compare Bell to Frederick Douglass, the leading Afro-American spokesman from the 1840s until his death in 1895. Lacking Douglass's oratorical abilities, Bell dedicated himself more fully to journalism. After he stopped publishing his paper in 1863, Douglass held numerous high offices, while Bell struggled on in comparative obcurity, continuing the *Elevator* and attempting to galvanize Afro-Americans. Though Douglass's accomplishments are overwhelming, Bell's remain impressive. Bell's free-born status made his rise to prominence less dramatic than Douglass's, and the lack of an autobiography has also hindered appreciation of Bell's achievements. But the quality and longevity of Bell's newspapers, spanning five decades, offer valuable documentation of his thoughts on politics, race relations, and the Negro's progress in the nineteenth century. They are also invaluable for studying Black social and cultural life of that era.[36] Like Douglass, Bell kept the abolitionist heritage alive when the nation's thoughts were elsewhere. Unlike Douglass, a diplomat, confidant of presidents, and occupant of federal offices, Bell—like a number of Blacks—never reaped large rewards. Bell's poignant final years underline both American society's neglect of Black talent and the nation's appalling lack of interest in racial and humanitarian issues during the Gilded Age.

Bell was clearly the most talented Negro journalist in the United States in the nineteenth century. His rival, Peter Anderson of the *Pacific Appeal,* lacked Bell's experience, political following, and connections. Few newspapermen were able to surround themselves with capable writers, organizers, and orators, as Bell was; and Bell in turn gave his loyal following a number of opportunities to hold offices and serve as correspondents. While the *Pacific Appeal* closed with Anderson's death, Bell's journal continued under the leadership of James B. Wilson until it merged with the *Pacific Coast Appeal,* published by William H. Blake and George Watkins.[37]

In the late nineteenth century there were several Black-published journals in San Francisco. They lasted for only a few years, and not many issues remain, but their very existence in a city of a mere sixteen hundred Negroes highlights the importance Blacks placed on having an op-

portunity to plead their cause. James E. Brown, a pioneer resident and one
of the few regular Democratic party supporters in the 1880s, edited the
*Vindicator.* In the 1890s, Augustus A. Collins and R. C. O. Benjamin
published the *Sentinel.*[38] As the twentieth century approached, racism and
a felt need caused a number of leaders to emerge in the field. Beginning in
1894, J. S. Francis and J. L. Derrick published *The Western Outlook,* and
noted that for Blacks, journalism was "a hazardous undertaking at best."
But the publishers of the several organs in San Francisco and the East Bay
were talented, and they had the support of their readers. The *California
Voice* of E. A. Daly and his wife began in the 1920s and continued under
their guidance for five decades, when new management assumed control.[39]

Although she did not have her own newspaper, Delilah Beasley
established a reputation as a journalist in a field dominated by men. She
wrote for the Cleveland *Gazette* and Cincinnati *Inquirer* before migrating
west around World War I, and then for the Oakland *Tribune.* Besides
playing a leading role in colored women's clubs, Beasley sought out the
Black pioneers and their descendants, collected their nineteenth-century
newspapers, interviewed aged residents, and wrote a history of California's
Negroes. The first work of its kind, it remains the most important
secondary source on the topic sixty years after its appearance.[40]

Focusing on leaders has some shortcomings. While Black people
viewed these individuals as "representative," they mainly exemplified self-
flattering qualities which were thought to be lacking in the group. This
approach, often criticized as "elitist," can be said to throw little light on the
average Black. Another criticism is that many leaders were only temporary
residents who came when they were mature and often left after a few years.
But the accomplished urbanites do help us understand the values,
aspirations, and strategies of the group's institutional life. Yates, Bell,
Collins, and Beasley were praised as leaders and were approved models for
children. And transients—among them Reverends Moore and Walters
(and the white journalist Samuel L. Clemens)—were common at that time.
Newcomers, transient or otherwise, usually worked with existing leaders
and institutions to galvanize members and concentrate the group's
activities on a specific objective; they rarely launched a new organization in
a different direction. Their ability to organize lasting institutions is an
accomplishment that, besides justifying treatment of their origins and
activities, requires us to examine their organizations.

The formation by Blacks of several organizations and a newspaper
before 1860 indicates the dynamic energy of the less than two thousand
citizens. The perpetuation and expansion of churches and Masonic orders,
and the formation of new institutions in the East Bay and along the coast,
reveals the love for associations that is frequently attributed to other

Americans. Continuation of the pioneer churches and fraternal organizations into the late twentieth century, despite fires, earthquakes, migration, and death, and support of two Black newspapers from the Civil War years, indicates the talents and abilities of the pioneer urbanites.

The number and variety of race improvement organizations from the 1850s indicate constant attempts by Afro-Americans to deal with the most frustrating aspect of their condition. They formed conventions and societies to combat injustice at the city, state, and national levels. San Francisco sent eighteen delegates (out of a total of forty-nine) to the 1855 Colored Convention in Sacramento; conventions were also held in 1856, 1857, 1865, 1873, 1880, and 1882. In what ranged from dignified formal affairs to tumultuous political caucuses, Afro-Americans formed committees, delivered speeches, introduced resolutions, issued reports, circulated petitions, organized local and state societies, launched newspapers, inveighed against gambling and immoral behavior, and urged citizens to struggle for their rights.[41]

In addition to working for the right to testify in court, supporting political candidates, and requesting jobs for their votes, Black city dwellers sent aid to freedmen and Black soldiers in the Civil War era. In late 1889, Bay Area pioneers met in A.M.E. Zion Church, along with "not a few" whites, to discuss the condition of the freedmen. They formed the California Protective League, "a political organization," to coordinate the state's Afro-Americans, to advance the interests of the race, to protest the outrages against southern Negroes, and to seek aid from the national government to secure the rights of their group. Its probable successor, the Afro-American State League (later Congress) of California, was formed shortly thereafter; continued interest in national affairs was indicated by its intent "to unite fraternally all persons of the Negro race," by its support of Booker T. Washington and Tuskegee Institute, and by its efforts to raise Black volunteers for the Spanish-American War. In later years the NAACP of Northern California concentrated on both local and national concerns.[42]

By seeking redress at the city, state, and national levels, San Francisco's Negroes showed their reformist as well as their humanitarian sentiments. Their efforts also indicated the close bonds among Afro-Americans wherever they resided and the breadth of their interests. The California Colored Conventions, for example, were concerned with forming educational institutions and collecting statistics, besides petitioning to overturn unjust laws. Similarly, the Afro-American League, headed by T. B. Morton and J. C. Rivers, undertook to improve the race's condition in several areas: to "give moral and material aid to its members," to educate them "socially, morally, and intellectually," to advance the interests of its members politically, and interestingly, "to carry on and conduct a general merchandise business for the benefit of its members." Prejudice affected so many areas of life that Blacks thought a broad range of activities was necessary to halt its effects.[43]

The organizations collected statistical information on Black numbers, prosperity, and equality. For evidence of "thrift among our people," the California Conventions gathered data on Black-owned personal property and real estate in the Bay city and in various California counties. They pointed out the contrast between their political inequality and the fact that they were expected to pay California taxes. In 1865 the Colored Convention formed a Committee on Statistics to collect information on illiteracy, the number of children and the percentage of them enrolled in school, the proportion of individuals supported by benevolent societies, the assets of Black institutions and businesses, the holdings of libraries, and the occupations of workers. The convention published this data for several cities and counties, so the world could assess Black talent and compare the Black condition to that of other citizens. Like many modern scholars, Black Californians believed that racism could be stemmed with accurate information.[44]

The most durable institutions lasted over a hundred years, occupied impressive physical structures, and were also most indicative of Black pride. Besides illuminating the Afro-American religious impulse and doctrinal heritage, church life highlights other social facts. W. E. B. Du Bois, E. Franklin Frazier, and Melvin D. Williams all emphasized churches as social centers of primary importance. In San Francisco, as elsewhere, they were all-purpose, housing political and civic meetings, benefits, and fairs, besides providing a host of leadership positions.[45] The church structures themselves tell much about the pioneers' views of themselves, because church-building was an outlet for Black ambitions; church committees competed to raise funds and vied with one another to construct the most elegant temple. By examining attempts to build, remodel, and refurnish churches, we learn of the institution-founding objectives and organizational skills of Black San Franciscans.

When the Reverend T. M. D. Ward became pastor of the A.M.E. congregation, it occupied the St. Cyprian Church on Jackson Street. The parishioners moved to the Scott Street Church after Reverend Ward reorganized the sect in 1856. Six years later, the congregation paid $5,500 for the property known as Grace (or Powell Street) Church.[46] The A.M.E. parishioners desired a physical structure that matched their aspirations as the leading lights of the "Pacific Israel." The ornate temple symbolized the achievements of the devout urbanites. The "stately building, . . . with gothic piers and handsome gilding" inspired the small but energetic congregation to make an even more impressive showing of its religious zeal. Ninety-two parishioners completed payment of the debt in 1864, and then undertook extensive repairs in early 1865.[47]

Over the next three years, Reverend Ward and his congregation held fund-raising affairs and collected $6,600 for remodeling. The bells, belfry, and organ contributed a refined quality to the religious services and surprised a visiting New Yorker, William P. Powell, who attended Sunday services in 1874. "Well, I never! In all my travels I never saw the like— colored worshipers *rung* to church and *bell'd* to prayers."[48] The energy, zeal, and organizational talents of the Bethel A.M.E. Church members were matched by the two other Black congregations. In 1864, the parishoners of the African Methodist Episcopal Zion Church purchased a "very commodious house," seating eight hundred, twice the size of the rival A.M.E. temple. "Either church is large enough for both congregations," a San Franciscan noted in 1869; and the *Christian Recorder* remarked, "The colored population of San Francisco is not destitute of abundant church accommodation."[49]

Besides the impressive physical structures, the interior furnishings and locations underlined Blacks' attachment to the symbols of a refined life. They installed carpets, bells, cushioned seats, and an artificial pool for baptism in the Third Baptist Church. The structures were located "in the most popular neighborhoods and thoroughfares." The small congregations did not limit the dimensions of the churches. The Black city folk, dreamers like many westerners, built temples to mirror their aspirations, which knew no limits.[50]

But by the time of the earthquake, the oldest churches were eclipsed in number and size of congregation by younger ones. In 1904 Los Angeles's two A.M.E. Churches had 400 members each, while San Francisco's one listed only 60. Oakland's A.M.E. Church also surpassed San Francisco's, with 150 members. In subsequent decades the new institutions continued to grow, as both Oakland and Los Angeles sustained large increments in Black population while San Francisco's contingent remained relatively small, despite substantial proportionate increases.[51]

Through the churches and newspapers, San Francisco's Black leaders worked to instill a sense of historical tradition and race pride in their followers. In Emancipation Day celebrations, speakers reminded audiences of their heritage. Particularly in the nineteenth century, slavery and the race barrier were usually presented as the causes of Blacks' unique situation and of their need to organize. In May 1862, the *Pacific Appeal* requested that its readers donate old copies of the *Mirror of the Times* "to make up a complete file." This would preserve the pioneer heritage. Along the same lines, the *Appeal*'s premier issue carried articles from the *Mirror* on the California Colored Convention of 1857, and the *Elevator* reprinted articles on Hannibal of Carthage and Martin R. Delany.[52]

Black orators, singers, and amateurs who gave recitations displayed their knowledge of Black history in the West Indies and in places as distant as Africa. At an Emancipation Day celebration the Reverend T. M. D. Ward spoke of a glorious African heritage, displaying an impressive knowledge of history. He discussed the uniqueness of the African heritage, its antiquity, and most significantly, its comparative superiority to the European traditions: "For ten successive centuries they [Africans] lifted along the torch of science to a darkened globe and philosophy traveled, awe struck pilgrims, to learn wisdom of the obelisks and temples." In the same vein, Ward reminded his audience of the importance of their heroes by recalling the contributions of John Quincy Adams, William Lloyd Garrison, Denmark Vesey, Nat Turner, Abraham Lincoln, and John Brown.[53]

The leaders stressed history in order to cultivate race pride. Every ethnic institution promoted pride insofar as its successes were the result of the ambition, cooperation, and striving of Negroes. Besides stressing race pride in their speeches, Blacks marched en masse in Fourth of July parades and participated in other civic celebrations as a proud, distinguished group. In 1894 a Colored American Day at the Midwinter International Fair in San Francisco allowed them to demonstrate appreciation of their historical and cultural tradition through speeches, songs, and a dance in the evening. The very names of such organizations as the "Drill Squad and Fancy Drill Corps D'Afrique" or the uniforms of the Lincoln Zouaves, modeled after the Corps D'Afrique of the French army, paid homage to the members' African heritage. The names of both the Sojourner Truth Club of the 1920s and the Phyllis Wheatley Dance of 1925 evoked the history and the race pride of these Americans.[54]

Despite this emphasis, some Blacks felt ambivalent about a separate identity. For example, Negro city dwellers objected to Colored American Day as a needless drawing of the color line. Similarly, Blacks debated the desirability of an appellation that set them apart from the general American citizenry.[55] But San Francisco still supported a surprising number and variety of ethnic organizations that afforded the opportunity to belong in a society that denied participation in politics, economics, and social life. The civil rights organizations promised the chance to participate as equals. The leaders provided examples of character and zeal that were needed to combat prejudice. Ministers, editors, and Masonic officers interpreted the historical and cultural tradition so as to inspire the descendants of slaves and support their self-esteem. Finally, the leaders and their institutions gave pioneers the opportunity to dominate Black social life.

Because of their numbers, wealth, and talents, Black San Franciscans exercised considerable influence in Afro-American affairs on the west coast in the nineteenth century. In the Colored Conventions, for example, they always comprised the largest contingent of delegates. The city's leaders often headed state, as well as local, organizations. William Yates and William H. Hall were presidents of Colored Conventions. John A. Barber, a pioneer San Franciscan, held the highest California office among Prince Hall Masons in the nineteenth century. Reverend T. M. D. Ward was the first regularly ordained A.M.E. minister in the far west; at the end of his stay in California, he was episcopal superintendent for the region. In 1870, San Francisco's influence was so great that "whichever way . . . San Francisco decides, we believe that it will control, in a great degree, the colored citizens in every city and town in the State—because the largest body of colored citizens are [sic] concentrated here. The heads of the churches are in this city, or the controlling influence at least; as also every political movement that has ever been made among us has had its head centre [sic] here."[56]

The establishment of Black institutions in California cities and towns often depended on leading San Franciscans. Reverend A. B. Smith, of the San Francisco A.M.E. Zion Church, was credited with erecting a branch church in San Jose in 1862. In 1864 Reverend Ward raised $2,000 at the dedication of a Virginia City church, and also laid the cornerstone for an Oakland edifice. Reverend R. C. O. Benjamin traveled in the interior of the Pacific slope in 1890, attending to church business and establishing Afro-American Leagues.[57]

San Franciscans were frequently invited to cultural events to deliver speeches or promote interest in various projects. When Afro-American residents of Virginia City, Nevada, celebrated the ratification of the Fifteenth Amendment in 1870, they invited William H. Hall, "California's eloquent orator" and a former San Franciscan, to deliver the key speech. When Stockton Negroes held a "Grand Cake Walk and Southern Jubilee," a Black San Franciscan came to arouse interest in the dance competition for a two-storied cake.[58]

But the power and influence eventually shifted to southern California. This was due in part to simple numbers: By 1904 Los Angeles's Blacks outnumbered San Francisco's two to one. Like the churches already mentioned, political and race improvement organizations came to find their power based in the south. This was indicated in 1906, when the Afro-American Congress met in Pasadena.[59] The noise and numbers of the recent arrivals finally overshadowed the history and achievements of the pioneer era.

The pioneers had managed to establish and maintain institutions with little outside interference. They had guided western affairs, and given aid to slaves, freedmen, and the families of lynching victims in the south. Black leaders had extended their aid to whites as well, as in the recruiting and intelligence activities of Philip Bell. The conventions expressed regrets and commiseration for the failed revolutions in Hungary and Poland; and, despite Black competition with the Irish in America, they gave "cordial approbation" to the Irish effort to expel the British from their homeland.[60] Their error probably lay in stressing form, style, and proving Blacks were fit for civil rights, while whites were not required to do so; in fact, if anything, the enslavement of Blacks and the denial of the rights of the free Afro-Americans offered concrete evidence that whites lacked the qualities necessary to make democracy a reality.

The well-known San Franciscans left speeches, letters, and institutions that shed light on their democratic ideals, on their unusual abilities, and on the condition of the pioneers. The numerous institutions indicated that the leaders and their followers were as association-minded as the typical American. This inclination was heightened by three factors. First, the very rootlessness of life in a distant and new city encouraged the formation of churches, military societies, fraternal orders, and benevolent associations to give a sense of order and identity. Then the lack of ordinary familial relations heightened the social needs of urbanites. Finally, race prejudice served to draw together Negroes of different national, regional, cultural, and social origins. The leaders of Black society interpreted these factors and provided directions for the pioneers.

Race prejudice, frequently seen as the causal agent behind the behavior of Black folk, is only one among a number of variables. Although it has been important for Afro-Americans, its impact varies with time, place, and area of life. When it is the main causal agent, Blacks are often viewed as passive subjects incapable of responsibly initiating actions. But when we view discrimination as one variable among many—one that stimulates humanitarian sentiments in a highly individualistic and competitive society—we add a significant dimension to the lives of anonymous urbanites.

Because even the more noteworthy leaders are absent from traditional popular and scholarly histories, we must question conjectures about the lives of ordinary Negroes in the far west until considerable research is done. By combing written and other documents, we can ascertain contemporary popular opinions of Afro-San Franciscans and their place in the urban society, and compare the popular opinion to the Blacks' own conceptions of themselves.

# 8

# Cosmopolites

*The walls of such a [reading] room might be adorned with the
photographs of the champions of freedom, on whose achievements
our ministers of religion and teachers would be pleased to lecture
for the benefit of their kindred.*
San Francisco Elevator, *August 18, 1865*

*The Committee should make extensive arrangements for a large
procession—employ musicians, procure cars, banners, chariots,
and all the necessary paraphernalia to give* eclat *to the occasion.*
San Francisco Elevator, *February 25, 1870*

Whites' images of Blacks in newspapers, reminiscences, and history
books often contrast with Blacks' images of themselves. Sometimes
favorable, frequently paternalistic, whites' descriptions focused on colorful
idiosyncracies. Unlike their southern counterparts, San Francisco's
Negroes were rarely accused of being stupid, vicious, and beast-like.[1]
Rather, the pioneers were frequently portrayed as one group among many
that, because of complexion or stylish dress, gave the city a colorful and
cosmopolitan character. Soulé's *Annals* noted "single dandy black fellows,
. . . who strutted as only the negro can strut, in holiday clothes" among
other pedestrians in Portsmouth Square. The Negro coachman of a Nob Hill
millionaire impressed a San Francisco belle with his "suit of white cloth
with black velvet buttons as large as butter-dishes, and orange-topped
boots." On Morton Street, lined with brothels, "women of every race and
hue, white, yellow and black, hung from window-ledges, in various stages
of undress," waiting to snatch men's hats, daring them to enter and retrieve
them. The fame and nickname of "Uncle Sam," a Black San Franciscan
popular among the city's children, derived from his red, white, and blue

suit. He sang, sold candy to children, and threatened to "punish bad" youngsters with a long whip; he could be found on the city's boulevards in the late nineteenth century.[2]

Non-Black travelers and reporters rarely discussed Afro-Americans in detail. They were content to note their presence, describe their clothing or function, and move on to other subjects. In the 1850s an observer, commenting on the carriage of a notorious New Orleans murderer, mentioned that he was "drawn by two magnificent black horses with a Negro groom in livery in the smart rear 'tiger' seat." Similarly, in describing the popular entertainment area on Market near Fourth Street in the late nineteenth century, Evelyn Wells found "negro minstrels sitting on [the] . . . wagon bed" of Pawnee Bill, the Wild West showman.[3] Blacks were noted in other characteristically "Black" jobs, often lending humor to a scene. "Two burly Negroes" labored before a large audience at an auction in 1895 where unclaimed articles of baggage were sold. "No matter what the size, style, or description of the package being shown, the two porters invariably groaned and grunted when it was being lifted from the floor to the bench. . . . After the article was sold one of the porters would take it in his left hand and carelessly toss it ten or fifteen feet, where it fell lightly as a feather."[4]

But aside from their dress or function, Blacks were rarely recognized as individuals or as important actors in city life. There were some exceptions: Mary Ellen "Mammy" Pleasant was particularly well-known because of her reputation for power and intrigue; Major Waters, a leader of East Bay parades, and "Deacon Jones," a bodyguard, also won distinction; "Muffin Tom," an old man who came to work in the Palace Hotel kitchen in 1875, was singled out from the Black workers as one "the fame of whose egg-muffins and corn-bread has made him the aristocrat of his race for the last half-century from Charleston to Long Beach"; and "Blind Bob" Jackson, a former jockey, was "known to thousands of San Franciscans during more than a quarter of a century."[5]

Some variations occurred in the images of Blacks, reflecting variety among Negroes as well as degrees of racism among observers. Occasionally reporters were quite complimentary, lacking the Negrophobia characteristic of many southern journalists. One late nineteenth-century reporter revealed an uncommon eye for feminine beauty when he noted "several shapely Afro-American young ladies [who] rode to the [Midwinter] Fair grounds on their bicycles . . . jauntily attired in knickerbocker costumes." The procession that took over the grounds on Colored American Day was described, surprisingly favorably, as "a composite picture of dignity, grace, and color as it moved around the court of honor."[6]

Other descriptions reveal the paternalism underlying the racism of even well-intentioned whites. While "Uncle Jerry" Peterson of the Palace Hotel was heralded as "in a sense, a veritable aristocrat of his race and condition," the title "Uncle" evidenced both familiarity and condescension. When he died in 1902, a newspaper obituary identified him as a Negro—"as the affectionately familiar title might indicate." Jerry Peterson had stayed on at the Palace "solely because of his popularity with the guests" after white workers replaced Negroes. He was described as a "cheerful, courteous, soft-speaking, darky," as "discreet, ever courteous, kindly, obliging, and in every sense of the term a gentleman." These were ideal qualities for a servant, although the modern reader might wonder what went on in the mind of a man who was privileged to view what one scholar referred to as "the seamy intimacies of high life." Peterson's death notice leads to the conclusion that he was a victim of an American apartheid, even in death; his obituary ended with the happy speculation that he had gone "where all good darkies go."[7]

Black San Franciscans were denigrated in such other ways as daily minstrel shows. San Franciscans could not get enough of the nineteenth century's most popular entertainment. In 1862 a Black resident complained about the "Jim Crow Exhibitions and Negro Extravaganzas" that occurred nightly in the Bay city. "Pernicious men" staged these exhibitions "at the expense of the poverty and ignorance of an oppressed, long-outraged and downtrodden people." "Ridiculously highly exaggerated similitudes" performed by white men were bad enough, but the entertainments "assumed a new phase" in San Francisco (and in the nation) in the Civil War era. "Men, naturally black, . . . have been induced, through ignorance, lack of principle, or sheer cupidity, to be a party in representing by public entertainment, their own degradation and that of their unfortunate race." James Madison Bell, a poet and plasterer, wrote: "This, Mr. Editor, is by far 'the unkindest cut of all.'" Another Black citizen, commenting on a Negro-performed minstrel show held in the former St. Cyprian Church building in 1859, noted: "Truly we have an uphill road in endeavoring to elevate some of our people to a commonsense standard."[8] In the early twentieth century Blacks were confronted with Thomas Dixon's novel *The Clansman* and D. W. Griffith's technically innovative film adaptation of it, *Birth of a Nation*. The problem was compounded by Afro-American participation. For example, Bert Williams and George Walker disliked using blackface and minstrel stereotypes when they started in San Francisco in the 1890s, but at that time it was the only form of entertainment that was popular, acceptable to whites, and lucrative.[9]

Racist stereotypes were also featured in both white and Black newspapers. A cartoon that appeared in the World War I era illustrates the legacy of minstrelsy. "Kelly Pool—Winners and Losers" depicts a poolroom scene in which the winner counts his take while his cronies make excuses for losing, and one hanger-on contemplates getting a loan from the winner. A Negro in a white coat cleans the pool table and amiably chatters to the winner. None of the cartoon characters are nobly portrayed; but while the white men are clearly individuals, the Negro looks and talks like a man in blackface.[10]

A cartoon that appeared in the Black *Pacific Coast Appeal* in 1904 shows a Negro laundry woman explaining that she borrowed her mistress's fine clothes to attend a cakewalk. She speaks in what passed for Negro dialect and is depicted stereotypically, while the mistress appears to be a refined upper-class society lady. In 1915, the San Francisco *Western Outlook* carried a cartoon of a well-dressed Black couple, both very dark with full lips. The caption read:

She—Go on, niggah, I doan want none ob yo' lip.

He—It's plainly obvious, mam, dat you doan need none ob it.[11]

The turn-of-the-century Black newspapers got as much as half of their material from a syndicate, so they sometimes appear to be no different from any white newspaper. This perhaps accounts for the degrading material, although it remains ironic and tragic to see these cartoons in journals that regarded themselves as instruments of race elevation. This was the dilemma for Afro-Americans: they sought acceptance from a society convinced of white superiority.

Culture-conscious Blacks, sensitive to their appearance as evidence of quality, joined societies and clubs to acquire social skills and poise. They believed that images of refined Negroes could counter the stereotypes, so positive images were invariably featured in Black-written newspaper articles, in dances and processions, and in obituaries. Flattering images of the urbanites were also projected in photographs. The pioneers preferred to see themselves as refined cosmopolitans whose lives were a constant program of balls, parades, festivities, celebrations, concerts, fairs, and exhibitions. These images present to us the Afro-Americans as they wished to be seen and remembered. San Francisco's cosmopolitan character encouraged the pioneers to project themselves in certain ways. Costumes and stylish fashions distinguished them from anonymous residents, and imparted an identity that contrasted pleasingly with their humble origins. The city's many nationalities and ethnic groups, and its tradition of anti-Negro prejudice, only increased the need to be readily identifiable as a cultured citizen of the metropolis.

Before eastern cities attracted large numbers of foreign-born migrants, San Francisco housed "a population more mixed than one finds anywhere else in America, for Frenchmen, Italians, Portuguese, Greeks, and the children of Australian convicts abound there side by side with Germans, negroes, and Irish."[12] This variety fascinated residents and visitors, but it also posed a problem: What form of behavior should serve as the model for the many different city dwellers? Fashions in dress and recreation answered the question.

When roller skating appeared in San Francisco it was popular among Blacks, suggesting the degree to which they were stimulated by urban fads. There is no evidence that Blacks participated in the first wave of rink skating in 1866, but when the fad returned in the early 1870s, they showed familiarity with and accomplishment in that form of entertainment. In the late summer of 1871, a group of Black San Franciscans, including William H. Blake and James B. Wilson, managed the First Grand Masquerade Skating Carnival of the New Pavilion Skating Club in Platt's Hall. The event was eagerly anticipated: "All the *elite* had been on the *qui vive* for some time past, and all desired for it a success."[13]

The day-long affair consisted of a number of scheduled events. "A grand operatic overture" by the orchestra opened the carnival. The leisured urbanites, masked and dressed as "Sailor Boy," "Red Riding Hood," a "French Cook," a "Chinese Mandarin," and the like, skated in a Grand March. An hour later they competed for prizes. After an exhibition by an accomplished rink performer, the best skaters displayed their poise and skill by executing a Grand Quadrille. Upon receiving prizes and unmasking, they put on their street shoes and danced through a program of quadrilles, waltzes, a polka, and a mazourka until nearly four in the afternoon.[14] The day's events indicated mastery of skating, and the masquerade demonstrated a measure of refinement. It was a serious occasion; only those who practiced at the New Pavilion Club could compete in the "Grand March and all the Fancy Skating," and, to prevent claims of unfair judging, the managers obtained officials who were "entire strangers to the participants."[15]

Life in San Francisco was itself a charade, for appearances counted as much as origins. While roller skating, pioneers could exhibit their skill; and masks and costumes allowed them to perform, to conceal, and to reveal as they wished. The well-dressed Negroes around Portsmouth Square were like the masqueraders. Because appearances and wealth were the mark of quality, dress, style, and manners were of prime importance. San Francisco was full of newcomers and strangers who often sustained sudden changes of fortune and who wished to exaggerate their importance and obscure humble backgrounds.

San Francisco must have particularly appealed to Blacks, for there many races mingled, and the low-born won distinction. But a Black readily identifiable as such suffered reduced opportunities and, sometimes, exclusion from a Bay Area residency. So when Blacks dressed in fashion, or demonstrated dancing or skating skills, they enhanced their urban identity. Acceptance of them occurred in spite of race prejudice. This was proof of an equalitarian, or at least non-racial, strain in San Francisco society, and bolstered Blacks' faith in it.

"Passing" as non-Black was another way to dodge racism. Colored city dwellers often emphasized the variety of their racial strains to challenge the argument that, as Africans, they belonged to an inferior race. Occasionally Black biographers gave European and Indian (as well as African) ancestry to their subjects.[16]

Philip A. Bell, aware of the absurdity and injustice of the American race system, emphasized multiple racial strains. Tall, gaunt, and light-complected, Bell was particularly sensitive to this matter. Possibly because he differed from the popular image of the Negro, he often noted Blacks' complex racial make-up. He described himself as possessing eyes, skin, and hair of a "dull yellow" hue. In an editorial on prejudice, he wrote, "The colored people of the North are more of European than African lineage," and maintained that "probably some eight or ten generations back a remote ancestor on one side may have come from Africa, but the majority are as much European descent as the White American."[17] Although he probably exaggerated the remoteness of the African strain, there was some substance to Bell's point of view, for contemporary photographs clearly show the mixed racial origins of pioneers.

Many observers noticed that Negro San Franciscans ranged in color from nearly black to the lightest shades found among humans. Samuel Clemens commented on this in 1863, and a decade later a visitor to the San Francisco colored school remarked that the students' "natural complexions, and the texture of that which adorns their throne of reason—all, all represented the would-be Anglo-Saxon race."[18]

"White" Negroes could never be certain when they would be recognized, embarrassed, and even worse, denied employment or social advantages. They emphasized the American and San Franciscan aspects of their identity, concealing their Afro-American background when it would disadvantage them. Sometimes it was only necessary to apply for a position with the confidence and directness of a white person, while on other occasions Negroes simply assumed that acquaintances and employers knew they were Black.[19]

In San Francisco and Oakland, as in many large cities, it was easy for a Negro to confuse residents. Dress, deportment, and physical appearance were important, for racism often depends on visual perception. Afro-Americans were not always readily identifiable, especially when they did not resemble minstrel figures. Even Chinese might be confused for

Negroes. In the 1850s a writer claimed that Chinese women resembled Black women: Although the Chinese had complexions "in some instances approaching to fair, their whole physiognomy indicates but a slight removal from the African race." A few years later, the *Elevator* reminded readers of the absurdities of American racism by reprinting an account of how a Black woman passed as Spanish. "If a person of African descent, being passably light, can only mutter some foreign language as Spanish, French, Portuguese, etc., they can enjoy American hospitalities." Ironically, "*the more perfect their English tongue and manners*, the more certain they are of being treated with American barbarity." Most city dwellers were used to variations among Europeans, but the nuances among people of color were unfamiliar. An early twentieth-century portrait of city life claimed that the city's populace included the dark-skinned Italians, Mexicans, Peruvians, Pacific Islanders, and "others in whose embrowned and bearded visages it was impossible to recognize any especial nationality."[20]

Black pioneers took advantage of this by cultivating a foreign accent, giving an Italian or Portuguese name for employment purposes, and affecting foreign manners. A Spanish, American Indian, or Hawaiian identity led to greater freedom in the city. Black folk relied upon cultural and linguistic differences among Blacks, learned a foreign language, and depended upon American ignorance, thus compounding the problem of identification. This created confusion both for racists and for innocent residents, while it allowed a measure of latitude for Negroes. In 1862, shortly before California permitted Negroes to testify in cases where whites were accused, a remarkable incident showed how far whites might go to identify Blacks. The conviction of the white murderer of George W. Gordon, a prosperous Black barber, hinged on the testimony of a light-skinned Negro. To determine the man's race, the judge called in two "hairologists," southerners who claimed they could identify an Afro-American from his hair and nails. After performing their examination, they concluded that the witness for the prosecution was one-eighth Negro, making his testimony inadmissible.[21]

Although race sometimes caused problems and inconveniences, most San Franciscans did not usually scrutinize others so closely, so that Blacks who wished only to blend in and be left alone delighted in the freedom. As at masquerades and costume balls, citizens assumed new identities for a variety of reasons. Policemen blackened their faces and hands, imitating Negroes in order to enter and raid illegal gambling houses. Negro entertainers impersonated Hawaiians or West Africans when a production required it, refining the chameleon-like quality that was so convenient off as well as on the stage.[22]

Passing aside, the Afro-San Franciscans envisioned themselves as pioneers, adventurers, cosmopolitans, sightseers, workers, prosperous city dwellers, revelers, denizens of the sporting world, and so forth; they had both an urban and an ethnic identity. This duality is similar to that described by William E. B. Du Bois, who singled out a national (American) and an ethnic (Black) identity. But in 1903, when his *Souls of Black Folk* appeared, the emphasis was rural and southern, and many people overlooked Blacks' American traditions, stressing instead their "backwardness" or, at best, their quaint ethnicity. Du Bois had to underline the Black national character to remind both races of what they shared.[23]

The Bay Area welded different city dwellers into a cosmopolitan group despite, and partly because of, their varied origins. In 1852, William H. Hall married in New York City after returning "flush" from a California sojourn. "The splendor of the occasion was, perhaps, without a parallel in 'the history of colored society in New York'"; its magnificence mirrored the standards of both the old east coast metropolis and the new Pacific slope city.[24] In the winter of 1860, a San Francisco banquet was also favorably compared to New York affairs. Hosted by the wife of "one of our prince barbers," the event was described in an understated manner: "As you are aware of the doings in Fifth Avenue on such an occasion, I need only convey your ideas to that locality, for a favorable comparison, without encumbering your columns with the details of this most splendid affair."[25] Black folk also staged ceremonies that matched those of sophisticated white San Franciscans. When Wellington C. Patrick, a barber, married Mrs. Sarah Anderson in 1867, a crowd gathered outside the event. Strains of operatic music played by the Black Pacific Brass Band held the curious and attracted other passersby. "The whole arrangement was displayed with such grand simplicity and dignity, that the doubt was created as to whether there are colored persons among us that could be so refined." Brief glimpses of Negroes in "black broadcloths, white vests, silks, satins, etc." were visible when the door was opened.[26]

Social events were held frequently, so that different clubs and cliques could compete. The Blacks on the Palace Hotel crew were swept up in a whirl of social events shortly after their arrival in the city late in 1875. E. T. Lewis said that "during the short time we have been in your city, it has been a continued 'go' with us from one place of entertainment to another; and so abundantly have we partaken of the hospitality of your residents that we feel obligated to you for the many social favors." A few months later, another hotel worker testified to the number of social entertainments, although in a critical tone. Since their arrival, hardly a day had passed without "some catch-penny entertainment held by those claiming to be the *elite* of colored society in this city; indeed, the truth is, they have been so frequent that the greater portion of us have long since looked upon them as little less than a nuisance."[27]

The numerous events permitted Blacks to assume refined, idealized roles. Women enjoyed opportunities to plan elaborate programs and to vie with one another for acclaim as "the belle of the ball and queen of the evening." The newspapers carried picturesque descriptions of their elaborate dress and compared their jewels and stunning gowns. Reports of celebrants in the 1870s mentioned "the longest court train in the hall," a "cherry colored tarlatan trimmed with white lace," and "the Masonic jewels of her late father, . . . consisting of the Rite of Memphis, KADOSH, or the Star of Sirius, and the Rose Cross on beautiful purple silk trimmed with mauve." Hair was decorated "*a la Francaise*" or "*a la Pompadour*," and other styles were similarly described: women were "tastefully attired in a rose-colored *moire antique*, with spangle illusion overskirt, *en train*," or were "in pink tarlatan, and train *a la Anglais*." Citizens discussed these events and contested the decisions of judges or reporters on the best-dressed women.[28]

Such programs continued well into the twentieth century. In 1915, the San Francisco Women's Club sponsored a cosmopolitan, though not lavish, program, at the home of a member at 1962 Pacific Street. A "Japanese social" was featured, in addition to a "carefully prepared paper on 'women.'" Prizes were awarded for the best Japanese costume. After World War I, the Cosmos Whist Club changed its name to the Cosmos Social Club, elevating the tone of its social life. After an elaborate dinner and ball in 1922, the *California Voice* claimed the club had "set a precedent toward the uplift of the morale and standards of our western civilization. . . . The whole affair was perfect and that tone of refinement permeated the air."[29]

In a city of strangers jockeying for social status, a refined demeanor opened doors and made possible contacts and friendships. For ex-slaves or their descendants, a refined, urbane life style symbolized the heights an Afro-American could attain, thus proving the equality of Black folk. This refinement has since been repudiated as pretense, but Negro urbanites of San Francisco had little trouble identifying with the most aristocratic citizens of American and European metropolises. Leading Black scholars, notably W. E. B. Du Bois, James Weldon Johnson, and Alain Locke, and Black heroes from Frederick Douglass to Jack Johnson, emulated these ideals.

Elite social affairs permitted image-conscious Afro-Americans to equal more privileged citizens. The *California Voice* was serious when it claimed the Cosmos Social Club affair uplifted "our western civilization." Other citizens would view the Black guardians of culture as equals as a result of their refined events. Initially the Cosmos Club probably did not regard itself as a means for social elevation, but when members refined the group's activities, the club became "a necessary medium, through which a higher status for its members—the communities in which they live, and the pursuits in which they engage,—may be reached." These new heights offered proof positive (in the cloyed language of the time) "that 'Souls as Pure,' and 'Hearts as True' are to be found in human beings [regardless of color]."[30]

Naturally, the refined Afro-San Franciscans believed it necessary to separate the respectable from the rabble, and resented the fact that all Afro-Americans were lumped together in the popular imagination. Like whites of the nineteenth and early twentieth centuries, they viewed class divisions as necessary and desirable, and found loathsome "the conglomeration of vice and virtue, reputable and disreputable characters" at social events. In 1890 the *Sentinel* argued that "some sort" of distinction was necessary at their affairs. "Disreputable characters . . . and strangers with nothing to recommend them, and without references," should be excluded in order to protect "mothers, wives, and sisters of our little community."[31]

Moreover, a respectable demeanor, not color, should be the sole basis for admission to public facilities; Blacks resented the color barriers that prevented even clearly proper and refined citizens from participating in urban life as they desired. When "two of our most respectable females" were ejected from a city railway car in 1863, the *Pacific Appeal* argued that there had been no valid reason to refuse service. The other passengers did not object to the women's presence, evidently believing that their "appearance indicated propriety and respectability," so the employee's action was particularly reprehensible. The same position was frequently taken by Black newspapers and citizens.[32] Racist whites tended to make all Afro-Americans their victims, but Blacks still attempted to distinguish themselves in dress and manner, clinging to the belief that genteel behavior, proper manners, and a refined appearance increased their chances of acceptance.

The concern with appearances resulted from the nature of San Francisco. In a city of anonymous souls, new clothes and manners made for a new identity. When two Jamaicans arrived from the West Indies dressed in the latest Caribbean fashions, they immediately sought out another West Indian; the latter advised them to purchase new suits so that they would not look ridiculous. John A. Somerville termed learning to dress in "proper attire" "our first lesson" in American life. It was also their first lesson in urban living.[33]

Masonic dress and band uniforms gave urbanites a special identity, as well as fraternity with fellow members and admiration from others.

Anonymous residents paid particular attention to the styles, appearances, and exploits of the city's heroes; this helped some lose sight of their own humble status. A military, Masonic, or band uniform, or a stylish suit of clothes, made identification easier and enabled residents to distinguish the city's heroes—successful veterans of battlefield and counting house campaigns—from ordinary urban dwellers. A military uniform allowed the raw recruit to rank with the veteran in the eyes of average urbanites. The appearance of manliness and prosperity mattered as much as actually having those qualities.[34] Black military organizations projected images that met their members' deepest needs. Prestige, dress, and bearing of course varied with rank and insignia, but all men in uniform were differentiated from the anonymous souls that walked the streets in ordinary garments, in search of themselves and of companionship.

Sergeant W. H. Carney was a Civil War veteran who fought with the 54th Massachusetts Regiment, which won a distinguished reputation for its valor and steadfastness in battle. In 1867 he received one of the highest tributes that pioneers bestowed upon their heroes. The veteran was appointed Grand Marshall of the Day in the Fifth Anniversary Celebration of the Emancipation Day Proclamation, the most important festivity for far western Afro-Americans in 1867. He was responsible for directing the grand procession that wound its way through the streets. Like a general on the field, he gathered information on the route, conferred with aides, and delivered orders with the punctillio that the occasion demanded.[35]

Veterans and youth won acclaim by participating in the volunteer military organizations that were popular after the Civil War. The first such society in San Francisco was organized in 1866, and after three years the Brannan Guards—named for a California pioneer who helped them purchase uniforms—consisted of forty-five men. They maintained an armory on Pacific Street above Powell, meeting for drill—sometimes in full uniform—every Wednesday evening in 1869.[36]

The Brannan Guards, the Sumner Guard, and the Moore Cadets, a youth organization, acquired and perpetuated the skills and values of soldiers and developed military zeal among Negroes. A veteran who viewed an exhibition by the Black cadets in Dashaway Hall in early 1866 expressed the pride that many Negroes felt as they watched the youngsters' drills: "I never in my life saw a better drilled company than these juvenile soldiers." Black youth thus learned and demonstrated how to present a manly image and combat racial oppression.[37]

The military societies ranked among the most popular voluntary organizations in the late nineteenth century. The zeal with which colored men joined these companies was exhibited in 1874, when a new society was formed. Beverly Dodson was Sergeant-at-Arms, George W. Bell was secretary, and James H. Riker chaired the meeting called to form the company. "A most spirited election" was held, and three ballots were needed to elect the captain. The men competed for prestigious offices to such an extent that a reporter observed, "It was with some difficulty that the judges could maintain their equilibrium for producing fair play in the matter." Following the election and drill practice, they satisfied their thirst and their desire for camaraderie in nearby saloons, which were reopened especially for the occasion. For many, the urge to join was irresistible: "The number of young men already enlisted is 67," the *Elevator* commented, "and from the manner in which the 'fever' works, more is [sic] expected."[38]

In the spring of 1872, the first picnic of the season, held at Scheutzen Park in Alameda, permitted a glimpse of Black social life and of the role of the Brannan Guards, who sponsored the affair. The seventh annual target excursion began when about twenty of the Guards marched through San Francisco from their armory to the wharf, where they boarded a transbay steamer. After disembarking and taking a train to the park, the Guards and groups of Black picknickers "indulged in dancing out the programme, whilst others thought that skating, swinging, riding on hobbies, shooting, racing, sparking, wooing, and eating were all the pleasures necessary to give merriment to a Picnic." Fifteen Guards competed for prizes, firing their weapons at the bull's-eye from 153 yards. Ex-Captain John Jones, the previous year's winner of the Company's Gold Medal, presented the prize to Ex-Lieutenant William H. Ferguson. One of the speakers for the occasion, Nathan Porter, complimented the Guards "on their success, and the brilliant efforts and heroic achievements of the Black soldiery during the late war." He hoped the Guards would continue "to bear that independent spirit and action that has characterized it since its organization." Porter "paid a glowing tribute to the departed heroes" of the Civil War, eulogized Abraham Lincoln, and "at the close of his remarks he was heartily cheered with 'a tiger.'"[39]

The pioneers' traditional heroes were soldiers, ex-slaves, and anti-slavery men; as the slave and abolitionist generation passed, American military conflicts created new heroes. A chance to fight in Cuba, in the Philippines, or in Europe engaged the imaginations of Afro-American males and prompted them to join the Black regiments—the famous Ninth and Tenth Cavalry or the Twenty-Fourth and Twenty-Fifth Infantry Divisions.[40] The arrival of the Twenty-Fourth Colored Infantry in April 1899 dramatically depicted the military tradition of Negroes. The several companies stayed at the Presidio and on Alcatraz Island for three months. "Heroes of the Fight at Santiago," as the local press designated them, they reminded city dwellers of the valiant deeds of Black men in Cuba.[41]

As both southerners and northerners became increasingly racist and violent, Black city folk desired tangible evidence of their manhood. These soldiers fit the bill, especially since their sojourn on the coast was "a reward of merit" for valor in the Caribbean. The *Call* remarked that there were "no braver soldiers there of any color than they, and they won more glory than they could carry home." Despite the hardships, and despite the fact that in Cuba they sustained more illnesses and deaths from yellow fever than white troops, the colored soldiers' valor was unquestioned.[42] Their presence had a tangible impact on the lives of Black westerners they befriended. When they sailed for the Philippines in June 1899, a "big crowd of relatives and friends" saw them off from the Pacific Street wharf. Some 150 volunteers joined the regulars, and another large contingent of recruits sailed with the remaining companies of the Twenty-Fourth on the following day.[43]

Patriotism undoubtedly encouraged many to enlist, on this occasion and on others. But the campaigns in the Pacific, or in Europe during World War I, also provided recruits with opportunities to measure and prove their worth as men—at a time when society afforded few chances for them to do so. Like the military and fraternal societies, the army allowed Afro-American males to band together, to trade knowledge and insights, to develop unity, and to project a heroic image, while the city excluded them from such quasi-military positions as policemen and firemen until the 1920s. Under military discipline, a Black man could both test himself and continue the tactics and skills developed during the Civil War and Indian campaigns. Service encouraged courageous actions that served just as well in fighting prejudice and injustice at home.

The Black men's enthusiasm for order, dignity, and fraternity accounted for the existence of three Masonic lodges in San Francisco alone from the mid-1850s. Hardly any social organization was as popular; if pioneers' obituaries are any indication, nearly every respectable Afro-American male joined a fraternal order, and many belonged to several. These societies have never received the attention they deserve from scholars. Through fraternal orders, many Black men found fellowship, perpetuated values, learned traditional masculine and heroic roles, and projected the sense of dignity and self-worth that often is not seen in Afro-Americans.[44] Male societies provided camaraderie for lonely strangers. Splendid uniforms evidenced worth and stature, while oaths, insignia, signs, and countersigns bound members together. The societies dealt with certain human needs. Single men distant from friends and relatives depended upon their comrades to care for them when ill, and finally, to bury them with the ceremony befitting their rank.

The cultured gentleman was another exemplar of Black ideals. He stemmed from a tradition that originated among European aristocrats, combining education and erudition with chivalry. In San Francisco particularly, a gentleman thought of himself as cosmopolitan; moreover, he admired martial qualities, thus reflecting contemporary traits. He read the classics, presented a stolid front to the business world, and belonged to a men's club; he exalted fencing or boxing. In the business arena and in sports, he developed desirable qualities. The genteel tradition that urban gentlemen upheld is particulary apparent in photographs, where the most flattering self-conceptions are presented. The subjects wore fine suits, stood straight and stiff, and sported Van Dyke beards and long or short moustaches, depending on the fashion. Facial hair gave men an individual stamp, as head hair was invariably short, unless it could be worn long and wavy. In the photographer's studio, pioneers presented their idealized selves, exhibiting the look of supreme confidence, dandified styles and poses, Masonic pins, and canes which distinguished gentlemen from unfortunate ne'er-do-wells, the unemployed, and common citizens. Equally important, these images contrasted starkly with the stereotypes portrayed in newspaper cartoons and in minstrelsy.[45]

Dark suits and a formal bearing bespoke the gentleman in the same way that military uniforms evidenced manly achievements. For urbane Black males, social skills were a basis of pride and of a cosmopolitan identity. They learned the "Fine Art of Dancing" at Seales Hall in 1865 where, for three dollars per month, they attended the evening school run by Simon P. Clark and Shadrack Howard. Black gentlemen exhibited their competence at the numerous promenade concerts, "hops," and balls. Women as well as men learned the science of "Vocal Music"; as enthusiastic singers or as appreciative listeners, Black residents enjoyed the choral jubilees and grand operatic concerts that were popular in the nineteenth century. In 1872 they heard a choir of two hundred vocalists, an orchestra, and a military band execute the American, English, French, and German national anthems and selections from European composers in Pacific Hall. They attended the exhibit of the Black sculptress, Edmonia Lewis, who visited the city in 1873, and participated in amateur dramatic productions. The latter allowed them to assume the roles of stage heroes and to display the poise, diction, and presence of mind valuable for success in a competitive city. Philip A. Bell's Shakespearean readings and William Blake's musical presentations have been noted. In 1904, J. C. Rivers, an ex-slave who was active in the Afro-American League, formed a dramatic company named after Charles H. Tinsley, who was a bellman, butler, and waiter.[46]

Black gentlemen also cultivated and perpetuated knowledge of Greek, Latin, and English authors, and valued the parliamentary and oratorical skills of the European tradition. The list of officers of the San Francisco

Literary Institute, formed to discuss and disseminate knowledge, read like a Who's Who of colored urbanites in 1862. The president, James Madison Bell, was a poet and plasterer; other officers included James R. Starkey, Philip A. Bell, James E. Brown, and William H. Blake—all active leaders in the social, cultural, and political affairs of the Bay Area. Such men emulated the leading actors of classical European literature and the politicians of England and the United States when they held meetings or discussion groups. Their erudite speakers quoted Solon and d'Alembert. They attended lectures on the political rights of Blacks, the condition of freedmen, and such subjects as "The Nation concedes to the Colored Race the right to be Men." They believed that an educated and informed populace was a prerequisite for equality and a sense of manhood.[47]

While such behavior may strike modern readers as peculiar, few Americans questioned these values until the twentieth century. The success of Blacks (or of any other race) was believed to depend upon the attainment of standards considered the goal of civilized man. If not everyone could quote the classics, all could at least develop knowledge of the world and acquire respect for the desired way of life for all humanity. Reading, reflection, and knowledge of the world—or at least of the U.S. and Europe—were as essential to refined urbanities as marksmanship was to soldiers. Leading residents used words in editorials, petitions, and orations much as soldiers used bullets. They warred against discrimination, vice, and immorality—those practices considered to be at odds with a civilized condition. Black city folk developed skills needed to project refined images in public meetings and councils of the race. They sought to attain heroic stature in public forums and on the dance floor, to reveal knowledge and skills that distinguished them from ordinary citizens.[48]

Blacks frequently wrote about the importance of "good manners"—the standards that prevented one from offending refined sensibilities. Manners were particularly important in San Francisco, because proper behavior increased the likelihood of acceptability in a city where individuals were often unsure of their status. Misunderstandings could offend sensibilities or even provoke physical violence; "no man or woman can mingle in polite society without the polish of refinement." The code of manners prevented, or at least lessened, social friction, and was in theory accessible to mechanics as well as gentlemen.[49]

Rather than proving effeteness, good manners and gentility enabled a humble resident to associate confidently with leading citizens. A measure of democracy characterized relations among urbanites as leading San Franciscans, Palace Hotel waiters, members of gentlemen's clubs, and prize fighters mingled as equals. "Unruly elements" and "hoodlums" who mixed with well-mannered city dwellers were also held to these standards.

When white men broke the rules of the Somerset Social Club entertainment by smoking cigars, they were rebuked by the manager of the affair. The *Elevator*, in reporting the difficulty, suggested that white men should not be admitted unless a member of the club spoke for their good behavior. Many leading Blacks would have concurred with the *Sentinel*'s contention that "refinement is one of the many essentials of gentility," a trait that "may be very easily acquired," even by those not born with it. The best way to learn it was through "cultivation of refined people."[50]

In nineteenth-century San Francisco, the gentlemen's code permitted Afro-American males to attain heroic stature and to rank with the most respected city folk. A Black boxer could win not only fame and money, but also the respect and friendship of residents who valued manners and muscle more than color. Because he mixed "with men of the world," Peter Jackson possessed "a polished manner" that, with his fighting prowess, won the respect of the California Athletic Club and many San Franciscans. He was the first of a new kind of hero that mixed with the sporting crowd but exhibited the gentility of refined residents.[51]

With increased urbanization and leisure time, Americans and Europeans devoted themselves to new kinds of recreation. Organized sports gained in popularity at the end of the century. Among the masses of new urban residents, athletics became the rage for spectators and prospective sportsmen. Clubs were formed to foster athletic ideals, aid sportsmen, teach discipline, and mold "character."

Champions of "the manly art," boxing, were models of health and masculinity during the late nineteenth century. After John L. Sullivan, boxers often displayed genteel manners, proving that they could be refined as well as combative. They became the idols of the sporting crowd, and leisured citizens appreciated their skills and endurance. Champions were monuments to physical conditioning, strength, and agility at a time when the nation seemed to value mechanical and literary skills more than brawn. In the late nineteenth and early twentieth centuries, champion boxers found the Bay Area congenial, because its residents delighted in boxing exhibitions and had the money to support fighters. Their every physical dimension was measured, commented on, and compared with those of other fighters.[52]

Peter Jackson, a West Indian, became a boxer in Australia, won the heavyweight championships of the British Empire and, by rights, of the United States (John L. Sullivan refused to fight him). In 1894, the *Call* publicized Jackson's measurements and manners so he could serve as a model for San Franciscans. The journal noted that his sixteen and three-quarter inch neck, thirty-nine inch chest, and thirteen (left) and twelve and one-half (right) inch biceps helped produce "one of the most finished boxers that ever stepped into the ring." Standing six feet and one-half inch and weighing two hundred and ten pounds, he was a rather large man for that time and for that matter a good sized heavyweight for the twentieth century. "The symmetrical body, lithe and sinewy muscles, carried about on a pair of spry, active legs, used to be the delight of the lovers of the pugilistic sport," the *Call* noted at the end of Jackson's career.[53]

Such fighters as Peter Jackson or Jack Johnson (or the white champion, "Gentlemen Jim" Corbett) represented a new type of nineteenth-century urban man. They combined the code of the gentleman with a measure of fine-tuned brawn and violence. With their popularity and their entourages, the champions ranked with European royalty. Moreover, they appealed to city folk, who delighted in physical encounters but, concerned with civilized standards, also desired a scientific exhibition. Boxers frequently personified the scientific style and degree of sportsmanship thought consonant with civilized life.[54]

Athletes were popular because their skills allowed them to excell, to surpass opponents in exhibitions, and to live independently. A few years before the earthquake, Jack Johnson was the hero of Oakland's Black citizens. The *Chronicle* observed he had "struck a congenial atmosphere in West Oakland, where his race abounds and [he] has been crowned king of them all." Moreover, "the colored population of all ages has thronged his quarters, until there was scarcely room left for him to work." The heroes were followed by a string of young aspirants. In June 1900, Young Peter Jackson, a Black fighter who possibly adopted the name of his hero, returned to San Francisco from Denver "bedecked in diamonds" that proclaimed recent successes. He had left the Bay city an unknown two years prior, but since then had lost only one bout—a disputed one at that.[55]

In an age of monopolistic enterprise, a champion athlete or leading entertainer could live in the style of the plutocrat. As various "sports" became known as scientific players and refined men, gentlemen took interest in athletics. Refined Bay Area citizens followed the sporting set, attended and gambled on boxing matches and horse races, and admired champions. Men of "culture" and "breeding" found a rough but pleasing sort of fraternity in the sporting crowd, much as they enjoyed the camaraderie of the gentlemen's club with their peers. Like men of humble origins, gentlemen exulted over athletes' muscle and nerve (just as Theodore Roosevelt or Jack London adored the strenuous life). They took pride in the fact that there was no necessary contradiction between a gentleman and a sportsman, even though some guardians of traditional culture thought otherwise. The male San Franciscan admired Peter Jackson's sheer stamina when he fought Jim Corbett for sixty-one rounds to a draw in 1891. He also admired the worldly manner that Jackson acquired through association, his "quick wit," and his skill as a "clever, well-informed conversationalist."[56]

In accordance with the gentleman's tradition, Jackson never belittled an opponent; nor would he discuss his own prowess. After retirement and numerous heavy drinking bouts that possibly hastened his early death, Jackson staged a comeback in early 1898. Though his drinking lost him popularity among some followers, and though they ridiculed the comeback of the Black athlete who found the racism of American boxers an unconquerable opponent, he refused to lambast his critics. "Until I am whipped my wish is that the sporting people of this city will refrain from cauterizing me because I may have not lived an abstemious life." Jackson's eloquence testified to the existence of gentlemanly ideals in fight circles, where previously champions had gained a reputation for little more than brutality and coarse language.[57]

San Francisco, by the way, was the western hub of the sporting world, and from the rise of Corbett in the 1890s to that of Jack Johnson shortly after the earthquake, it contributed more boxing winners than any other city. Aside from civic pride, the desire for money and love of competition caused northern Californians to follow prize fights, horse races, and other contests with the same devotion they paid to stock prices. The need to challenge opponents also promoted participation in different sports.

The competition of the business arena and the heroism of the battlefield merged in sports, which became a major business enterprise in the late nineteenth and early twentieth centuries. Urban dwellers emulated their heroes. For Black city folk in the late nineteenth century, sports permitted a champion like Jack Johnson to defeat the "white hopes" put forth by a racist society. Black winners in sports were kings among a people denied opportunities in business and politics. Physical competition could enable Blacks to stand out, to win money, and to attract adulators. When Jack Johnson won the heavyweight championship of the world in 1910, he proved that white men were not invincible. What was true in the ring might also hold in economic and political affairs. His victory presaged the gains for Blacks as well as the losses for whites that the twentieth century held in store.[58]

Whatever its source, an urban identity gave Blacks a perspective on racism. As the *Pacific Appeal* defined it in 1863, racism was "simply a mental hallucination, without reason or common sense," the "culmination of the chivalry sentimentalism engendered by the hell-born demon of slavery in the matrix of distorted minds."[59]

This sophisticated view indicates the frame of mind that enabled Blacks to survive in San Francisco. Slave heroes and antislavery speakers convinced them that chattel slaves were men capable of valorous action.

Black soldiers were gallant fighters who competed with white men as equals, engaged in life-and-death struggles, and killed their enemy on battlefields in the south and in Europe. Black champion boxers, like Black soldiers, were proof that whites could be defeated, and suggested that white domination could be brought to an end by the valorous efforts of Negroes. Black fighters who gained renown had qualities thought to be exclusive to whites. Black urbanites who won in games of chance and who developed oratorical skills offered evidence that Blacks deserved the civil and social rights accorded white males.

Negro pioneers sought and attained manhood through roles as athletes, urbane gentlemen, hoodlums, soldiers, fraternal officers, and eloquent orators; this reflected the opportunities of the urban world. Competition for fame and fortune was exacerbated by the congregation of large numbers of womenless men in a region fabled for its opportunities. Besides assuming new roles and proving their possession of manly attributes, Blacks perpetuated these values to prepare their youth for life in a racist society.

Negro city folk depended upon parades and military drills, in addition to barroom brawls, to teach each other how to conduct themselves, to instill discipline, and to foster martial values. To instruct youths, they held celebrations, pageants, and amateur stage productions, and related their exploits of the early years. Newspaper editors extolled the virtues of Afro-San Franciscans as they related tales of the underground railroad or the deeds of Frederick Douglass and Nat Turner. By emulating their heroes, the Black urbanites ranked with other residents, and contradicted monochrome portraits of Blacks as "Samboes" and "Uncle Toms."[60]

The city created many diverse roles that afforded opportunities for Blacks in search of a place to realize their ambitions. Bay Area Blacks were among the first Americans to experience this diversification; their creativity and organizational skills distinguished them both from other city dwellers and from inhabitants of rural areas. Passing as white or Spanish also gave Afro-Americans a sense of success. Passing not only made possible a job or access to housing or public accommodations, it also proved that Blacks could shed their racial identity, which was considered the antithesis of being cosmopolitan. The desire to escape not so much the race as the injustices inflicted on the race made Negroes ambivalent. Their churches, Masonic orders, and celebrations promoted race pride, but their desire to be accepted as soldiers, gentlemen, refined ball-goers, or "sports" were important non-racial poles. Analysis of these citified aspects of Black identity, which have not been fully appreciated, should clarify our understanding of how racial and non-racial aspirations influence Black urban life.

The reliance on passing indicates how far manners and deportment alone could carry Afro-Americans. Passing seems to have been practiced most frequently by people looking for work, indicating that being a heroic ex-slave or ex-soldier was not highly valued in the marketplace. That well-mannered Afro-Americans were subjected to racial prejudice shows that proper connections were valuable along with credentials as a cosmopolite or veteran.

Their high regard for European, elitist culture prevented Black San Franciscans from critically evaluating the Afro-American economic condition. Their meager numbers and cultural attainments were no match for the rise of Jim Crow. Nor did their proper manners matter to the thousands of Negroes who settled in New York, Chicago, and Los Angeles around World War I. Concern for genteel manners, refinement, and certain styles of entertainment encouraged Black urbanites to lavish money on expensive clothes and masquerade balls. This served only to divert money from business enterprises and to emphasize the distance between the prosperous citizens and the majority of Blacks.

The pioneers' heroes and elitist values indicate that nineteenth-century Black urban culture differed from that of the twentieth-century ghettos. The emergence of their own distinctive urban culture awaited the mass migration of the 1940s, when large numbers of southern-born Negroes brought uniquely Afro-American values to the Bay Area. Because they were often laborers or skilled workers, the newcomers of the Second World War years also possessed different kinds of skills. But before this development, early Bay Area residents experienced some success; and while they received little attention, they ranked with the pioneers who won praise for their roles in western settlement and urban life.

# 9

# Rounders

*Jack Johnson used to train over in Oakland in a place called Link*
*Dennis's. . . . Link had a big room in the back of his saloon over*
*there and that's where Jack used to train. . . . And Jack had an*
*automobile cut way down, way up high there. He would cut way*
*down like this, you couldn't see him. Just see his head. And this big*
*old four cylinder car used to come chucka-chucka. . . . Smiling.*
*Chucka-chucka. . . . Go down San Pablo Avenue every night.*
*Around six o'clock. Go right down to Fourteenth and Broadway*
*and then he'd speed back. The cops would get after him and have*
*him arrested. They'd get him a fine of five dollars. And he used to*
*ride on the side of his car on the—foot—boards, you know, they had*
*steps on the machines then. . . . . They'd stand on that and hang on*
*and Jack would speed up right fast past the. . . (inaudible)[place*
*where] the cops [were] hanging out. . . . . And old Jack, he used to*
*cruise back, chucka-chucka-chucka—lean way down. Waving at*
*everybody, everybody he saw (inaudible) marching past. . . . . . All*
*you could see is the head. Get way down. And all you could see was*
*the head, if you're looking, coming towards you. You had that*
*golden smile. Chucka-chucka—I can see that now.*

*Alfred J. Butler*

In 1933, a Negro newspaper nostalgically recounted how a well-
known Black resident of Berkeley took in the Panama-Pacific Exposition
of 1915. He cranked up his Buick and drove to "Link" Dennis's place, a
gathering spot for railroad men and local rounders near Seventh and
Willow streets in West Oakland. After a drink, he drove to San Francisco,
where, in addition to visiting the fairgrounds, he stopped at Lew Purcell's,
the famous Barbary Coast resort where Black jazz musicians, dance girls,
and patrons cavorted. Before returning home, he stopped off again at Link

Dennis's for a last round. The evening was in the San Francisco tradition, for it glorified the sophisticated pleasure of a night on the town.[1]

Night life is an integral part of any urban scene, and rounders, as the revelers were called, came from all walks of life. After a day's labor, workers retired to a saloon or a club, dined in a cafe or restaurant, and sought companionship; the affluent and bored entertained themselves by slumming—visiting the haunts that, to them, possessed a forbidden aura; and theatre people, athletes, musicians, and underworld characters enjoyed visiting the best spots and meeting the celebrities.

In San Francisco, activities and life styles that were invisible in daylight appeared in the late afternoon, quickened as the sun set, and intensified still more at night. Residents appreciated the way different classes mixed more freely after sundown, learning new dances, the latest music, and the slang of the underworld and sporting life. A Black newspaper noted in 1915 that local youths wore hats to look "tough" and danced "suggestively." "Notice the language of your son, the inflection of his voice, the snap of his fingers, the expressive English. He only needs the bones and tambourine." Cultural syles that were considered bohemian and immoral or criminal were an expression of the freedom that residents valued, and constituted powerful lures for urbanities.[2]

Just as the city was transformed at nightfall, so were its inhabitants. The glow of lights against the dark sky created an enchanting, festive air, as we see in a Black newspaper's description of the night life in Market Street near the Tenderloin: "Altogether the street is like the fairway of an enormous circus or carnival. Color, lights, crowds, music, candy, hawkers, ballyhoo—everything is there but the elephants and the sawdust." Among the passersby were thousands of varied faces of every race, creed, and color. "Hindoos, . . . Japanese . . . Black men [with] wide shoulders, slim hips, loose relaxed gait. . . . noisy Jews, Swedes, . . . Spaniards, fat Chinese, lean Englishmen mingling in the drift, physically together, yet retaining their individuality in a gesture or expression."[3]

From the Gold Rush era, the city was famous as the place where miners, lumbermen, traveling businessmen, and sailors went on sprees alongside the city's many unmarried wage earners, who had money as well as time to spend after a day's labor. Many San Franciscans lived in hotels and boarding houses instead of single-family units, and even the well-to-do who built homes still conducted their business from offices and hotel rooms. Dining out was customary for married couples as well as single souls because of the varied and inexpensive meals available in the restaurants. The resorts also were places for the married and unmarried alike to find companionship.[4]

From the Gold Rush era, the city of single transient men also became known as a vice center, which conformed to a common view of man and of the city. Brothels and lewd shows were necessary to pander to man's "base" instincts, just as other forms of entertainment met "refined" and "civilized" needs. Because it accommodated all, San Francisco was ranked with London, New York, and Paris as a "gay capital of international society."[5] The city's vice districts were matched only by New Orleans's Storyville. A prostitute testified to this during a 1917 anti-vice crusade: "It's the only wide open town except New Orleans, in America," she claimed. "We're all right. The police wink at us."[6]

San Francisco was said to be the last major American city where "commercial society and vice were frank and open commodities." Even during Prohibition, many San Franciscans continued to drink openly in cafes and night spots. In 1924, one federal official claimed that the "eighty-five percent wet" city was "the principal market for smuggled liquor on the West Coast." Not only did the city's residents refuse to support Prohibition, juries refused to convict.[7]

In other cities, such as Chicago, the dipomacy of a Johnny Torrio or the terrorism of an Al Capone made for a wide open city. In San Francisco, a long-established reputation as a pleasure or sin city permitted the night life to thrive without gangland violence, although there was municipal corruption. Landlords profited when their tenants paid exorbitant rents with profits from illegal activities, and politicians gained in votes and bribes. This state of affairs persisted despite reform, because the night life met the needs and won the support of mobsters, politicians, show folk, and patrons. As the *Examiner* observed in 1917, "The real root of this evil lies in the fact that the underworld can muster 20,000 or 25,000 votes in an election which are cast practically *en bloc*. The politicians need these votes."[8]

Why did the tradition of glamorous wickedness win the support of such a variety of San Franciscans? It permitted city dwellers to express interest in such activities of questionable propriety as drinking, dancing, slumming, mixing with Negroes, and having affairs. Knowledge of these forbidden pleasures distinguished the sophisticated from the prudish and provincial. The sporting districts and the bawdy shows ranked among the sights that the worldly should see. Frequent attendance of the popular resorts gave urban dwellers a sense of belonging.

For Afro-Americans, the night life served these and other important functions. Competition among club owners and entertainers allowed Black residents to prove their worth as individuals and as a group. Exclusive Black social clubs held balls and cotillions to prove that Afro-San Franciscans were "second to none" in the social realm. The fame won by successful show people made narrow job opportunities less significant.

Generally, the night life was a satisfying world that made racism seem less important.[9] Entertainment figured large in Black life. Because many fundamentalist Protestants viewed popular music, dance, and show business as frivolous if not downright sinful, entertainment roles were appropriate for an outcast group like the Blacks. This buttressed and continued a cultural tradition in which music and dance were central and in which even distinguished citizens were likely to cultivate their ability to perform.

Music and dance were prominent in Black San Francisco's cultural heritage. Blacks' love of entertainment was noted as early as 1859 by a San Francisco correspondent. "Withal religion and morality don't seem to be much sought after from the legitimate source by the majority of our people, as the theatres and other places of amusement get their usual share of Sunday nights' attendance." Because they valued entertainment so much, and because show business promised significant opportunities, Afro-Americans sometimes performed as minstrels, a mode of expression that made Black folk appear ridiculous.[10]

San Francisco's fame as a show town gave Negroes further incentive to acquire musical and dance skills and to join up with vaudeville or minstrel groups. This work was non-threatening because it accorded with stereotypes of the Negro. Because racism prevailed in both daytime work and nighttime entertainment, Afro-Americans found similar frustration in either arena, and consequently felt freer to choose a profession according to their inclinations. Their need for song and dance expressed itself everywhere one turned. In the 1860s a piano was purchased for the colored school, and concerts were held where pupils displayed musical talents. "Promenade concerts"—dances or balls—often followed dinners, bazaars, and celebrations. Ministers complained because churchgoers could not easily refrain from dancing. Music punctuated the addresses at nineteenth-century Emancipation Day celebrations. When the United Negro Improvement Association of Marcus Garvey, the Jamaican Black nationalist, held a meeting in the Bay Area in the 1920s, the program featured as many vocal solos, anthems, and hymns as it did speeches.[11]

Afro-Americans seem to have appreciated dances at night more than erudite speakers and literary entertainment at afternoon ethnic celebrations. In 1864 Samuel L. Clemens, then a reporter for the *Call*, noted that the dancing at a West Indian Emancipation celebration was not "a brilliant success." Though the Black dancers know little about the "formal" aspects of the art, "they 'let on' magnificently, as if the mazes of a quadrille were their native element, and they move serenely through it and tangle it hopelessly and inextricably, with an unctuous satisfaction that is surpassingly pleasant to witness."[12] Week nights as well as weekends were occasions for festivity. Shadrack Howard and Simon P. Clark held their "Grand Dress Ball" on May Day Night in 1865, which fell on a Wednesday evening. The 1868 West Indian Emancipation celebration took place on a Monday night. In 1915, an "All Night Southern Ball" occurred on a Monday night, and a few months later the Panama Canal Dance, sponsored by Harmony Court No. 167, a fraternal lodge, at Magnolia Hall in Oakland, was held on a Wednesday night. Aside from weekdays (usually Wednesdays), social affairs were commonly held on Saturday night. In August 1926, Black patrons danced to three different Bay Area Negro bands at an all-night masquerade ball.[13]

Of course there was criticism. Some leading pioneers felt that the time and money spent on dress balls, parades, dances, and the glittering regalia of fraternal orders was wasted. These social activities, it was argued, took money which should be saved and invested in such productive enterprises as real estate and business.[14] To keep some of this money among Afro-Americans, and to maintain Black social organizations, entertainments were sponsored by various societies, clubs, and civil rights groups. The churches, particularly, sponsored bazaars, fairs, dinners, and exhibitions to entertain Blacks and to raise money. All of these organizations competed with the saloons and billiard parlors that were the heart of the night life.

One popular resort, George Smith's Magnolia Saloon, was located in Apollo Hall, 808 Pacific Street, near Stockton. Opened in 1867, it offered colored city dwellers wines, liquors, cigars, and a fine billiard table. In 1869 the Magnolia became the Golden City Club, with William Freeman as the proprietor. It featured a "New French Carom Billiard Table." In 1869 a city dweller could frequent the Grant Invincible Billiard Saloon, at Powell and John Streets. Its advertisement in the *Elevator* read: "Walk in Gentlemen, sit down at your ease, Pay for what you call for, call for what you please." Later in the century, colored urbanites gathered south of Market Street in the saloon and private club rooms of the Aurora at 649 Mission Street or in the Acme Saloon of Manus D. Davis and Charles A. Jamieson. The Acme was taken over by Samuel F. King around 1890, and by the turn of the century King formed a partnership with Louis V. Purcell, whose name became associated with several Black clubs in San Francisco.[15]

Purcell's Elite Cafe was regarded as the most important Black night spot on the west coast in the early twentieth century. Slummers frequented the place often. A new dance, the "Turkey Trot," originated in Purcell's So Different Saloon at 520 Pacific Street. The So Different "was furnished only with a bar, a few rough tables and chairs, and a score or more wooden benches which faced a splintery dance floor." Bouncers were on hand to eject rowdies as well as mere spectators. The proprietor of Spider Kelly's, a place next door, reportedly lined the back of his bar with iron boiler plates to keep the bullets shot by Purcell's patrons from ripping through the walls.[16] After Purcell's death, Lester Mapp, a West Indian by birth, managed a string of San Francisco resorts, including Purcell's Elite Cafe and the Olympia Cafe, rising to prominence during and after World War I. Mapp employed "quite a number of men, probably more than any other colored man in Northern California."[17]

The colored night clubs were more prominent than their number or size would indicate. The resorts were termed black and tan, meaning they catered to white as well as Negro revelers. The photographer Arnold Genthe described "the most famous, as well as the infamous" Barbary Coast resort, the Olympia. Frequented by the "dregs of many countries," it was "a vast palace of gilt and tinsel with a great circular space in the center and around it a raised platform with booths for the spectators." The tom-tom, cymbal, horn, and banjo made a "barbarous sound" while "a medley of degenerate humanity" danced "weird dance steps." It attracted well-to-do city dwellers and foreign visitors, and such Afro-American bands as Lester Mapp's Jazz Dogs or Sid Le Protti's Crescent Orchestra provided the music. These bands won acclaim in the Bay Area, reflecting the emergence of an entertainment world in which Afro-Americans played an increasingly significant role.[18]

Not long before World War I, Black folk had depended upon white or mixed bands with white leaders for their social affairs. With the increased popularity of ragtime, jazz, and blues, the Negro entertainers who created these forms gained greater influence. In 1914 the Oakland *Western Outlook* noted: "Today white people are much in the same position that we were in a few years ago." Afro-American musicians were popular because "the white-light districts simply clamor for colored manipulators of the rag-time muse."[19]

To meet the demand, Black musicians and entertainers formed clubs, and colored night club men afforded regular jobs for bands and showmen. In San Francisco, as in New York and New Orleans, Black show folk organized in accordance with modern business practices. A Colored Entertainers' Club that combined economic and social functions opened in San Francisco in 1915. Located on the two floors of a building at 107 Columbus Avenue, near Jackson and Kearney in the heart of the Barbary Coast, and organized much like New York's exclusive Clef Club, its topmost floor featured refreshments and lounge chairs for entertainers, as well as a large polished floor for dance rehearsals. The lower floor contained the manager's office and reception and dining rooms. Each dues-paying member had his own key. A *Western Outlook* reporter who surveyed the resort noted, "It was a surprise to us and we must say it is the swellest club of its kind in the city."[20] The club indicated the Black entertainers' affluence and popularity. Membership and possession of a key highlighted the almost familial ties that developed among Black show folk. Finally, the club reflected concerted efforts to take advantage of the opportunities offered by entertainment.

Individual pioneers enjoyed quite a measure of freedom in the sporting world. Its support of John Tuers, a pistol marksman and minstrel man accused of killing a well-known theatre manager in the course of a brawl, has been noted (Chapter 6). Nearly half a century later, Olympia proprietor Lester Mapp also won an acquittal because of his close ties with the San Francisco Police Department. He was arraigned for violation of the Mann Act, prohibiting transportation of women across state lines for immoral purposes, and his conviction seemed almost certain. The testimony of railroad officials and witnesses mounted during the trial, giving the federal government a case it seemingly could not lose. But then nearly a dozen policemen affirmed his spotless character and the upstanding nature of the Olympia. When incredulous officials attempted to check police records against the testimony, they found the files had disappeared. Mapp won this case, just as shortly before he had won another on a technicality.[21]

Some creative Afro-Americans won acceptance in the bohemian, cosmopolitan entertainment milieu, which encouraged individual eccentricities and new styles. The most talented artists met, worked together, and developed both showmanship and fraternity. Their shared experiences and goals as artists also united the races, providing a defense against a hostile world.

Despite such camaraderie, at various times urban dwellers disagreed on what constituted proper entertainment. In the nineteenth century particularly, Irish, French, German, and British residents were more tolerant of a wide range of activities than many Americans. The newer Pacific coast cities emphasized their wholesome, family-oriented qualities, and reform-minded citizens believed that, in rebuilding after 1906, San Francisco should strive to match the character of Oakland and Los Angeles. Before considering the alarm of some twentieth-century San Franciscans at the city's night life, I should note certain developments that affected entertainment by the time of the First World War.

In the late nineteenth and early twentieth centuries, a relatively multi-ethnic urban culture emerged in the United States. Eastern and southern European immigrants introduced their distinctive attitudes toward politics, work, leisure, and consumption of alcohol. Joining with the earlier German, Irish, and French arrivals, the new immigrants popularized the use of spirits, wine, and beer, promoting the growth of a major liquor industry. This new enterprise, and the foreigners' customs, politics, and poverty, disturbed many Americans.

The Great Migration also threatened urban whites, as the Black newcomers enriched American culture with ragtime, jazz, and blues, as well as dances new to whites. Both the songs and the dances were shaped by African-derived rhythms. The dances were copied by whites, including Vernon and Irene Castle. The new recording industry distributed the music throughout the nation in the 1920s, so that it too spread into white culture.[22]

Whether San Francisco Blacks had a distinctive style of music and dance before 1900 is unclear. As in New York and New Orleans, some Blacks in San Francisco played European music and gave operatic concerts featuring American and particularly European composers. Colored San Franciscans danced the quadrille, waltz, schottische, and other European-derived folk dances, not those of the slave quarters. No evidence suggests that spirituals, blues, or traditional Negro folk songs were popular; probably the pioneers, like their eastern counterparts, shunned these art forms as relics of slavery.[23] But there is some evidence that Black San Franciscans knew of a distinctively Afro-American musical tradition, which some artists drew upon as early as the mid-nineteenth century. A Black San Franciscan "jazzed" or "ragged" traditional songs long before Americans accepted the practice; the habit of improvising appeared in San Francisco a few years after the Civil War.[24]

In the unlikely setting of a Grand Operatic Concert, the Afro-American pianist Arthur C. Taylor played in a fashion that the *Call* found most objectionable. "If he would drop the very unmusical habit of elaborating his accompaniments by adding little runs and arpeggios, [he] would really entitle himself to high praise." Like the musicians of New Orleans's Storyville and Chicago's South Side in a later era, Taylor was reluctant to let the composer have the final say. Admittedly, the popular custom of permitting virtuosos to vary the notes of a composition encouraged Taylor, who felt that his distinctive rendition and embellishments were of primary importance in presenting the music. The *Call*'s criticism indicates that embellishing was not an accepted practice. "The composer is generally the best judge of what the accompaniment should be, and is entitled, at least, to a faithful rendering of the music."[25] Nearly twenty-five years later in Stockton, a Black singer from Oakland added an embellishment to a traditional song that suggested Taylor's musical outlook. At the end of "Swanee," Oscar T. Jackson, a barber, improvised a new touch, "adding a higher bar at the finish, uncommon to the regular way of singing the old familiar song." The Stockton *Evening Mail* concluded that this change was "Mr. Jackson['s] own make up."[26]

While this does not prove the existence of a Black San Francisco style of music before 1900, it does suggest that Afro-American elements existed in the far west. After the turn of the century, travelers brought the music of New Orleans and New York to San Francisco. Black San Franciscans, it seems, played mainly the standard east coast and southern ragtime and jazz. They were familiar with the latter term by World War I, if not earlier.

Though the evidence is inferential, Black musicians in the Bay Area held their own among their peers. Jelly Roll Morton, who lived in San Francisco during the First World War, characteristically criticized Negro musicians in other towns, maintaining that they knew very little about ragtime or jazz, but he never said anything about San Francisco artists. Tom Stoddard has observed that the omission is significant, because Morton rarely missed an opportunity to contrast his abilities with those of local musicians. This suggests that Bay Area Negroes were accomplished in, and played, the latest style. Also, Morton did not comment on a distinctive west coast music, suggesting that his did not differ from that of the Bay Area.[27]

If San Franciscans did not evolve a style of their own, they at least shared in and presented the developments that transformed popular music. Ragtime appeared in San Francisco at least as early as the 1890s, when it received written notice in other urban centers. About this time Bert Williams learned to play ragtime accompaniments in San Francisco's saloons. At the end of the decade, sheet music spread the songs throughout the United States, and ragtime became a fad. The ambitious started schools for playing ragtime; one of the first in San Francisco was founded by Axel W. Christiansen in 1909. Apparently the term "jazz" was used in the Bay Area to denote dance styles before it was current in New Orleans or Chicago. Art Hickman, a white bandleader who is generally credited with first using the term, was influenced by Blacks. "As a feature Hickman included a banjo player in his orchestra—some one said he got the notion from watching one of the Negro orchestras at Purcell's on the Barbary Coast."[28]

It took several years for ragtime (later jazz) to become popular, because most people associated it with brothels, waterfront dives, vice, and Negroes. Even in 1917, the ragtime that respectable whites listened to was only an "imitation" of "the real Simon Pure cabaret ragtime."[29] The "real" ragtime or jazz was a genuinely American style that blended African rhythm, Afro-American melody, and European tradition and instruments to execute popular songs. It was appreciated by those who were familiar with different kinds of music, but not culturally Eurocentric. Played properly, it impelled people of all social classes and ethnic backgrounds to mingle in cafes and saloons and to delight in the African rhythms by dancing to and singing the songs.[30]

The communion the music encouraged was described in a romantic turn-of-the-century portrait of city life, in which three bohemians went to Sanguinetti's, a "saloony-looking restaurant" on the waterfront. A one-eyed, bullet-headed, bull-necked bartender served drinks, and patrons ate New England, Italian, and French cuisine. A policeman and his date, the captain of a bay schooner, and a Tenderloin politician sat among the patrons. "A buxom lass" danced to the popular Stephen Foster song, "Old Black Joe," while "several misses" sipped maraschino, sang "coon songs"—ragtime—and looked worldly. "Everybody joined in the songs; everybody called to his or her neighbor sans ceremony." The conviviality resulted partly from the continental decor, the cuisine, and the alcohol. But the most important ingredient was the music, which was an artful, cosmopolitan synthesis of national and ethnic traditions. Although it possessed European elements, this American urban music was often written and played best by Afro-Americans because of their command of the polyrhythms that were essential to the music. The two Black musicians at Sanguinetti's played banjo and guitar, "singing the while hilarious coon songs."[31]

Because it was so appealing, jazz frightened some city folk, especially when it became popular outside of the vice districts. Traditionalists objected to the Barbary Coast and Tenderloin dives because of the music, which they could hardly view as a legitimate art form. The dances, too, startled many Americans, who thought the hip movement that is essential to African and Afro-American dance was licentious. Around World War I, the *Western Outlook* maintained: "Our young men and women have no other thought but dancing"; worse yet, "the most indecent dances seem to be the most popular."[32]

From pioneer days on, Black San Franciscans danced at nearly every social event. They changed their style in the early twentieth century; the Grizzly Bear, the Turkey Trot, and the Texas Tommy were among the popular styles said to have originated in San Francisco. Slummers attempted to learn these new steps; even the famous Russian ballerina, Anna Pavlova, was captivated by the music and dance of the Barbary Coast resorts, particularly Purcell's. But others condemned the shimmy and the tango, which were thought "to invite the vulgar and immoral performances . . . [that] appeal to the lust" of youth. The fear of dancing was so strong that resorts were required to have licenses specifying what night of the week dancing was allowed. "Dance is the one indispensable feature" of the afternoon cafes and nighttime cabarets, the *Examiner* claimed.[33]

In 1926, a visiting minister spoke on jazz music and dance. Dancing has a "psychological effect" on the nervous system, he felt, and the bright lights in the resorts affect patrons' "emotional nature," while the physical contact of dancers causes changes in the atmosphere and in behavior. The beautiful colored dresses lure men in the same way that bright colors facilitate mating in nature. Combined with jazz, the concoction "breaks down the most stubborn wills," and "pure" women become "damaged goods." He denounced the new music and dance as "damaging, devilish, and damnable."[34]

The presence of women in the resorts was another appalling aspect of urban culture. The new freedom of American women recalled that of San Francisco adventuresses of an earlier era. During and after the first World War, in San Francisco and other cities, young unmarried women and housewives frequented cafes and night clubs where they smoked, drank, danced, and flirted with attentive males. In the nineteenth century discreet women had avoided such resorts, even in San Francisco, preferring the closed rooms of French restaurants, which provided privacy but which became obsolete in the twentieth century. As the *Examiner* noted, women frequented the afternoon cafes, where they made friends and, if they wished, exchanged phone numbers. Timid women mixed with bolder females, and youngsters were also present. Some married women became involved with the underworld, leaving their phone numbers with houses of assignation. For reformist ministers, women's club leaders, and Progressives, this represented a threat to home and society. They sought to prohibit afternoon dancing to deny women their "questionable pleasures," as the *Examiner* referred to them.[35]

The questionable pleasures compounded other concerns: the shortage of church-going women, the lack of home life, and the number of womenless men. The new urban culture might have been tolerated in the Bay Area, regardless of the reform movements in other American cities, except for this factor. When women approached the license traditionally accorded men, cafes and cabarets became intolerable. Men's entertainments—gambling, drinking, and sex—were no longer their exclusive domain. Fearful of these developments, the reformers joined forces, first in 1913 and again in 1917, to close the San Francisco resorts and to prohibit the sale of alcoholic beverages in restaurants.[36]

Sexual liasons among white rounders were bad enough, but the opportunity for white women to dance and mingle with Black men and other non-whites was even more abominable, and provoked reformers to single out certain clubs for close observation. Racism intensified dislike of these nightly gatherings. When asked why he denied the New Fillmore Workers Center a dancing permit in 1932, a San Francisco police captain replied, "You wouldn't want your sister to dance with a nigger."[37] While black and tan clubs were popular in New York City in the 1920s, they appeared in San Francisco and New Orleans some years before, and the chance to dance and have affairs with members of other ethnic groups made the latter cities especially attractive.

The reformers who sought to close the resorts included clubwomen, leading ministers, concerned churchgoers, and newspapers such as the *Examiner*. They desired "clean" entertainments, supervised recreation, and traditional music and dance, and sought to uphold contemporary standards. Their attempts to halt developments in urban American culture highlighted the differences between the contending groups. Reformists surveyed the resorts, interviewed call girls and patrons, and published their findings in the newspapers to mobilize support. Their descriptions of what repelled them, together with their arguments, were designed to create a sense of outrage and thereby to promote the cause of reform. The *Examiner's* articles of September 1913 and January 1917 reveal how disturbed residents were by the cafes and resorts where alcoholic drink flowed, Black music pulsated, and entertainers and customers danced in a loose-hipped style. If gambling and bribery of officials perturbed San Franciscans, these aspects of the new urban culture alarmed them even more.

National prohibition was one of the reformers' goals; they thought they had succeeded in 1919, when the Volstead Act was passed. By curtailing drinking, the Progressives, as the reformers were called, thought they could deal with alcoholism, saloons, and boss rule—problems associated with the new immigrants. The new city folk had ideas about patronage and government which were viewed as being at odds with American democracy; and they drank beer and wine in the course of a normal day. The crusade against alcohol, like the restricted immigration of the 1920s, was directed against the Europeans who helped strengthen the new urban culture.[38]

San Francisco's reformers hoped prohibition would seriously weaken the resorts. But the custom of consuming alcohol at every opportunity was so ingrained in traditional San Francisco life that enforcement of the Volstead Act proved merely to be a basis for harassing resort owners and their patrons. Thwarted for a time in closing the Barbary Coast, reformers were horrified when they learned that leading San Franciscans and fashionable society women frequented certain Negro night spots.

A number of Black resorts, including Purcell's, the Jupiter, and the Olympia, were harassed by police from 1917 to 1921. They were all black and tan clubs. The Olympia cafe was closed permanently after Christmas in 1921 when police found, according to a captain, "fashionably dressed white women . . . dancing with negroes and . . . white men . . . waltzing on the floor with colored girl entertainers." A few days later, the captain told the court that this was the reason for the raid, in addition to the fact that dancing took place on nights when it was not permitted. An *Examiner* reporter also said that the mixing of whites with Negroes was behind the closing. About the same time W. H. Wilkerson, another Black cafe man, was put out of business for similar reasons.[39]

In late summer of 1913, the *Examiner* led a temporarily successful campaign to close the Barbary Coast; the crusade marked the beginning of a battle that extended through the First World War years. As if to affirm the hollowness of the reformers' victory, San Francisco's rounders turned the last official night of the Barbary Coast's life into a celebration. "The strident voice of the Coast was lifted in a final crescendo of wild, untrammeled gayety [sic]," producing "a revel such as it had seldom seen before." In the last few hours, nearly ten thousand people entered the district to celebrate the occasion and to relive the glorious nights of an historical era.[40]

In fact the crusaders had not succeeded, for in 1917 they joined with the *Examiner* to close the resorts once again. After a fifteen-day grace period in February 1917, San Francisco police surrounded the Barbary Coast. Their attitude reflected the war mentality prevalent in a period of world conflict, labor unrest, and socialist revolution. Upon blockading the oldest and most infamous vice district in the far west, officials demanded that all resorts close and that the Coast's inhabitants leave the city. Police estimated that 1,400 prostitutes, musicians, cooks, and other resort workers left the district.[41]

Advocates of clean living were more successful after the United States entered World War I, and under Prohibition many notorious resorts vanished. A few remained, enduring thanks to connections with the underworld and with police officials.

Lester Mapp was said to be the "colored lieutenant of the McDonough brothers," two well-known residents who were allegedly "chieftains of the redlight district." In 1917 he won a liquor-license violation case on a technicality; in 1921, when he was acquitted of federal charges, his victory was celebrated joyously in the Olympia, in the very heart of the moribund Coast. Friends of Mapp, entertainers, slummers, and some of Mapp's police cronies drank and danced together. On Christmas night of 1921, police officials raided the Olympia twice because entertainers and patrons were dancing in violation of a city ordinance; they arrested Mapp on their first visit, demanded that the dancing cease, and returned a few hours later to make arrests when it resumed again. Eventually a series of police raids closed the Olympia, one of the last Barbary Coast night spots, and Lester Mapp went to Chicago.[42] Some resorts survived by following their patrons to the suburbs, where they located and behaved discreetly. They persisted despite attempts to segregate them away from residential areas, to regulate drinking and dancing, and to close them altogether.

Some San Franciscans, like the residents of New Orleans who created

Storyville, thought that vice segregation was the answer to the evils of city life. Just as race segregation kept whites from having to accommodate themselves to Black neighbors, vice could be contained in districts away from ordinary men, women, and children. But whether reformers used segregation, regulation, or complete shutdown, they failed to prevent the resorts from persisting, spreading, and influencing the young. The dispersal of vice resorts was a major concern by the late 1920s. The *Western American,* a Black Bay Area newspaper, commented on the spread in 1928, several years after the passing of the Coast and the enactment of national Prohibition. Women of "ill-repute," chased out of the vice districts, rent or buy new places anywhere they can and post rental signs. Then "they by some turn or another get acquainted with the next door neighbor and pretty soon she will accept a glass of wine and all else follows nine times out of ten. . . . Your wife or your daughter soon gets a touch of wild life and the end is near."[43] The same happened with bootleggers.

How San Franciscans worked to realize their conceptions of the city reflects the changes that followed the earthquake and fire of 1906. Vice resorts adapted to suburban locations, and San Francisco changed its ideas about amusement. Underlying the reform movements were the lower train fares and industrialization that brought working men with families and larger numbers of women to San Francisco. Because these new migrants went to Oakland and Los Angeles in even greater numbers, San Franciscans decided that it was time to create a "clean" city. Vice districts had a "deadening influence" on businesses, homes, social life, and respectable night life. The upcoming Pacific-Panama Exposition in 1915 spurred residents to present the proper image to tourists and their families.[44] The City Beautiful Movement found residents of San Francisco, Oakland, and Los Angeles attempting to outdo one another in the construction of new civic buildings, municipal projects, and parks. In San Francisco, closing the Coast was just one phase in the drive to establish a modern and progressive city that could stay apace with the new Pacific coast cities.[45] The increased number of women in San Francisco also influenced the reformers, who believed the reputation for wickedness should be killed to accommodate respectable young women and their beneficial cultural and social influences. Otherwise, prospective brides would favor Los Angeles, whose reputation stressed wholesomeness and health. Moreover, reformers argued, the city's home life would suffer if women were permitted to frequent cafes and cabarets.

But the real issue was which city dwellers should entertain themselves, and how; and reformers, whose crusades were efforts to transform a men's city of rounders into a city of families, thought entertainment should reflect the change. Wholesome recreation would attract foreigners, tourists, and businessmen to expositions and civic events. Ragtime and jazz music and dance were suitable—if limited to a certain area or transformed into something more acceptable to Protestant tastes. San Francisco would be an excellent place to live if the influences of the east would tame the city. Dancing should be restricted to certain nights in licensed resorts, just as working conditions and hours should be regulated. Reformers responded to competition from other cities and new developments in social thought with organizations such as the Y.M.C.A. in which whole families could participate.

The Y.M.C.A. and the Y.W.C.A. afforded sports and social activities to urban dwellers. Blacks, often excluded from these organizations, formed their own dance clubs and a community center after World War I. The Social Dancing School furnished "good, wholesome amusement for . . . young people." Parents were invited to attend one Friday evening dance in April of 1922 "and be satisfied that [their children] are being taught the value of good, clean dancing."[46]

In the 1920s the Booker T. Washington Community Center, at 1433 Divisadero in San Francisco, offered "wholesome" recreation, because Afro-Americans needed a place for "clean, legitimate fun." A group of Black clubwomen, and some leading men, sought to provide entertainment of "the kind that builds healthy minds and bodies, that offsets weary hours of humdrum toil with wholesome, needful recreation." Classes in sewing, singing, piano playing, handwork, and folk dancing were offered to meet the needs of a growing populace that included the largest proportion of married Black couples the city had ever known. Skills developed in the night life were used in the community center. Organized and supervised recreation drew people interested in the opportunities of cabarets. In the center's weekly program, the Glee Club, largely teenagers, sang "semi-classics and ballads," after which there was "social dancing." After October 1926, the club replaced this with a program of "diversified vaudeville production."[47]

The center was probably the first Black secular community-wide institution to provide recreation in several phases, in a continuous program, in addition to employment and child care services in the Bay Area. This reflected the influences of women's clubs and the settlement house movement, as did the make-up of its staff—mostly female volunteers who feared that unsupervised recreation led "to the juvenile court, the prison, and not infrequently to an early grave."[48] The sociological thought which emphasized social environment as well as human frailties also contributed to the nature of the center. Its social workers and volunteers counseled mothers through the Mothers' Fidelity Club, aided job seekers, and advised youth in juvenile court cases. Social programs at the center, like those at the churches, represented respectable Blacks' alternative to the night life and vice districts. They allowed people to gather and to develop their skills within a respectable milieu instead of an underworld environment.[49]

Nonetheless, the social service organizations and churches maintained certain cultural standards that frustrated some participants. They praised European-derived culture over Afro-American, and social workers and volunteers supervised artists instead of allowing them to follow their own thinking. The societies were ultimately like the reformers who wished to impose European music and dance and the standards of eastern cities on the western metropolis. The Glee Club occasionally performed spirituals, but refrained from encouraging interest in jazz, blues, or Black dance music. The societies could not hold an artist with bohemian proclivities, or a recently arrived southern laborer and his family, for any length of time. Because of a concern with proprieties and the law, they also lacked the conviviality that results when alcoholic beverages are consumed freely. Meanwhile, the night life continued to attract Blacks and whites because of its illegal and forbidden character and because of the restrictive nature of conventional culture and morals.

Any consideration of American entertainment must include the central role of the Negro. In the ante-bellum south, Blacks traditionally entertained whites. In the north, free Blacks became famous for their fine bands. The ubiquitous Black street or carnival entertainer served as the basis for Jim Crow, who with Jim Dandy was one of the two stock figures in American minstrelsy.[50] Nathan Huggins has observed that this form of entertainment permitted whites to express instincts forbidden by their Protestant ethic. As minstrels, white men could, through assuming Negro stereotypes—speaking incorrectly, walking and standing improperly, eating with gusto, and so forth—do everything forbidden by proprieties and refinement.[51]

Slumming served a similar function. For an evening whites could consort with Negroes, dance to their music, sing their songs, and become as intimate as they dared. In some respects, Purcell's and Mapp's resorts were like minstrel shows or Jim Crow sections of trains in the south. They were among the few places where a person could relax in a milieu that contrasted sharply with the restraints of the everyday world.[52] Laws were also relaxed—for some. Whites were usually not prosecuted when arrested during police raids. Sometimes the license meant involvement in illegal activities. In terms of Black women, music, and dance, colored resorts like the Jupiter and the Olympia had a monopoly that permitted their continued existence, until unceasing harassment forced them to close.[53]

Blacks also enjoyed a measure of freedom in their own cabarets, for they too were constrained by the same standards as whites. This is often missed by scholars who emphasize only the distinctiveness and "pathology" of Afro-American life. A group as acculturated as the Black residents of the Bay Area felt the same constraints as white residents, and were familiar with the standards observed by gentility. While white rounders enjoyed some of the pleasures of being a Negro on a Saturday night, Blacks could be themselves. Black folk also took pride in the homage that white slummers paid to their culture. In the resorts, Negroes could meet affluent and influential San Franciscans and develop contacts in a racially relaxed atmosphere. The polyglot nature of the clientele afforded chances to meet and learn about different residents and their lives. The presence of emancipated women represented another aspect of the new urban culture which Black residents could enjoy along with others.

The uniquely Black music performed in the resorts awakened Negroes to the folk forms of the Black southerners who came to the Bay Area after 1910. In the process, they acquired a broadened identity that was reinforced when they traveled to the south. In addition, all Afro-Americans found a unity that did not exist before the dispersal of Black southerners to every major American city. Development of their art forms was a source of pride, and also enabled them to win non-Black friends and sympathizers.

The Black night spots contrasted with those settings in which Blacks had previously entertained whites. When, in the early 1880s, Alexander D. Sharon, manager of the Palace Hotel, organized a Black orchestra, in "gay uniforms" for "reveling occasions," the entertainers were kept in their proper situation, where a degree of decorum could be maintained.[54] Conduct in the Negro clubs far exceeded proper behavior. Cabaret folk violated every canon of the workaday world; they repeatedly flaunted municipal ordinances; they had friendly ties with both the police and the underworld. They threatened the established order, for their existence would only perpetuate the music, dance, and practices for which they were known. The political power of Black cabaret men and underworld leaders would increase, influencing larger numbers of people. Interracial liasons that began in the clubs also threatened some urban dwellers' sense of proprieties. The racism underlying police raids (and public support for them) indicated the non-equalitarian basis of Progressive and fundamentalist reforms.

Imposing eastern standards on San Francisco during the First World War years was one of the first steps in remaking an area that had always lacked the restraint of the east. The raids on Black clubs showed the influence of the south, where segregation was enforced by law. Such segregation was also at odds with San Francisco's nineteenth-century tradition, since the city had no Black ghetto and no laws requiring discrimination in public places. San Francisco's reformers also drew strength from national organizations, which exercised increasing influence in the western metropolis.

The city's night life revealed the cultural differences between Progressives on the one hand, and the many San Franciscans who valued their city's unique reputation on the other hand. The former viewed the reform movements in other urban areas with a sense of satisfaction that morality and civilization could triumph over sin and decadence. The latter wished to preserve the city's unique character and looked to Paris and other European capitals for their ideal of a cosmopolitan metropolis. They believed that city dwellers should be free to consort and dance with one another, especially if it enriched their businesses and culture.

Rounders and slummers were significant for periodically abandoning their parents' mores. They danced with Blacks, listened to Black music, and frequented Black cabarets. This mixing heralded an order in which Black music and dance, enjoyed by various city dwellers, created a world more nearly equalitarian than any other in the Bay Area. Slummers found inspiration in the life as well as the song and dance of Negro cabarets; they paid homage to a people generally regarded as pariahs.

Despite its opportunities and excesses, the Black cabaret world reflected the problems of the larger society. Slummers broke only temporarily with the workaday world, and they entered the Coast for fun, not to learn about its denizens. They carried the dominant society's racism with them, and regarded Negroes as fascinating exotics with an inborn talent to entertain them.[55] The exploitative nature of the workaday world penetrated the nighttime, when Blacks performed for the benefits of whites. The night life was modeled along lines familiar to the modern student of Afro-American history. After all, Lester Mapp was only a "colored lieutenant" whose operations depended upon his relations with the McDonough brothers. The Apex Club, opened in the 1930s, featured a "sepia revue" and was owned by a wealthy white.[56] It is doubtful that slummers attempted to modify the relationship between Black entertainers and white patrons, or Black proprietors and white financial backers, in a way that would threaten the age-old institutional relationship between the races.

Nevertheless, the Negro cabarets and night life were significant for allowing an intimacy between Blacks and whites that was permitted in few other public places. Love of the music and dance also provided a basis for companionship among people otherwise reluctant to recognize similar interests. The opportunity for men and women of different colors to consort was one of the first steps in the emergence of a society that allowed residents to enjoy cosmopolitan life.

San Francisco permitted this freedom in the nineteenth century, more so than most other American cities. But it was limited to men and to women willing to risk losing their reputations, although the persistence of its wide-open character in the twentieth century meant that even conventional women could enjoy its opportunities. Even if it carried the problems of the workaday world, the night life offered the hope that, some day, urban dwellers might arrive at a better understanding of themselves, of each other, and of their city.

# 10

## Newcomers

*The colored people now living in the northern part of the State and around San Francisco remind one much of persons living around Boston and other New England towns; they are so fond of their own little corner of the world; they are so self-satisfied.*

*Delilah L. Beasley*

*Yet it has everywhere been manifest in the long run that while a part of the negroes were native-born and trained in the culture of the city, the others were immigrants largely ignorant and unused to city life. . . . Thus the history of the negro in Northern cities is the history of the rise of a small group growing by accretions from without, but at the same time periodically overwhelmed by them and compelled to start over again when once the new material had been assimilated.*

*W. E. B. Du Bois*

Black residents of the Bay Area loved the city that was so intertwined with their history, identity, struggles, and success. By the 1920s the connection sometimes extended back through their parents' to their grandparents' generation; and by the 1970s they had children, grandchildren, and great-grandchildren in the Bay Area or in California. The older (pre-World War I) generations are most aware and appreciative of the link between their family and personal histories and that of the metropolis.

The Bay Area was liked for various reasons. Ethel Terrell, pianist-leader of a vaudeville band, lived in New York City practically all her life, having been "born right across the river in New Jersey." She loved San

Francisco because it reminded her of home. She recalled her feelings on first seeing the western metropolis: "Even the skyline coming from Oakland to San Francisco on the ferryboat . . . I just got an uplift feeling that I'm coming home. I've always felt at home in San Francisco." New Yorkers like Ethel Terrell and James Weldon Johnson often had this feeling.[1] A Texan, Martel Meneweather, dreamed of moving to California when, as a school girl, she read about the state in history and geography classes. Jim Crow made California even more appealing: "I never liked the south. I didn't like the tradition and to me, south was like slavery. . . . I wanted to find a place where I'd be free to bring my children and my children would be reared as free citizens." Her husband thought the same way, so they migrated to California during the World War I years. After several decades' residence, Mrs. Meneweather said of San Francisco: "To me, it was heaven. It was just like coming from hell to heaven. That's how I felt about it." Her children "could run up and down the streets and play and they wasn't called nigger and all this kind of stuff. And they wasn't denied the privilege to play in front of white people's yards and so on like that. And I love that, I love that freedom."[2]

While they did not leave race discrimination, or even segregation, behind them, San Francisco-bound southerners managed to escape Jim Crow laws and humiliation. When Matt Crawford was a child en route to California from Alabama, he was so struck by the freedom to sit anywhere on the train after leaving the south that in his 70s he still recalled it vividly. Racism intensified as the number of white and Black southerners increased in the twentieth century, but compared to the rural, segregated, fundamentalist Protestant, tradition-bound south, San Francisco still symbolized freedom as much as Harlem or Chicago's South Side.[3]

And San Francisco seemed free of the poverty and tenements of New York or Chicago. Martel Meneweather said that New York was too crowded for her. Urania Cummings, who came from St. Thomas in the Virgin Islands, migrated to New York and lived there around World War I, saving her money, before choosing the west coast port city over its eastern rival. "Oh, in New York I was caged up. New York is a congested city and anybody that had lived in the outdoors, like I coming from a big farm—I was pent up." In terms familiar to the contemporary resident of northern industrial cities, she continued: "You just get frustrated and then you're scared to open your door and I was just so happy to live in a place where you—Of course, today [1976] it's almost as bad out here in Berkeley, but I mean in San Francisco, you can stay with your doors open." One can debate the last point, but what is more important was her reiteration: "That's such a beautiful city. I still love San Francisco. . . . In New York, it's all right if you like crowded cities. I like fresh air."[4]

The Bay Area offered locales to appeal to a variety of people. San Francisco had all the attractions and problems of an industrial metropolis, while the East Bay lured those who preferred a suburban setting. For southerners, West Indians, and San Franciscans with families, Oakland and Berkeley fulfilled childhood dreams. Urania Cummings, who moved to the East Bay in the 1930s, pointed out that San Francisco was getting too crowded. "So I wanted to get in a place where I had space . . . I always dreamt of having space for my children like I had when I grew up as a girl on the big farm."[5]

Prosperous Blacks who disliked San Francisco and Oakland's crowds, congestion, and ethnic immigrants could reside in Berkeley, a small and pleasant city of homes. The Black inhabitants of the university town grew to nearly four thousand by 1940, and on the whole were "more economically secure and better educated than average." In a survey conducted after World War II, eighty-seven out of ninety-one Black families in Berkeley owned homes—showing both their prosperity and the scarcity of rentals. Also, there was a certain amount of solidarity and a measure of homogeneity among the various citizens, including the Afro-Americans. "Berkeley used to be like a big family," Mrs. Cummings recalled. "Everybody seemed to get along nicely together because I think everybody owned something and we—and we had pride in what we owned."[6]

An Oakland native, in explaining why she preferred the Bay Area, emphasized the belief that the west is less class-conscious and stratified than the east. Eleanor Watkins said that "anytime I've visited the east, I've never been impressed with the east as a place to live." The west coast's lack of rigid stratification and its racial and cultural heterogeneity also appealed to her: "This is a more relaxed society and we associated with people from every strata," while "in the east it was pretty rigid as I understand it."[7]

As the Great Migration reached the Bay Area, the pioneers' descendants gradually became more aware of the differences between life in their isolated urban communities and in the east and south. Race-conscious and frequently well-educated individuals—Martel Meneweather, Elbert A. Daly, Lillian Dixon, Ida Jackson, Vivian Osborn Marsh, Alvin D. Nurse, Tarea Hall Pittman, C. L. Dellums, and World War I-era migrants—formed organizations and agitated for reform. Then during World War II, the Great Migration transformed the Bay Area much as it had radically transformed northeastern cities a generation earlier. If the older residents' feelings about the Bay Area remained much the same, their relationships to other kinds of Blacks and whites changed. As Du Bois noted (see the epigraph to this chapter), the sense of family among the Black residents was strengthened by differences with the newcomers, and was redefined because of similarities with the migrants.[8]

An increasing number of southern arrivals from the late nineteenth century heralded what was to come in the 1940s. Most of the newcomers of World War II migrated from the western region of the south—Texas, Louisiana, and Arkansas—to meet the needs of the expanding war economy in California. Henry Kaiser, the industrialist who built ships for the war, "brought Blacks here from all over the south—every state—and he brought them in train loads. He brought one to three train loads every day for six months." Like the northbound migrants of World War I, the westbound Blacks were recruited by industry, while the pioneers of the nineteenth and early twentieth centuries were rarely brought west by industrialists.[9]

Expansion of industry during the war accelerated changes that had begun at the turn of the century. Matt Crawford, a resident of Oakland from childhood, observed "an uprooting of thousands of people who were totally unfamiliar with the [Bay] area." As in World War I, labor shortages meant that "they were accepted for many types of work previously all but closed to them," especially in industry.[10]

The Black population's increase throughout the Bay Area, after nearly a century of remaining comparatively small, affected every area of life. Thanks to Kaiser's efforts and Executive Order 8802, which prompted industrialists to hire Negroes, the Bay Area's Black population more than tripled between 1940 and 1944 alone (see Table 8). "West Oakland overflowed," recalled John Watkins; "that's what built up East Oakland. That's what made North Oakland completely Black. That's what built up Richmond."[11] Matt Crawford explained, "Their coming exacerbated all of the latent racist and discrimination problems in the community: housing,

*Table 8*
*Growth of the Bay Area Black Population, by City, 1940–1950*

| City | 1940 | | 1950 | | Percentage Increase |
|------|---------------------|----------------------|---------------------|----------------------|------|
|      | Black Population | Percentage of Total | Black Population | Percentage of Total | |
| San Francisco | 4,846 | 0.8 | 43,460 | 5.6 | 800 |
| Oakland | 8,462 | 2.8 | 47,610 | 12.4 | 463 |
| Berkeley | 3,395 | 3.9 | 13,289 | 12 | 291 |
| Richmond | | | 13,374 | 13 | |
| San Francisco-Oakland Metropolitan Area | | | 147,223 | 6.1 | |

NOTE: Figures have been rounded.
SOURCE: U.S. Census.

employment, participation in community affairs, and government." Before the war, job discrimination excluded Blacks from "the major municipal facilities like streetcars, bus drivers, [and there were] very few Black policemen, . . . but all of this began to [change with the]. . . struggle for jobs and involvement in the community life."[12]

Crawford became active in the trade unions and was assistant director of the CIO Minorities Committee, a part of the state CIO Council organization. His involvement in unions and in California political affairs reflected changes that occurred among Blacks as a group. "Total community life began to take place." Struggles to open unions to Blacks, to secure better jobs and job security, and to move into new neighborhoods produced the modern racist responses: segregated union locals and "urban renewal. . . . Whole sections of West Oakland where Blacks were concentrated were torn down." A new section in an outlying area of Oakland developed. "People were really forced out into East Oakland." Crawford took part in a research survey conducted by the Black sociologist Charles S. Johnson, and observed migration's effect and the newcomers' adjustments at first hand. Johnson and the old residents realized that, as a result of the influx of job-seeking Black southerners, urban life in the Bay Area (and Los Angeles, which experienced similar growth) would never be the same.[13]

Money attracted the newcomers, just as it had attracted the individualists of the pioneer period. The desire for better jobs and higher salaries, and the understanding of what they meant for Negroes, made it possible for the pioneer residents to identify with the new migrants.[14] Suddenly there was a dramatic difference in the kinds of jobs available. Blacks had broken into the civil service in the Bay Area in the 1920s, and the war permitted them to secure better and more jobs in this area as well as in industry.

The change was so dramatic it produced a scholarly document. Charles S. Johnson's *The Negro War Worker in San Francisco: A Local Self-Survey* was based on a sample of nearly three hundred Black families. Like many contemporary studies of urban Afro-Americans, it focuses on the adjustment problems of the newcomers and their impact upon the city. It was carried out with an end to affecting policy, particularly job and union discrimination, segregated neighborhoods, and inadequate housing. Most importantly, the study compares in detail 123 non-migrant families (residents in 1940, the descendants of pioneers, and recent arrivals) to 149 migrant families; it sheds light on such topics as Negroes' changing job patterns, and the specific nature of those trends in the early 1940s. Unfortunately, no such analysis exists for the East Bay.[15]

Ship and aircraft construction expanded considerably during this period. Because of the labor shortage, federally required nondiscriminatory hiring, and on-the-job training, Afro-Americans moved into positions that were previously closed. It is noteworthy that during the war, San Francisco's Blacks, largely new arrivals, included five times as many skilled workers as the national average for Blacks. Migrants were more likely than non-migrants to hold industrial jobs. More than three-fourths (77.1 percent) of the newcomers worked in industries, and most of them (two-thirds) were "nearly evenly divided between the skilled and the unskilled." Only a few were service workers (12.1 percent), and still fewer were proprietors, professionals, or semi-professionals (5.9 percent).[16]

As noted in Chapter 3, the pre-war urbanites rarely worked in industry as skilled craftsmen or as laborers. By 1943, however, nearly half of the Black residents of 1940 (non-migrants) were in industry, and less than one-fourth were skilled. The proportion of service workers was much higher than among migrants (26.8 percent versus 12.1 percent). Ten percent of the 1940 residents were proprietors, managers, professionals, and semi-professionals, reflecting the benefits of lengthy residence. These advantages caused older residents to hesitate before entering industrial positions, and many avoided temporary but lucrative work for more secure positions. Also, the pre-war residents were less likely to be employed for their skills as craftsmen than were newcomers.[17]

The evidence controverts the popular image of the unskilled southern migrant having difficulty adjusting to the city because of his own job inadequacies. The newcomers to the San Francisco Bay Area were more highly skilled than the nation's Negroes and the old San Francisco residents, though they lagged behind the entire San Francisco population. It was clear to the researchers, however, that Blacks' concentration in ship-building and construction, combined with their recent arrival and the racism of employers, constituted disadvantages which resulted in job losses and high unemployment after the war. Afro-American newcomers were skilled in a sense which contrasts with the usual portrait of ghetto pathology. The gains older residents and migrants made during the war suggested their potential progress in a non-racist, peacetime society. In either situation, the San Francisco experience differed from the typical mid-twentieth-century preconceptions of eastern ghettos, suggesting either a western variant that is unique, or a need for closer comparison of older residents and new arrivals in other American cities.[18]

Like those who came north during World War I, San Francisco's new Negroes responded to the promises of recruiters, to the letters of friends and relatives, and to reports of high wages. Like the newcomers to Harlem a generation earlier, they were young and married, with large families; more than half (51 percent) arrived as family units. If spouse and children were left behind, they followed shortly afterwards.[19]

The character of the migrants comes into sharper focus upon comparing age-sex ratios, educational levels, and incomes of the newcomers with those of the earlier inhabitants. Johnson's 1943 study and a 1948 University of California study permit some comparisons between the new migrants and old inhabitants. When possible the characteristics of the inhabitants of 1900 will be recalled to give greater clarity to similarities and differences.[20]

In the 1940s, 53 percent of Blacks in San Francisco were females; this figure is comparable to those for California, eastern cities, and Negroes in the U.S. This differed from the figures for San Francisco in the nineteenth century and in 1930, when men were in the majority. Thus Black San Francisco acquired a feminine cast, making it much more like Oakland and Los Angeles.[21]

While San Franciscans viewed the Black migrants of the 1940s as poorly educated, their average grade level (8.3) indicates that this was not the case; old residents averaged nine years' education in 1943. The higher proportion of young citizens, more likely to have benefited from formal education, accounted in part for the educational level of the migrants. Davis McEntire and Julia R. Tarnopol note in their University of California study, "The educational attainment of the wartime in-migrants in 1948 approximated that of the Negro population of the San Francisco–Oakland metropolitan district in 1940." Also, an increased proportion of college-educated Negroes inhabited San Francisco after the war. Admittedly, these levels of education say nothing about the quality of schooling in the Jim Crow south.[22]

Differences between the pioneers and the newcomers can be clearly seen in housing accommodations and locations. To understand the peculiar problems faced by the migrants, we need to review the housing shortage in wartime San Francisco, the racism behind it, its manifestation in restrictive covenants, and the inferior housing allotted to Black newcomers. The need for adequate housing was the single most pressing—and most frequently articulated—problem of the migrants.

San Francisco experienced the housing problems felt by the northeastern cities during the Great Migration of World War I, and the Black newcomers suffered the most. It was not merely a question of the tremendous growth of the Black population in a few years; "because of the restricted housing market for minority populations, and particularly the Negro, during periods of growth, shortages are felt most acutely by them." If the World War II years had been unmarked by racial tensions and hostilities, the housing problem would not have been so severe.[23] But during the war, race riots in Detroit, New York City, and Los Angeles—where they were thinly disguised as "zoot-suit riots"—increased whites' fears, and caused Blacks to view whites with greater suspicion and hostility.

In addition, the spread of white as well as Black southerners to northern and far western cities meant that southern racial attitudes penetrated every urban center.[24]

The same antipathies that excluded Chinese immigrants and placed Japanese-Americans in concentration camps operated to contain Afro-Americans in urban ghettos. One San Franciscan remarked: "We don't want to go soft in the head like France on these matters and collapse"; another equated Blacks with the residents of the city's oldest and largest slum: "The mere fact that there is a Negro or Chinese family in a block immediately depreciates property values. It also diminishes property sales, and the area becomes undesireable [sic]." Still another claimed: "Negroes are lazy and dirty. It's bad to have them living around white girls." Also, city dwellers did not always distinguish one class of Negroes from another, or even permit exceptions for Black celebrities. "I wouldn't even want Marian Anderson as a neighbor."[25]

Restrictive covenants played an important role in preventing migrants from locating in certain neighborhoods of the city. White property owners agreed not to sell to non-Caucasians, in covenants that were part of an old San Francisco tradition, first developed to keep the Chinese in Chinatown. After the Japanese left the city in early 1942, white San Franciscans became especially concerned about preventing "invasions." According to Johnson, "that a concerted effort is being made by neighborhood groups, merchant associations and improvement clubs to restrict the area of living for Negro families to the present boundaries of the Fillmore district . . . seems fairly evident."[26]

Racist attitudes, restrictive covenants, and the sudden influx of Black migrants created the ghettos near the San Francisco shipyards at Hunter's Point and along Fillmore Street. As noted, in Oakland urban renewal forced Blacks into East Oakland, the site of today's ghetto. After occupying the crowded, dilapidated, or temporary structures, Negroes found it more difficult than other Americans to find suitable housing in desirable locations. "The presence of a hardened, set attitude against Negro families having access to more and better living opportunities in areas now occupied by whites" prevented the newcomers from a share in the advantages of residency in San Francisco. These attitudes also kept Blacks from advancing in their jobs after 1945, and even from maintaining their World War II-era gains in industry.[27]

The quality of the migrants' housing revealed the unusual disadvantages they suffered. Before World War II, Afro-San Franciscans inhabited the areas with the highest proportion of substandard housing. In 1939, 95 percent of the Negroes (compared to 98 percent of the Chinese and 83 percent of the whites) rented San Francisco accommodations; Black families were more likely to double up in a single dwelling than other San Franciscans.[28]

The urban poor use a large proportion of their income for rent, and in this respect the Negroes were even worse off than the Chinese, as well as the white residents.[29] As noted, this was the case before the 1940s; comparing the housing of old residents and migrants, it becomes clear that Black newcomers suffered from this tradition of California racism.

The housing shortage forced unrelated Black families to live together. "Almost half of the family dwelling units sampled were occupied by two or more groups of persons." As many families lived this way as in separate units.[30] Newcomers living with one or more migrant families were more likely to be related to them than were older residents in similar situations. Johnson believed this was a form of mutual aid among the migrants, and maintained that it was a carryover from the extended kinship arrangements typical of accommodations in the south. In addition, more migrant families in multiple households were not related to the household head or his or her spouse. This was one of the few ways migrants could obtain housing—by renting from older residents.[31]

Some unmarried Black residents took advantage of the plight of the newcomers by obtaining and then renting houses and rooms, in what Johnson regarded as "a mild form of racketeering and profiteering." Nearly four times as many old residents (over 11 percent) as newcomers (3.3 percent) did this.[32]

The migrants' inferior accommodations were reflected in the number of rooms available to them in each dwelling. In 1943, many Black San Francisco families lived in five- to seven-room apartments (42.6 percent); this included nearly 60 percent of the non-migrants, but only 30 percent of the migrants. Nearly as many migrants (28.9 percent) occupied one room as five, six, or seven rooms, while only 2.5 percent of the old Black residents lived in a single room. In fact, 50 percent of the migrants lived in three rooms or less, compared to only 12 percent of the non-migrants. Finally, many families that occupied dwellings of six or seven rooms actually lived in only one or two.[33]

Also striking were differences between old and new residents in the average number of rooms per family and in average family size. Migrant families averaged 3.3 rooms and five persons, compared with 5.12 rooms and 4.7 persons for pre-war families. Newcomers also lacked the access to bathroom and kitchen facilities possessed by old residents.[34]

Both groups earned approximately the same income, although migrants had larger families and more children. Despite their needs, newcomers averaged almost $13.00 rent per month more than old inhabitants (the former paid $43.52, the latter $30.70). Thus more money bought less for Black migrants, a problem typical of the poor.[35]

Relations between the groups and the attitudes of each toward the other shed more light on the old residents, the migrants, the character of their urban life, and on the nature of their adjustment to the city. The southern migrants viewed the older residents with favor. But the non-migrants' attitudes toward the newcomers were at times as unfriendly as the traditional attitudes of natives toward migrants in any American city or region. According to the old settlers, the newcomers hindered their opportunities in San Francisco; 82 percent of those interviewed by Johnson, and 69 percent of all old Black resident families, believed this.[36]

Yet few Blacks felt the migrants should be sent back south. Most of the old residents were born in the south themselves, and had since leaving that region lived elsewhere for many years before arriving in San Francisco. Nearly half of those in Johnson's study had lived in San Francisco fifteen years or more. Those who expressed negative views about the migrants were usually female renters, either housewives or domestics, and lived on Lyons, Post, Pine, or Geary Streets in the Western Addition.[37]

Most people I asked about the migrants saw differences that sometimes illuminated their own attitudes as well as the newcomers' situation. Aurelious P. Alberga, a San Francisco native, saw "quite a bit of difference." In particular, "a great deal of timidity" characterized the southern migrants. The former boxer, soldier, and aide to a well-to-do businessman explained that they "didn't have no confidence in themselves. . . . [or] in anything that they done." Their speech further diminished the self-confidence that Alberga thought was a prerequisite for success. "Well, their English, naturally, was very, very bad. And they took—quite a bit of repeating, almost, on all—nearly all occasions, to understand what they were endeavoring to try and impress you with." Unlike the proud pioneers whose photographs proclaim their sense of worth and confidence, the newcomers manifested what Alberga interpreted as uncertainty. It may well have been that the migrants were alert and curious, but the San Francisco native claimed: "Their demeanor in their way of walking down the street here. . . . They walked with that attitude, as though something was behind them." They were conspicuous: "You could pick them out from among all the others. Just like that (snaps his fingers)," and they needed seven, eight, or nine years "before they seemed to get Americanized." The last term suggests how foreign the newcomers seemed to a native San Franciscan.[38]

Freddie McWilliams, a dancer and master of ceremonies on weekends and federal employee during the week, had difficulties adjusting to the southern ways of the newcomers. He lived in the Italian section of North Beach and in West Oakland, and was an altar boy in a Catholic church though his parents were Protestant. As a teenage athlete in the 1920s, he used to run from downtown San Francisco to Cliff House, on the ocean, and back, or accompany his white friends on hikes in Muir Woods in Marin County. Occasionally he told the Blacks of these activities. But when he "started running with all Black kids," he "never did fit in." He also had difficulty understanding the southerners. "They sounded like foreigners to me. . . . They thought I was crazy. . . . 'What you mean, "Go hiking"?' . . . They thought I was crazy and they laughed at me because I put on some shorts to run to Cliff House. They'd say, 'Man, have you lost your mind to run that far?'" Interestingly, instead of stressing the migrants' need to assimilate, McWilliams emphasized his adjustment to them. "It took me quite a while to become assimilated with them. It just took me quite a while to get accustomed to this style of living. . . . It was foreign to me. I wasn't reared that way, that's all."[39]

An Oakland native, John Watkins, also noted the differences. He felt like a tourist whenever he went to downtown Oakland, because there were so many newcomers and they were so different from anything he knew. Old residents and newcomers were "just like two different peoples." They were a spectacle "to the extent of where we used to go down on Seventh Street [in Oakland], sometimes just [to] stand and watch them." Watkins, sitting in his hillside El Cerrito home, remembered them as "beautiful people, you know, but they had different ways or modes of dress and dialogue and—just their being. Living down in all those hovels and seemingly very happy to be out here working on good jobs. You see them down in department stores with overalls on, trying on fur coats and stuff like that. You'd never see any of these things before."

Like Freddie McWilliams, Watkins also had to adjust to the ways and slang of the migrants. He explained how once he and a friend went to what would today be called a soul food restaurant. Watkins asked for a second helping of potatoes, and so did his friend. Though their meals were identical, Watkins was charged a dime more. His friend explained that Watkins had asked for "potatoes," whereas he had requested "tatoes." Watkins's word suggested pretense, arrogance, and superiority—failure to acknowledge the customary "tatoes"—and from the perspective of the help this called for a higher price.[40]

The incident underlined the cultural differences between the two groups. Spitting in public, trying on new clothes when dressed in overalls, shooting birds from telephone wires, asking to rent garages for housing— all these highlighted variations in background and custom as well as the poverty that became increasingly apparent to old residents.[41]

Eugene P. Lasartemay, a Black who migrated to San Francisco from Hawaii in the 1920s, thought the cultural differences were downright embarrassing to the older residents, who had certain ideas about refinement and decorum and who "conducted themselves on a higher plane." The officer of the East Bay Negro Historical Society and his family and friends were "surprised to see people coming from the south that would be eating hamburgers openly on the bus; and baloney, and loud talking and fighting on the busses. . . . That never happened in those early days."[42]

Their manners and behavior embarrassed and alienated pioneer Blacks and undoubtedly many newcomers as well. Urania Cummings expressed her ambivalence about the migrants by noting how Berkeley changed for the worse. The town "used to be like a big family. Everybody seemed to get along nicely together because I think everybody owned something and we—and we had pride in what we owned. The people that came in here were looking for places to live and they just didn't understand. I don't know just how to put it in words, but they were different, because they didn't have a pride like we had in our little city."[43]

Some older residents thought prejudice increased as a result of the migration of southerners. A professional pointed out that Blacks were few and spread out before World War II. "That's why there wasn't any prejudice. We never had any prejudice until late years when the Negroes started the flack and flocking in here and raising hell." Before, "we all just— we didn't know we were Negroes or anything. Never heard the word 'Negro' mentioned." Although few others went so far as this, a number of other informants thought white racism became worse during and after World War II.[44] Like Charles S. Johnson and other scholars, some informants stressed the need of the newcomers to adjust and their difficulties in doing so. Mrs. Meneweather said that "on the whole they were fairly friendly," but to a woman who grew up in Marshall, Texas, where Black colleges emphasized self-help, restraint, and refined behavior, "some of them [the migrants] were kind of backwards."[45]

Also, they lacked the familiarity and independent spirit necessary for life in a free city. Mrs. Meneweather explained, "I understand they came from plantations"—a common belief which was not entirely true—"and they weren't used to a city and it was a long time before they learned how to take the—living in a city. A lot of them haven't learned yet. . . . The majority of people that's been reared on the plantation was told what to do, how to do it, and when to do it." As a result, "when you get to a city where you're free, well, then, it takes a long time to learn that I got to stand on my two feet laboring for myself and make my own decisions. . . . Their children . . . weren't used to having the things that they have in the city."[46]

Some old timers were more generous. Matt Crawford felt that "basically they were no different" from old residents. Although Eugene Lasartemay noticed different conduct, "as people, they just were people struggling to make a living for themselves." Moreover, he did not believe there was a considerable difference between old residents and migrants in terms of educational attainments or level of skills. Martel Meneweather also noted an educated class capable of taking advantage of the city's opportunities among those who were so poorly prepared.[47]

Vivian Osborn Marsh, active in various civic organizations and women's clubs for several decades, empathized to some degree with the migrants. A Texan by birth, she said, "I don't blame the Negroes for leaving [the south]." Also, "some of them came out here and worked for a while and then would lay off for a while. You know, we do have—to be perfectly frank about—we have all types in our race." Newspaper publisher E. A. Daly, though critical in other respects, sympathized with the World War II migrants. Someone once asked Daly what would happen to them after the war. The Alabama-born Daly, a migrant himself in the 1920s, responded, "If you were in prison and the doors were suddenly opened for you to go out, you wouldn't volunteer to go back in it, would you?"[48]

A number of informants admired the southerners, detecting spunk or pride where others saw timidity. John Watkins felt that the migrants resented older residents because of communication problems and the newcomers' assumption that the pre-war urbanites "thought that we were better than they." The higher bill in the restaurant reflected this distance from the old timers as well as the newcomers' sense of pride in the integrity of their speech and customs. Watkins believed that "a lot of the people that came out had a little more of a chip on their shoulder than the people out here did."[49]

Watkins's wife, Eleanor, also found the migrants not at all timid. I had heard this opinion a couple of times from informants, so I asked her about it. "I think they were more aggressive, really, in many ways [than the older residents]. Less friendly. They tended to be more suspicious of whites," which she thought was understandable because of their experiences with Jim Crow. They were "a little unpleasant in . . . the remarks they made about whites and that sort of thing," she recalled. Mrs. Watkins, who admitted that she did not have considerable personal contact with the migrants, nonetheless had reflected on their situation to the point where her analysis was as even-handed as any commentator's. She thought the descendants of pioneers should be grateful, for example, that southerners pointed out that the Bay Area was not so liberal as they thought. Educated Bay Area residents who had arrived around World War I, such as Martel Meneweather and Vivian Osborn Marsh, fought discrimination to win jobs for Blacks in the public schools, in hospitals, and other public places. Some pointed out that Bay Area Negroes suffered because Black history was not taught in the public schools as it was in the segregated south. They also claimed older residents neglected business opportunities by patronizing white shopkeepers while avoiding that profession themselves.[50]

Mrs. Watkins was very sensitive to the criticism Blacks and some whites made about the migrants. She saw them in terms of their background, their struggles, and their attempts to improve the lives of their children. These efforts overshadowed what others saw as "backwardness." A friend came up to her once and remarked:

"Eleanor—you must be—you colored people must be very disgusted with some of the people who have come here from the south and the way they act". . . and I said, "Well, Mrs. S., yes, some colored people are very disgusted, but as far as I'm concerned, the first thing I give them credit for is getting out of the situation they were in and coming some place where they could make some money. That's the first plus. Maybe they don't know how to dress or comb their hair or anything, but their children will and *their* children will. . . . [After all]—they came where they could make some money which was—you have to give them credit for it."[51]

Like Mrs. Watkins, the descendants of the Black pioneers came to see their similarities with the newcomers, while remaining aware of some differences. Old timers knew one another and had contacts with whites that often dated from childhood. Pre-war migrants were, consequently, often less suspicious of whites and somewhat less critical of discrimination than the newcomers. Work, cooperation in various organizations, the marriage of their children to one another, and other opportunities for association brought these two streams in Afro-America—old and new urbanites— more closely together. Besides adding a more complex dimension to the metropolitan existence of Blacks in the Bay Area, the sudden influx in mid-century made the history of the pioneer Blacks more remote, but not inaccessible.

# The Informants

*Honor and veneration to the dead and likewise to the living, who trailed and blazed the way for generations to come.*

Esther B. *"Hettie"* Tilghman

*We, unlike most Negroes, lived in a tradition of success, achievement, and hope for Negro liberation. With such sterling examples to guide us, surrender to prejudice seemed cowardly and unnecessary. Our goals were dictated by our past, we were obligated by our family history to achievement in our fight for individual and racial equality.*

Horace Cayton

Aurelious P. Alberga was born in San Francisco in 1884, the son of a Jamaican seafarer and of Ann E. Caines, a San Francisco resident. In his youth he was a successful boxer, losing one of about forty fights—according to his recollection. He admired Peter Jackson and Jack Johnson, heavyweight contenders of the late nineteenth and early twentieth centuries, respectively. Mr. Alberga worked at a number of jobs. As secretary for a blind millionaire, Louis Metzger, he handled a number of his employer's affairs, including managing some apartment buildings. He also owned a bootblack stand in the San Francisco Ferry Building and ran a bail bond business. Mr. Alberga worked in civil rights organizations and helped found the Booker T. Washington Community Center. He joined West Gate Masonic Lodge and the Golden Gate Lodge of the Grand United Order of Oddfellows. During World War I, along with the lawyer Oscar Hudson, he organized a regiment of Black volunteers, traveled to Des Moines, Iowa, for officer's training, and served as first lieutenant and acting captain in Company A of the 365th Infantry. Mr. Alberga attended Bethel A.M.E. and then St. Peter's Episcopal Church. At the time of the interview in the summer of 1976, he and his wife lived on Isabella Street in West Oakland.

Alfred James Butler, the son of John and Annie "Aunt Ludie" White Butler, was born December 22, 1888, at 1551 Brush Street (now 2151), Oakland. His father came from Baltimore, Maryland, and his mother from San Jose, where her father,

Alfred J. White, owned a barbershop. Walter Butler, the lawyer and NAACP leader, was the informant's uncle, and Mr. Butler identified him in a photograph in the Bancroft Library, thus solving a vexing problem for me. Mr. Butler attended Lafayette school and Oakland High in the East Bay. He obtained a job as a stock clerk for the H. S. Crocker Company through the influence of his uncle, Walter G. Maddox. He worked as a mechanic in a garage during World War I, then with two partners opened the Thirty-Sixth Street Garage at Thirty-Sixth and West Streets in Oakland. He recalled watching Jack Johnson drive down San Pablo Avenue every night, slumped down in the seat. This example prompted him, and his job enabled him, to purchase a car with an old friend, Dr. Earl Lenear. The two also frequently went to the Barbary Coast together. When I interviewed him in July 1976, Mr. Butler lived in San Francisco near the ocean, had considerable vitality and energy, and still enjoyed driving about the city. He died in 1979.

Matt Crawford was born in Anniston, Alabama, on May 18 or 19, 1903, one of several children in the family of a carpet-layer. The increasingly oppressive Jim Crow system caused his parents to move with their family to West Oakland when Mr. Crawford was a youngster. He attended Prescott School, helped his father—who was not able to work at his trade because of race prejudice—clean offices after school, and longed to escape such menial tasks and become his own boss. He worked as a clerk in an insurance office, but knowing there was no chance for advancement, went to chiropractic college. During the Depression, he traveled with Langston Hughes and a number of other young Afro-Americans to the Soviet Union. Racial oppression, his readings, and his travels led him to espouse socialism. During World War II he was quite active in the Congress of Industrial Workers and helped the sociologist Charles S. Johnson compile a report on the Negro war worker. Remaining active in Bay Area labor and race relations and politics, he worked for the Coop Credit Union in Berkeley until his retirement. A photographer, he installed a darkroom in his home in Berkeley, where he lived in the summer of 1976. He was one of the most knowledgeable, articulate, and philosophical of the informants.

Urania Cummings was born on St. Thomas in the Virgin Islands around 1889. In 1910 she left for Santo Domingo and then Puerto Rico, where she worked as a nurse taking care of American children. In 1918 she migrated to New York City, working as a domestic for eight years while saving her earnings. A cousin who was a train porter told her California was very much like the Virgin Islands, so she migrated once again. She was active in women's clubs and attended some United Negro Improvement Association meetings of Marcus Garvey. Mrs. Cummings married, started a family, and purchased a home in Berkeley during the Depression. After her four children were grown, she took courses in public speaking and art. Beginning in 1958, she exhibited a number of her paintings, many depicting West Indian scenes, and she has been featured in articles on her career and her art. She died in 1978.

Elbert A. Daly was born on November 16, 1891, on the campus of the University of Alabama at Tuscaloosa. His parents had a thirty-acre farm, raised sweet and white potatoes, peanuts, watermelons, cantaloupes, cotton, sugar cane, and corn while caring for the university grounds. He grew up on the farm, attended Talladega College, and lived in Atlanta and Pittsburgh before being drafted for the World

War. He was wounded in Europe; after he recuperated he became a school principal in Florida. He worked at a number of jobs, including stints as a chef on a steamer, as head of his own housecleaning business, as a janitor, and as a clothes presser. He migrated to California in 1922 and eventually went into the newspaper business with his wife, who had acquired considerable printing experience with her brother-in-law in Florida. Eventually they assumed control of the *California Voice,* a weekly which they ran for five decades. Mr. Daly was active in politics, registering voters and supporting candidates, and joined East Gate #44 Masonic Lodge and the Shriners. Shortly after the interview in August 1976, he turned the *California Voice* over to another editor.

Walter Leslie Gibson was born in San Francisco on November 27, 1895. His mother, Telazine Cornell, attended San Francisco's public schools and worked as a servant. Most notably, she preserved her school notebooks, a number of photograph albums, articles of clothing, and furnishings, which she handed down to her son. The Gibsons moved to Oakland around 1900. Mr. Gibson attended public schools, worked as a newsboy, and became a licensed "ham" radio operator. He worked in the Bethlehem Shipyards and then was drafted during World War I, serving in the 812th Pioneer Infantry. Afterwards he took a postal examination and passed it. He worked for the post office thirty-eight years, rising through the ranks to the position of supervisor. He was an officer in the American Legion and active in Acacia Masonic Lodge #7. Mr. Gibson successfully preserved a number of nineteenth-century photographs and artifacts and was kind enough to permit me to copy them. At the time of the interview he lived with his wife in their East Oakland home. He died in early 1979. His wife, Mrs. Veola Gibson, who has also passed, was close to her mother-in-law, and was consequently more informative about the people in the photographs than her husband.

Edward J. "Buster" Johnson was born in Oakland in 1906. His father migrated west from Montgomery, Alabama, shortly before the turn of the century. His mother grew up in Shasta County, in northern California, the daughter of a woman who came west as a slave around 1848. He lived in Berkeley, sold newspapers, and acquired carpentry skills in a musical instrument shop while attending Berkeley High. Like his father, he railroaded for a period of time, traveling all over the United States. In the 1930s he was doorman and then maintenance man for a number of apartments owned by an affluent San Francisco family. After a stint in the military during World War II, he worked as a redcap at the Ferry Building. Eventually he became a building contractor and built a parking garage in downtown Oakland. At the time of the interview in 1973, Mr. Johnson lived in the Berkeley home his father purchased shortly before World War I.

Eugene Pascual Lasartemay was born in the Hawaiian Islands in 1903. Of Puerto Rican and Basque descent, he migrated to California in 1923. Unable to get a good job in San Francisco, he went to sea for fifteen years. Starting as a fireman, he progressed through several positions as wiper, water tender, and deck engineer until becoming a licensed second assistant, and then first assistant engineer. His Hawaiian birthplace enabled him to join San Francisco's Marine Engineers and Beneficial Association Local #96, which like most unions rarely admitted Blacks. While ashore, he made extra money singing with a group of shipmates who were also Hawaiian. He grew up speaking pidgin English and Spanish, and still maintains ties with Hawaiian Islanders. In 1965 he helped found the East Bay Negro Historical Society, where he and wife could be found at the time of the interview in 1976. Mr. Lasartemay is also an accomplished photographer, a skill he acquired during his travels at sea, and a founder of Las Arts Camera Club, now known as Acorn Camera Club.

Born in St. Joseph, Missouri, in 1886, Dr. Earl Lenear was brought to San Francisco as an infant. His father, Dr. Reuben Lenear, was a chiropractor. The elder Lenear started a school to teach the profession, and his son followed in his footsteps. Dr. Earl Lenear frequented the Barbary Coast with his friends as a young man. He joined several lodges and was a charter member of Adonis Lodge. He maintained an office on Grove Street in Oakland when I interviewed him. On first seeing Dr. Lenear, I was struck by the fact that he could easily pass for white.

Freddie McWilliams was born in Vallejo, on the northwest shore of San Francisco Bay, January 26, 1904. His mother's family, the Clarks, were from West Oakland, and his father came from the south. As a youth Mr. McWilliams lived in Oakland, where he fraternized with Blacks, and in San Francisco, where he associated with Italian-Americans. For a while he was a messenger, then he started in vaudeville as a tap dancer. He was in show business for a number of decades as a dancer, a tap-dance teacher, and a coordinator of entertainment acts for local lodges and clubs, among other full- and part-time roles. He went on tour in the 1930s, visiting Hawaii, the Philippines, and China. In addition, Mr. McWilliams worked for the government until his retirement, after which he studied real estate and tax laws. One of the most spry of the informants, Freddie McWilliams demonstrated a number of dance steps in the course of the interview. He has also saved numerous photographs from when he was in show business. In 1976 he lived with his wife in North Oakland.

Mrs. Vivian Osborn Marsh was born in Houston, Texas, and came to the Bay Area in 1913. She attended Berkeley High and graduated from the University of California, Berkeley, where she studied anthropology and wrote a master's thesis on Negro folklore in the Americas. She was also a charter member of Kappa Chapter of Delta Sigma Theta, founded by Black students at the university. Moreover, Mrs. Marsh joined the Phyllis Wheatley club. She was an officer in a number of women's clubs and civic groups, played a leading role in Bay Area politics and social life, and traveled extensively. In the summer of 1976 she was still actively involved in civic affairs. A resident of Berkeley, she has also saved a number of photographs of her family and social life.

Martel Meneweather was born in Marshall, Texas, the daughter of college graduates. After attending college herself, she married and in 1919 moved to the Bay Area with her husband. She was not quite thirty years of age. They first lived in San Francisco, but, like many other Blacks, they moved to Oakland in the 1920s. She worked with a number of groups, such as the Garveyites, and helped organize the California Association of Colored Women. Besides raising a family, the informant was active in church, in politics, and in civil rights. She also worked to obtain jobs for Afro-Americans in Bay Area schools, hospitals, and other public institutions. In 1977, still active in civic affairs, Mrs. Meneweather lived in Oakland.

Ethel Terrell was born in Newark, New Jersey, near the end of the last century. The daughter of a railroad man, she learned to play piano and started a career in show business after completing school. She played for silent movies, toured with Sisseretta "Black Patti" Jones's group, and also traveled the vaudeville circuit with a show band, the Syncopated Seven. In the early 1920s the Orpheum vaudeville route brought her to San Francisco, where she decided to settle. She led her own band, the Franciscans, married, moved to the East Bay, and continued to play piano, though she stopped touring. Mrs. Terrell was active in women's clubs and during the 1930s supervised a WPA theatre group in the musical *Change Your Luck* as well as other productions. In the 1970s she played an advisory role in musical productions set in the 1920s and 1930s. She passed in late 1977.

Royal E. Towns was born February 10, 1899, in West Oakland. His father and mother had lived in the Bay Area for several decades, raising a large family before the birth of their last child, Royal. Besides attending the local schools and actively participating in sports, he inherited a family tradition that mirrored the history of the Bay Area. From his older brothers he learned the details of that history and acquired several photograph albums. Mr. Towns worked in industry and on the railroad before becoming one of Oakland's first Black firemen. He rose to the rank of lieutenant, fought to win better jobs for Afro-Americans, and was active in political, civic, and Masonic organizations. He founded and for eleven years edited the *Prince Hall Masonic Digest*, which chronicled the history and contemporary activities of the oldest Black fraternal order. He also studied photography, building a darkroom in his home to pursue the craft in depth; researched his family's history on the Pacific slope; helped found the East Bay Negro Historical Society; and remained involved in civic and social affairs in the 1970s.

Eleanor Carroll Watkins was born in Oakland in 1912. She attended St. Augustine's Episcopal Church. After completing public school at an early age, she enrolled in the University of California, obtaining a B.A. and a degree in Library Science. While at Berkeley she joined the Kappa Chapter of Delta Sigma Theta. Mrs. Watkins worked in the public libraries of the East Bay until her retirement. She saved a number of late nineteenth-century studio portraits and twentieth-century photographs from her family's collection. These records, her training, and her experience resulted in a historical consciousness that reflected years of residence in the Bay Area. In the summer of 1977 she and her husband lived in El Cerrito, a suburb north of Berkeley.

John Watkins was born in Oakland in 1910. Both his parents had lived in the Bay Area a number of years. He attended Oakland's public schools, where he played in the band, excelled in athletics, and planned to join the service to become an aviator. After graduation he encountered racial prejudice in the military and, consequently, worked in an insurance office and on the railroad. During the Depression he became a union organizer on the waterfront. In World War II he was a mechanic, then an instructor, and subsequently a planner in a defense plant. After working in the post office, he realized a lifelong ambition when he opened an equipment rental business in the suburb of Walnut Creek. Recently Mr. Watkins started studying photography, developing film and making prints in his El Cerrito home.

# Notes

## Chapter 1: Introduction

1. Richard Wright and Edwin Rosskam, *Twelve Million Black Voices: A Folk History of the Negro in the United States* (New York, 1941), p. 5.

2. Ibid.

3. Ibid.

4. The late Professor Elizabeth Parker, Ethnic Studies, University of San Francisco, interviewed Black San Franciscans. The San Francisco African-American Cultural and Historical Society has also undertaken an oral history project. In addition, the Oakland Museum interviewed a number of Bay Area Afro-Americans. Mary Perry Smith and the Cultural and Ethnic Affairs Guild of the Oakland Museum were kind enough to allow me to listen to the tapes, which broadened the bases of my insights and conclusions. I also consulted the interviews that are a part of the Earl Warren Oral History Project of the University of California, Berkeley. E. A. Daly, publisher of the *California Voice* (Oakland), C. L. Dellums, an officer in the Brotherhood of Sleeping Car Porters for several decades, Tarea Hall Pittman, an activist in the women's clubs, and California Assemblyman Byron Rumford were among the informants. One of the problems with incorporating material from other interviews, however, is the fact that different researchers have their own objectives and therefore ask different kinds of questions.

Recently historians have utilized the Works Project Administration's slave narratives, which have been published in George P. Rawick, ed., *The American Slave: A Composite Autobiography* (19 vols.; Westport, Conn., 1972–). Examples are: Eugene Genovese, *Roll, Jordan, Roll: The World the Slaves Made* (New York, [1974]); and Lawrence Levine, *Black Culture and Black Consciousness: Afro-American Folk Thought From Slavery to Freedom* (New York, 1977). Theodore Rosengarten, *All God's Dangers: The Life of Nate Shaw* (New York, 1974); Alex Haley, ed., *The Autobiography of Malcolm X* (New York, 1965); and William L. Montell, *The Saga of Coe Ridge: A Study of Oral History* (Knoxville, Tenn., [1970]) are other examples of what scholars might accomplish through interviewing.

Some of the methods and problems involved in oral history are discussed in Lewis L. Langness, *The Life History in Anthropological Science* (New York, [1965]); Willa Baum, *Oral History for the Local Historical Society* (Nashville, Tenn., 1971); Ramon I. Harris, et al., *The Practice of Oral History: A Handbook* (Glen Rock, N.J., 1975), pp. 1–4 discusses oral history's place in scholarship; Montell, *The Saga of Coe Ridge*, pp. vii–xxi, treats oral history, folklore, and the oral tradition; William W. Moss, "The Future of Oral History," *The Oral History Review* (1975), pp. 5–15 is also valuable.

5. Karen Becker Ohrn, "The Photoflow of Family Life: A Family's Photograph Collection," *Saying Cheese: Studies in Folk Photography* No. 12 (1975), p. 27. I would like to thank Professor John Vlach, Ethnic Studies and the Department of Anthropology, The

University of Texas at Austin, for informing me of this publication. Examples of scholars' contributions to the study of society and culture through photography are: Gregory Bateson and Margaret Mead, *Balinese Character: A Photographic Analysis* (New York, 1942); and Margaret Mead and Paul Byers, *The Small Conference: An Innovation in Communication* (Paris, 1968).

6. John Collier, "Photography in Anthropology," *American Anthropologist* LVIX (Oct. 1957), 849, 853, 857–58; John Collier, *Visual Anthropology: Photography As A Research Method* (Stanford, Calif., 1967). Also, see Richard Rudisill, *Mirror Image: The Influence of the Daguerreotype on American Society* (Albuquerque, N.M., 1971); William Stott, *Documentary Expression and Thirties America* (New York, 1973). On the history of photography, see Robert Taft, *Photography and the American Scene: A Social History, 1839–1899* (New York, 1938), and Michel F. Braive, *The Photograph: A Social History* (New York, 1966). On the snapshot as a genre, Jonathan Green, ed., *The Snapshot in Aperture* (Millertown, N.Y., 1974). Particularly significant is *Studies in the Anthropology of Visual Communication* (SAVICOM) I (Fall 1974), which is a publication of the Society for the Anthropology of Visual Communication.

7. Ohrn, "Photoflow of Family Life," p. 31.

8. Gilbert Osofsky, *Harlem: the Making of a Ghetto, Negro New York, 1890–1930* (New York, 1966); and Allan H. Spear, *Black Chicago: the Making of a Negro Ghetto* (Chicago, 1967). For a classic which uses photographs to document the history and living conditions of Black folk, see Wright and Rosskam, *12 Million Black Voices*. For an excellent photographic record of Black urbanites in an eastern city, see Liliane De Cock and Reginald McGhee, *James Van Der Zee* (Dobbs Ferry, N.Y., 1973). Edith M. Dabbs, *Face of An Island: Leigh Richmond Miner's Photographs of Saint Helena Islanders* (New York, 1971) focuses on southern rural Blacks. Examples of how photography aided the conclusions of scholars on Black non-verbal communication are: Benjamin G. Cooke, "Nonverbal Communication Among Afro-Americans: An Initial Classification"; and Annette Powell Williams, "Dynamics of A Black Audience," in Thomas Kochman, ed., *Rappin' and Stylin' Out: Communication in Urban Black America* (Urbana, Ill., [1972]), pp. 32–64, 101–8. Richard Chalfen, "Introduction to the Study of Non-Professional Photography As Visual Communication," *Saying Cheese* No. 13 (1975), 19.

9. Richard Chalfen, review of Robert U. Akeret, *Photoanalysis,* in *Studies in the Anthropology of Visual Communication* I (Fall 1974), 58.

10. Ibid.

11. Howard S. Becker, "Photography and Sociology," *Studies in the Anthropology of Visual Communication* I (Fall 1974), 21.

## Chapter 2: Pioneers

1. For demographic and social changes in western towns and cities, see: Ralph Mann, "The Decade After the Gold Rush: Social Structure in Grass Valley and Nevada City, California, 1850–1860," *Pacific Historical Review* XLI (November 1972), 484–504; and Richard H. Peterson, "The Frontier Thesis and Social Mobility on the Mining Frontier," *Pacific Historical Review* XLIV (Feb. 1975), 52–67. On Seattle during the World War I years, see Horace Cayton, *Long Old Road: An Autobiography* (Seattle, 1963). On Los Angeles, see J. Max Bond, "The Negro in Los Angeles" (Ph.D. diss., University of Southern California; reprinted by R&E Research Associates, San Francisco, 1972); and Lawrence B. de Graaf, "The City of Black Angels: The Emergence of the Los Angeles Ghetto, 1890–1930," *Pacific Historical Review* XXXIX (Aug. 1970), 323–52. On the Bay Area, see the San Francisco *Chronicle,* Nov. 11, 1943, p. 5 on the housing and health of World War II migrants, and Dec.

10, 1944, p. 12 on the future of the Black San Francisco population; see also Charles S. Johnson, *The Negro War Worker in San Francisco* (San Francisco, 1944); Davis McEntire and Julia R. Tarnopol, "Postwar Status of Negro Workers in San Francisco Area," *Monthly Labor Review* LXX (June 1950), 612–17; Ottole Krebs, "The Post-War Negro in San Francisco," *American Communities* II (1948–49), 549–86; Barbara Sawyer, "Negroes in West Oakland," *Immigration and Race Problems* (1949–53), pp. 844–64; and Edward Everett France, "Some Aspects of the Migration of the Negro to the San Francisco Bay Area Since 1940" (Ph.D. diss., University of California, Berkeley, 1962). On the Great Migration, see Emmett J. Scott, *Negro Migration During the War* (New York, 1920); Louise V. Kennedy, *The Negro Peasant Turns Cityward: Effects of Recent Migrations to Northern Cities* (New York, 1930); and Florette Henri, *Black Migration: Movement North, 1900–1920* (Garden City, N.Y., 1976).

2. Frank Soulé, John H. Gihon, and James Nisbet, *The Annals of San Francisco* (New York, 1855), and Roger W. Lotchin, *San Francisco, 1846–1856: From Hamlet to City* (New York, 1974) for the city's early history. On the uniqueness of San Francisco and Denver, see Gunther Barth, *Instant Cities: Urbanization and the Rise of San Francisco and Denver* (New York, 1975). On San Francisco's population growth, see United States Census Office, *Twelfth Census, 1900: Population* (Washington, D.C., 1901) I: cxix, 430–33.

3. Lotchin, *San Francisco, 1846–1856*, pp. 45–46; *Twelfth Census, 1900: Population*, I: 430–33; John P. Young, *San Francisco: A History of the Pacific Coast Metropolis*, 2 vols. (San Francisco, [1912]), I: 322; II: 487, 670, 932, 976–77.

4. Young, *San Francisco*, I: 322; II: 939; "The City and Port of San Francisco, California," *San Francisco Descriptive Pamphlets* (San Francisco, 1896), pp. 2–3; United States Census Office, *Manufacturers of the United States in 1860* (Washington, D.C. 1865), p. 36.

5. Young, *San Francisco*, I: 272–73; II: 605, 716, 760; San Francisco *Call*, Jan. 16, 1887, p. 1; "City and Port," *Descriptive Pamphlets*, pp. 2–3; United States Census Office, *Negro Population in the United States, 1790–1915* (Washington, D.C., 1918), p. 93.

6. On the role of shipping in the city's development and economy, see Lotchin, *San Francisco, 1846–1856*, pp. 31–33, 45–48, 67–69. [United States Census Bureau], Original Schedule of the Eighth Census, 1860, San Francisco, California (hereafter cited, with the appropriate year, as Manuscript Census), lists Black crew members aboard ships in Ward One; *Elevator*, Aug. 18, 1865, p. 3, June 30, 1865, p. 3.

7. E. Berkeley Tompkins, "Black Ahab: William T. Shorey, Whaling Master," *California Historical Quarterly* LI (Spring 1972), 75–84; Delilah L. Beasley, *The Negro Trail Blazers of California* (New York, 1969 ed.), pp. 125–27; interviews, Eugene Lasartemay, July 23, 1976, Aurelious Alberga, July 27, 1976.

8. Manuscript Census, 1870. San Francisco *Call*, Aug. 5, 1893, p. 4; Oakland *Western Outlook*, July 22, 1916, p. 2; "Oakland Business Men," *The Colored American Magazine* IX (Nov. 1905), 648–50, and XII (Oct., 1907), 269–72.

9. *Pacific Appeal*, May 16, 1863, p. 4; Philip Durham and Everett L. Jones, *The Negro Cowboy* (New York, [1965]), pp. 170–71.

10. New York *Weekly Anglo-African*, Dec. 17, 1859, p. 3, Dec. 31, 1859, p. 3; *Elevator*, Jan. 12, 1866, p. 3; Beasley, *Negro Trail Blazers*, pp. 206–7.

11. Ann Charters, *Nobody: The Story of "Bert" Williams* (New York, 1970), pp. 20–25 discusses Williams and Walker's early years in San Francisco; Alan Lomax, *Mister Jelly Roll: The Fortunes of Jelly Roll Morton, New Orleans Creole and "Inventor of Jazz"* (New York, [1950]), pp. 167–69.

12. *Call*, April 8, 1899, p. 7, June 23, 1899, p. 7, Jan. 13, 1903, p. 10; *Chronicle*, Dec. 3, 1902, p. 5, Aug. 4, 1916, p. 9, Jan. 15, 1920, p. 8; San Francisco *Alta California*, Oct. 11, 1889,

p. 8; Beasley, *Negro Trail Blazers,* 278–300, discusses the military careers of a number of Black pioneers.

13. San Francisco *Pacific Appeal,* Jan. 27, 1872, p. 2; interview with Alfred J. Butler, July 29, 1976; San Francisco *Elevator,* April 7, 1865, p. 4, July 10, 1868, p. 2; "The Palace Hotel," *The Overland Monthly* XV (Sept. 1875), 298–99.

14. The Manuscript Census and published censuses give details on occupations. On the competition of whites and Blacks for hotel and restaurant positions, see *Call,* July 14, 1883, p. 1, July 18, 1883, p.1, Nov. 3, 1896, p. 1; *Alta California,* Nov. 9, 1889, p. 1, Nov. 10, 1889, p. 10; Beasley, *Negro Trail Blazers,* p. 149.

15. *Chronicle,* Feb. 7, 1904, p. 7, glorifies the opportunities in San Francisco and the achievements of its Black citizens; Oakland *Sunshine,* April 28, 1906, p. 1; *Twelfth Census, 1900: Population,* I: 18, II: 71–72; *Negro Population,* p. 140; *Sixteenth Census, 1940: Population* (Washington, D.C., 1943), part 1, pp. 599, 637, 657; Beasley, *Negro Trail Blazers,* p. 149. Informants invariably recalled narrow job opportunities for Black workers, and in the San Francisco *Examiner,* Aug. 2, 1968, p. 52, labor leader C. L. Dellums mentioned some of the difficulties of the 1920s.

16. *Tenth Census, 1880: Population* (Washington, D.C., 1883), I: 498, 538; conclusions on the origins and percentage of foreign-born Blacks were based on the Manuscript Census, 1860 and 1900, and the *Twelfth Census, 1900; Population,* II: 72. Gilbert Osofsky, *Harlem: The Making of a Ghetto* (New York, [1963]), p. 3.

17. Based on the Manuscript Census, 1860.

18. Based on the Manuscript Census, 1900. The Manuscript Censuses of 1860 and 1900 give residents' place of birth; the 1900 gives that of their parents, as well.

19. *Elevator,* Jan. 26, 1866, p. 2 indicates that two-thirds of all Pacific slope Negroes were literate; *Tenth Census, 1880: Population,* I: 919, 924–25; Monroe Work, *Negro Year Book, An Encyclopedia of the Negro, 1918–1919* (Tuskegee, Ala., 1919), pp. 80, 277; *Thirteenth Census, 1910: Population* (Washington, D.C., 1913), II: 181.

20. *Pacific Appeal,* June 7, 1862, p. 2 notes that a number of Blacks were educated "by the liberal school system of the Free States."

21. Henry G. Langley, comp., *The San Francisco Directory, 1871,* p. 11 provided figures for analysis of age distribution.

22. Computations based on Manuscript Census, 1860; *Eleventh Census, 1890: Population* (Washington, D.C., 1897), II: part I, p. 890; *Twelfth Census, 1900: Population,* II: 142–43; *Thirteenth Census, 1910: Population,* II: 180; and *Fifteenth Census, 1930: Population,* III: part 1, pp. 245, 248. For age/sex ratios of Blacks in other cities between 1890 and 1910, see United States Census Office, *Negro Population,* p. 156; San Francisco's proportion of males was uncommonly high among urban Black centers. Denver's was comparable in 1890, but only in that year. The only major cities that approached Black San Francisco's ratio (166 males/100 females) in 1910 were Oakland (112/100), Detroit (108/100), and Chicago (106/100). Also, other cities' female populations grew from 1920 to 1930; see *Fifteenth Census, 1930: Population,* II: 115.

23. Based on the Manuscript Census, 1860. Compare the changes in social structure in other California towns, as described in Mann, "The Decade After the Gold Rush." See notes 21 and 22. *Fifteenth Census, 1930: Population,* III: part 1, p. 248; W. E. B. Du Bois, *The Black North in 1901: A Social Study* (New York, rpt. 1969), p. 5.

24. Based on the Manuscript Census, 1860. *Eleventh Census, 1890: Population,* II: part 1, p. 890; *Twelfth Census, 1900: Population,* II: 344; *Fifteenth Census, 1930: Population,* II: 968; III: part 1, p. 248.

25. *Fifteenth Census, 1930: Population,* VI: 64.

26. Ibid., 59.

27. *Fifteenth Census, 1930: Population,* IV: 21, 38, 39.

28. Ibid.

29. Charles S. Johnson, "The New Frontage on American Life," Alain Locke, ed., *The New Negro* (New York, 1969 ed.), pp. 288–89.

30. *Pacific Appeal,* July 5, 1862, p. 2, Oct. 3, 1863, p. 2. See the account of a lecture, "Battleships of the U.S. Navy," in *Elevator,* June 11, 1898, p. 2. The lecture described in detail the construction and armaments of vessels, using a five-foot model of the *Oregon,* electric torpedoes, and the destruction of a miniature vessel by electric mines.

## *Chapter 3:* Optimists

1. Gunnar Myrdal, *An American Dilemma: The Negro Problem and Modern Democracy* (New York, [1944]), p. 186.

2. San Francisco *Pacific Appeal,* June 21, 1862, p. 3.

3. *Proceedings of the First State Convention of the Colored Citizens of the State of California* (San Francisco, 1855), p. 18; San Francisco *Elevator,* Feb. 21, 1874, p. 3; on Jonas Townsend, *Elevator,* Oct. 26, 1872, p. 2; and *Pacific Appeal,* Nov. 9, 1872, p. 2.

4. [United States Census Bureau], Original Schedule of the Eighth Census, San Francisco, 1860 and 1870 (hereafter cited, with the appropriate year, as Manuscript Census).

5. Quoted in Julia Cooley Altrocchi, *The Spectacular San Franciscans* (New York, 1949), p. 70.

6. San Francisco *Examiner,* June 16, 1889, p. 10; San Francisco *Chronicle,* Feb. 7, 1904, p. 7.

7. *Pacific Appeal,* July 12, 1862, p. 2.

8. Gunther Barth, *Instant Cities: Urbanization and the Rise of San Francisco and Denver* (New York, 1975); Oscar Lewis, *Silver Kings: The Lives and Times of Mackay, Fair, Flood, and O'Brien, Lords of the Nevada Comstock Lode* (New York, [1971]); and Neil Larry Shumsky, "Tar Flat and Nob Hill: A Social History of Industrial San Francisco During the 1870s" (Ph.D. diss., University of California, Berkeley, 1972) for the city's early economic history.

9. John S. Hittell, *A History of the City of San Francisco and Incidentally of the State of California* (San Francisco, 1878), p. 456; *Frederick Douglass' Paper* (Rochester, N.Y.), April 1, 1852, p. 3.

10. Hittell, *History of San Francisco,* p. 429.

11. On Phillips's life, see San Francisco *Pacific Coast Appeal,* May 3, 1902, pp. 4–5.

12. Mifflin W. Gibbs, *Shadow and Light: An Autobiography* (New York, 1968 ed.), p. 40.

13. Lucius Beebe and Charles M. Clegg, eds., *Dreadful California,* by Hinton Rowan Helper (New York, [1948]), p.59. Frank Soulé, John H. Gihon, and James Nisbet, *The Annals of San Francisco* (New York, 1855), p. 216. Delilah L. Beasley, *The Negro Trail Blazers of California* (New York, [1969] ed.), pp. 119–21; and *Examiner,* June 16, 1889, p. 10. William F. Rae, *Westward by Rail: The New Route to the East* (New York, 1871), p. 287.

14. Andrew S. Hallidie, "Manufacturing in San Francisco," *The Overland Monthly* XI (June 1888), 641; Oscar Lewis, ed., *This Was San Francisco* (New York, [1962]), pp. 180–81. Gibbs, *Shadow and Light,* pp. 43–44; Ira Berlin, *Slaves Without Masters: The Free Negro in the Antebellum South* (New York, 1974), p. 67.

15. Beasley, *Negro Trail Blazers,* p. 286; Manuscript Census, 1860, 1870.

16. Oscar Lewis and Carroll D. Hall, *Bonanza Inn: America's First Luxury Hotel* (New York, [1971]); "The Palace Hotel," *The Overland Monthly* XV (Sept. 1875), 298–99.

17. Oakland *Sunshine,* July 21, 1907, p. 2, at the East Bay Negro Historical Society.

18. Lucille Eaves, *A History of California Labor Legislation* (Berkeley, 1910), pp. 94–96, 90; Clyde Duniway, "Slavery in California After 1848," *Annual Report of the American*

*Historical Association for the Year 1905* I (Washington, D.C., 1906), 241–48; Delilah L. Beasley, "Slavery in California," *The Journal of Negro History* III (Jan. 1918), 33–34; Rudolph M. Lapp, *Blacks in Gold Rush California* (New Haven, Conn., 1977), pp. 130–35; Paul Finkelman, "Slavery and Law in California" (unpublished essay in the author's possession) discusses bondage in what was technically a free state; in the *Elevator*, Feb. 2, 1866, p. 3, William H. Hall reported that southerners were taking slaves through Mexico to isolated regions of the west.

19. *Pacific Appeal,* July 12, 1862, p. 2; *Examiner,* June 16, 1889, p. 10; Beasley, *Negro Trail Blazers,* pp. 119–21, 145.

20. Beasley, *Negro Trail Blazers,* pp. 119–21.

21. Ibid.; *Examiner,* June 16, 1889, p. 10; Manuscript Census, 1860, 1870, 1880; San Francisco *Spokesman,* Jan. 4, 1932, p. 2; *Pacific Coast Appeal,* Dec. 19, 1903, p. 4; Sue Bailey Thurman, *Pioneers of Negro Origin in California* (San Francisco, 1949) also provides information on Dennis; *Elevator,* June 20, 1874, p. 3, June 27, 1874, p. 2; on Daniel Seales, the "colored millionaire of San Francisco," Oct. 18, 1890, p. 3; March 17, 1877, p. 2.

22. United States Census Office, *Sixteenth Census, 1940: Population* (Washington, D.C., 1943), II: 114.

23. Manuscript Census, 1860, 1870, 1880, 1900 give job patterns; the Manuscript Census, 1870 provides information on personal and property wealth for that year.

24. *Thirteenth Census, 1910: Population* (Washington, D.C., 1914), IV: 600–601; *Fifteenth Census, 1930: Population,* IV: 209–11.

25. Ibid.

26. Ibid.; *Fourteenth Census, 1920: Population* (Washington, D.C., 1921), IV: 1227–30.

27. *Elevator,* July 21, 1865, p. 2. On the difficulties of recruiting white laborers for the railroad, see Oscar Lewis, *The Big Four* (New York, [1966] ed.), pp. 48–51.

28. *Elevator,* July 21, 1865, p. 2, Nov. 29, 1865, p. 2. The use of freedmen was first proposed by William H. Hall, a Black pioneer.

29. Doris Marion Wright, "The Making of Cosmopolitan California: An Analysis of Immigration, 1848–1870," *California Historical Society Quarterly* X (March 1941), 65–68.

30. *Elevator,* May 12, 1865, p. 2.

31. Ibid.

32. Oakland *Times,* Nov. 5, 1879, p. 2; and Chapter 4 of this work. Eaves, *History,* pp. 126–27; Lewis, *Big Four,* pp. 148–51; Alexander Saxton, *The Indispensable Enemy: Labor and the Anti-Chinese Movement in California* (Berkeley, 1971), pp. 60–66.

33. Occasionally Black residents (for example, Dawson Thomas and John Woodis) worked as ship caulkers. Woodis reported $15,000 in property in 1870 and ranked among the ten wealthiest Afro-San Franciscans. Such cases were exceptions. *Chronicle,* July 24, 1883, p. 7; *Pacific Appeal,* Dec. 19, 1863, p. 3; Manuscript Census, 1870; *Elevator,* March 18, 1870, p. 2. See Frederick Douglass on the prejudice of white workers, *Life and Times of Frederick Douglass* (London, [1969 ed.]), p. 287. Based on Manuscript Census, 1860.

34. *Elevator,* March 16, 1865, p. 2.

35. *Pacific Appeal,* Jan. 2, 1864, p. 3.

36. Gibbs, *Shadow and Light,* pp. 43–44; *Elevator,* March 7, 1874, p. 2.

37. *Elevator,* March 25, 1870, p. 2, June 4, 1869, p. 2.

38. *Chronicle,* June 6, 1894, p. 5.

39. William E. B. Du Bois, *The American Negro Artisan* (Atlanta, Ga., 1912), p. 108; "Colored California," *Crisis* VI (Aug. 1913), 194.

40. *Elevator,* May 15, 1868, p. 2; William M. Camp, *San Francisco, Port of Gold* (Garden City, N.Y., 1947), pp. 317–18. For background on the white workingmen's ideology and their struggles with the Chinese, see Saxton, *Indispensable Enemy.*

41. *Elevator*, March 16, 1866, pp. 2–3, Aug. 17, 1868, pp. 2–3.

42. Soulé, Gihon, and Nisbet, *Annals*, p. 369.

43. *Pacific Appeal*, May 6, 1872, p. 2, Jan. 29, 1876, p. 1; "Palace Hotel," pp. 298–99; *Pacific Appeal*, Dec. 28, 1878, p. 2, Jan. 29, 1876, p. 1.

44. San Francisco *Call*, Nov. 15, 1875, p. 3.

45. Henry G. Langley, comp., *The San Francisco Directory, 1886, 1893, 1895, 1905* (hereafter cited as *City Directory*); *Chronicle*, Feb. 7, 1904, p. 7; Harr Wagner, ed., *Notable Speeches by Notable Speakers* (San Francisco, 1902), p. 322.

46. *City Directory, 1876, 1878, 1895;* Beasley, *Negro Trail Blazers*, p. 127.

47. *Chronicle*, Jan. 18, 1878, p. 3; *City Directory, 1887;* Edward Paul Eaves, "A History of the Cooks' and Waiters' Union of San Francisco" (M.A. thesis, University of California, Berkeley, 1930), pp. iii–iv; *Chronicle*, Jan. 16, 1888, p. 8; on anti-coolie organizations, see Saxton, *Indispensable Enemy*, pp. 175–76.

48. *Call*, Aug. 13, 1883, p. 4, April 27, 1887, p. 2, Jan. 31, 1887, p. 1, Jan. 30, 1887, p. 6; *Chronicle*, June 15, 1886, p. 5.

49. *Chronicle*, Jan. 17, 1888, p. 8, Jan. 19, 1888, p. 8, Jan. 16, 1888, p. 8, Jan. 27, 1888, p. 8.

50. Ibid., April 20, 1889, p. 8; *Call*, June 27, 1889, p. 7, June 29, 1889, p. 8, May 3, 1889, p. 7; Beasley, *Negro Trail Blazers*, p. 149.

51. *Chronicle*, Nov. 9, 1889, p. 6. Lewis and Hall, *Bonanza Inn*, p. 51; Lewis and Hall discuss the strike (pp. 47–48) and quote a Black worker (p. 48). I was not able to discover the source of the quotation.

52. *City Directory, 1884, 1885;* San Francisco *Alta California*, Oct. 27, 1889, p. 1.

53. *Alta California*, Nov. 9, 1889, p. 1.

54. Quoted in *Chronicle*, Nov. 10, 1889, p. 16.

55. Ibid.

56. *Call*, Nov. 3, 1896, p. 14.

57. John C. Kirkpatrick to Francis G. Newlands, Sept. 9, 1896, Sharon Papers, Bancroft Library, University of California, Berkeley.

58. *Call*, Nov. 3, 1896, p. 14.

59. *Chronicle*, Nov. 10, 1889, p. 16.

60. *Elevator*, July 3, 1886, p. 3, and Sept. 11, 1886, p. 3; San Francisco *Sentinel*, Sept. 20, 1890, p. 2 discusses the decline of Black artisans in the south; see *Pacific Coast Appeal*, Jan. 3, 1903 on mistreatment by unions; Herbert G. Gutman discusses the narrowing job opportunities in other cities in "Persistent Myths about the Afro-American Family," *The Journal of Interdisciplinary History* VI (Autumn 1975), 205–7; a similar decline is noted by Robert A. Warner in *New Haven Negroes: A Social History* (New Haven, 1940), pp. 240, 250: "When eating places have been 'modernized,' the colored service has disappeared." On the other hand, progress was noted in Boston; see John Daniels, *In Freedom's Birthplace: A Study of the Boston Negroes* (Boston, 1914), pp. 328–29, 355–56.

61. Peter R. Decker, *Fortunes and Failures: White-Collar Mobility in Nineteenth-Century San Francisco* (Cambridge, Mass., 1978).

62. *Chronicle*, Aug. 3, 1916, p. 1 and Aug. 16, 1916, p. 3.

63. Ibid., Aug. 9, 1916, p. 9, Aug. 16, 1916, p. 3.

64. Ibid., July 14, 1916, p. 4 and July 19, 1916, p. 6; for the strike's settlement, see July 15, 1916, p. 1.

65. Ibid., Aug. 6, 1916, p. 3.

66. Beasley, *Negro Trail Blazers*, p. 149.

67. Judd Lewis Kahn, "Imperial San Francisco: History of a Vision" (Ph.D. diss., University of California, Berkeley, 1971), pp. 21–22, mentions an occasion in which Blacks were brought to work on the waterfront. For 1916, see Robert C. Francis, "A History of Labor

on the San Francisco Waterfront" (Ph.D. diss., University of California, Berkeley, 1934), pp. 115, 152; *Chronicle,* Jan. 15, 1920, p. 8, Jan. 16, 1920, p. 22, Jan. 17, 1920, p. 11.

### Chapter 4: Survivors

1. San Francisco *Pacific Appeal,* Sept. 20, 1862, p. 2.

2. Interview, Matt Crawford, Aug. 3, 1976.

3. Shadrack Howard was a sailmaker, a seamen, and a "victualer" in New Bedford before migrating west. He also had a reputation as an inventor. San Francisco *Elevator,* Dec. 1, 1865, p. 2, and *Pacific Appeal,* Sept. 19, 1863, p. 3. James Abajian was kind enough to provide information on Howard's early years. On Dyer, *Elevator,* April 7, 1865, p. 4, April 5, 1867, p. 4, June 18, 1869, p. 2; *Pacific Appeal,* Sept. 19, 1863, p. 3. Henry G. Langley, comp., *San Francisco Directory, 1868* (hereafter referred to, with the appropriate year, as *City Directory*). Another noteworthy business, the Cocoanut Pulverizing Company, was formed in 1874. *Elevator,* May 16, 1874, p. 3, Aug. 22, 1874, p. 2, Nov. 14, 1874, p. 3; Articles of Incorporation of the California Cocoanut Pulverizing Company, Office of the Secretary of State, California State Archives, Sacramento.

4. *City Directory, 1860* lists Peter Anderson as a tailor. According to his newspaper, the *Pacific Appeal* (April 19, 1862, p. 4), he was a "coat renovator" and "steam scourer"; [United States Census Bureau], Original Schedule of the Eighth Census, 1860, San Francisco, California (hereafter cited as Manuscript Census, with the appropriate year), lists Anderson as the proprietor of a clothing store; it also gives the occupations of Brown, Smith, and Cornish.

5. San Francisco *Examiner,* June 16, 1889, p. 10.

6. *Elevator,* May 14, 1869, pp. 2–3; New York *Weekly Anglo-African,* Nov. 19, 1859, p. 1, and June 23, 1860, p. 2. James A. Fisher, "A Social History of the Negro in California, 1860–1900" (M.A. thesis, Sacramento State College, 1966), ch. 4; Delilah L. Beasley, "Slavery in California," *Journal of Negro History* III (Jan. 1918), 44; *Elevator,* April 17, 1868, pp. 2–3; John Hope Franklin, *From Slavery to Freedom: A History of Negro Americans* (New York, [1969] ed.), pp. 240–41, 267–68.

7. Neil Larry Shumsky, "Tar Flat and Nob Hill: A Social History of Industrial San Francisco During the 1870's" (Ph.D. diss., University of California, Berkeley, 1972); and Oscar Lewis, *Silver Kings: The Lives and Times of Mackay, Fair, Flood, and O'Brien, Lords of the Nevada Comstock Lode* (New York, [1971]) analyze these developments.

8. The "Madame" prefixed to Mrs. Phillips's name indicates the high esteem in which she was held. *Elevator,* June 11, 1898, p. 1 notes that she won a gold medal at the California Midwinter Exposition; San Francisco *Pacific Coast Appeal,* Jan. 17, 1902, p. 1, and May 3, 1902, p. 4; Oakland *California Voice,* Dec. 18, 1925, p. 6; San Francisco *Spokesman,* March 16, 1933, p. 1.

9. *Pacific Coast Appeal,* Jan. 17, 1902, p. 1; Robert C. Francis, "A Survey of Negro Business in the San Francisco Bay Region" (M.A. thesis, University of California, Berkeley, 1928).

10. *Elevator,* May 2, 1885, p. 2; *Pacific Coast Appeal,* Jan. 17, 1902, p. 4; Peter R. Decker, *Fortunes and Failures: White-Collar Mobility in Nineteenth-Century San Francisco* (Cambridge, Mass., 1978).

11. Francis, "Survey," pp. 4, 40; Ivan H. Light, *Ethnic Enterprise in America: Business and Welfare Among Chinese, Japanese, and Blacks* (Berkeley, 1972), analyzes reasons for business failures among Blacks and compares them with other non-white groups.

12. *California Voice,* Aug. 6, 1926, p. 2; Francis, "Survey," pp. 18–19.

13. William E. B. Du Bois, *The Black North: A Social Survey* (Atlanta, Ga., 1901), p. 44; *Crisis* VI (Aug. 1913), 194.

14. *Pacific Coast Appeal,* Jan. 17, 1902, p. 4; on the growth in Fresno, see San Francisco *Sentinel,* Dec. 13, 1890, p. 2; and in Seattle, *Sentinel,* Sept. 29, 1890, p. 2.

15. *The Colored American Magazine* IX (Nov. 1905), 648–50, and XII (Oct. 1907), 269–72.

16. Oakland *Western Outlook,* Jan. 2, 1915, p. 2.

17. Delilah L. Beasley, *The Negro Trail Blazers of California* (New York, [1969] ed.), p. 54; and *Pacific Appeal,* April 5, 1862, p. 2; Rudolph M. Lapp, "Negro Rights Activities in Gold Rush California," *California Historical Society Quarterly* XLV (March 1966), 8–10; Mifflin W. Gibbs, *Shadow and Light: An Autobiography* (New York, 1969 ed.), p. 46.

18. Gibbs, *Shadow and Light,* p. 54; San Francisco *Chronicle,* Feb. 2, 1895, p. 7; the *Pacific Appeal* and the *Elevator* chronicle the civil rights and political struggles, summarized in subsequent paragraphs, of the 1860s and 1870s.

19. San Francisco *Daily Evening Post,* June 25, 1873, p. 1.

20. William H. Blake to Governor George B. Stoneman, Jan. 1883, California State Archives.

21. Petition of William H. Blake, March 25, 1903, California State Archives.

22. Brochure of the first meeting of Afro-American League, in the California Historical Society Library, gives this information.

Racist government officials were an obstacle to employment for Blacks. In 1894 the mayor of San Francisco attempted to fire the Black clerk in City Hall solely because of his race. *Chronicle,* Aug. 11, 1894, p. 5; Aug. 12, 1894, p. 15; a complaint on job patronage was also voiced by the *Elevator,* Feb. 21, 1874.

23. Clipping, "Appeal to Reason," dated late 1906, in Negro Pamphlet Box, Bancroft Library, University of California, Berkeley; *Elevator,* June 28, 1873, p. 2.

24. Interviews, Vivian Osborn Marsh, Aug. 16, 1976, Royal Towns, Aug. 30, 1973. Information on Ruth Acty is in the East Bay Negro Historical Society, Oakland. Maya Angelou, *I Know Why the Caged Bird Sings* (New York, 1971 ed.), pp. 256–63; Patricia Myers Davidson informed me of this book's section on San Francisco.

25. Interview, Royal Towns, Aug. 30, 1973.

26. Ibid.; Lillian Dixon expressed the same opinion in a conversation with me (April 3, 1975), as did Tarea Hall Pittman and other activists in the Oral History Collection of the Oakland Museum and in the Earl Warren Oral History Project of the University of California, Berkeley. I would like to thank Mary Perry Smith and the Cultural and Ethnic Affairs Guild of the Oakland Museum for permitting me to listen to its tapes.

27. Interview, Ed Johnson, Aug. 14, 1973.

28. Interview, Eleanor Carroll Watkins, July 30, 1976.

29. Interview, Royal Towns, Aug. 30, 1973.

30. Interview, Alfred Butler, July 29, 1976. Nat Love, *The Life and Adventures of Nat Love, Better Known in the Cattle Country as "Deadwood Dick" by Himself* (New York, 1968 ed.), p. 135; interviews, Ed Johnson, Aug. 14, 1973, Aurelious Alberga, July 27, 1976; *Western Outlook,* July 22, 1916, p. 2.

31. *Elevator,* March 16, 1866, p. 2, June 30, 1865, p. 3.

32. Oakland *Sunshine,* June 21, 1902, p. 6; *Western Outlook,* Nov. 28, 1914, p. 2.

33. Several informants said that passing was common, and at least one was so light-complected that I mistook his race on our first encounter. See Fannie Barrier Williams, "Perils of the White Negro," *The Colored American Magazine* XIII (Dec. 1907), 21–23, for a contemporary opinion on passing. Family albums and photographs at the East Bay Negro Historical Society reveal the wide variation in skin tones among Black pioneers.

34. Alex Haley, ed., *The Autobiography of Malcolm X* (New York, 1965) abounds with examples of hustling and "street smarts."

35. "Oakland Business Men," *The Colored American Magazine* IX (Nov. 1905), 648–49; interview, Ed Johnson, Aug. 14, 1973.

36. *Pacific Appeal,* April 26, 1862, p. 4; *Elevator,* July 5, 1867, p. 1.

37. *City Directory, 1869; Sunshine,* June 21, 1902, p. 5; *Elevator,* Feb. 12, 1869, p. 3, Feb. 19, 1869, pp. 2–3, Feb. 26, 1869, p. 3; *Sentinel,* Sept. 20, 1890, p. 3, Dec. 6, 1890, p. 1; *Sunshine,* June 21, 1902, p. 8; *Pacific Coast Appeal,* Jan. 4, 1902, p. 8, Jan. 18, 1902, p. 7, Dec. 19, 1903, pp. 6–7.

38. *Elevator,* June 22, 1872, p. 3; Beasley, *Negro Trail Blazers,* pp. 121, 194–95; *Chronicle,* Jan. 18, 1922, p. 14; Oakland *Western American,* Oct. 12, 1928, p. 1. Interviews, Royal Towns, Aug. 30, 1973, Eugene Lasartemay, July 23, 1976, Claudia Cheltenham, April 17, 1973.

39. *City Directory, 1865; Pacific Appeal,* Aug. 1, 1863, pp. 2–3. Beasley, *Negro Trail Blazers,* p. 54; Rudolph M. Lapp, "Jeremiah B. Sanderson, Early California Negro Leader," *Journal of Negro History* LII (Oct. 1968), 321; interview, Martel Meneweather, June 13, 1975.

40. Interview, Ed Johnson, Aug. 14, 1973. In times of financial hardship, his clientele was generous: "After they found out I had that trouble, my dad dying and everything, they . . . . people gave me, I think they gave me just because they heard I'd had my troubles . . . . I made $300 in November just before Christmas . . . . Every night they'd hand me something." Ibid.

41. United States Census Office, *Fifteenth Census, 1930: Population* (Washington, D.C., 1931), IV: 21, 38, 39; VI: 67; Amelia Neville, *The Fantastic City: Memoirs of the Social and Romantic Life of Old San Francisco* (Boston, 1932), p. 148. Anne Pindell, a music teacher, gave concert performances, did fancy needlework, and was an example of a versatile woman of the mid-nineteenth century; *Weekly Anglo-African,* Dec. 17, 1859, p. 3; *Elevator,* July 28, 1865, p. 3, Dec. 18, 1865, p. 4, Jan. 12, 1866, p. 3. Other women, such as Mrs. Irwin Johnson and Mrs. John A. Barber, at the turn of the century, and Ethel Terrell, in the 1920s, took in boarders; *Elevator,* June 18, 1892, p. 3; *Western Outlook,* Jan. 27, 1900, p. 3; and interview, Ethel Terrell, April 20, 1973.

42. *Fifteenth Census, 1930,* VI: 50, 64–65.

## Chapter 5: Scouts

1. Rudolph M. Lapp, *Blacks in Gold Rush California* (New Haven, Conn., 1977), pp. 12–48; San Francisco *Pacific Appeal,* March 21, 1863, p. 2; San Francisco *Elevator,* April 26, 1863, p. 3, Feb. 17, 1873, p. 3. Harold Cruse has claimed modern scholars do not recognize migration's central role in Black history; see "Black and White: Outlines of the Next Stage" (parts 1, 2, and 3), *Black World* XX (Jan., March, May 1971). Stephan Thernstrom and other scholars regard mobile urbanites differently from me. Thernstrom's *Men in Motion: Some Data and Speculation About Urban Population Mobility in Nineteenth-Century America* (Los Angeles, 1970) stresses the impersonal forces that cause workers to drift from city to city.

2. *Pacific Appeal,* Jan. 9, 1864, p. 3, Jan. 23, 1864, p. 3; *Elevator,* June 1, 1872, p. 2; also, see June 22, 1872, p. 1, Sept. 14, 1872, p. 2, Dec. 6, 1873, p. 3.

3. *Elevator,* Dec. 21, 1872, p. 3, Aug. 25, 1865, p. 3.

4. Theodore Hershberg, "Free Blacks in Antebellum Philadelphia: A Study of Ex-Slaves, Freeborn, and Socioeconomic Decline," *Journal of Social History* V (Winter 1971–72), 183–209, emphasizes the destructive impact of urbanization.

5. *Elevator,* June 20, 1874, p. 3, June 27, 1874, pp. 1–2, May 18, 1872, p. 2; San Francisco *Examiner,* June 16, 1889, p. 10; see *Elevator,* July 3, 1868, p. 2, June 26, 1868, p. 2 for other instances of their travels.

6. *Elevator,* March 19, 1869, p. 3.

7. Mifflin W. Gibbs, *Shadow and Light: An Autobiography* (New York, 1969 ed.), pp. 37–69; San Francisco *Chronicle,* Feb. 2, 1895, p. 7.

8. *Elevator,* April 16, 1869, p. 1.

9. Ibid., March 19, 1869, p. 3, April 12, 1873, p. 3, May 17, 1876, p. 3; Delilah L. Beasley, *The Negro Trail Blazers of California* (New York, [1969] ed.), pp. 191–97; *Examiner,* June 16, 1889, p. 10.

10. John Hope Franklin, *From Slavery to Freedom: A History of Negro Americans* (New York, [1969] ed.) and August Meier and Elliott Rudwick, *From Plantation to Ghetto: An Interpretative History of American Negroes* (New York, [1968]) are two standard texts by contemporary historians. On slavery, see John W. Blassingame, *The Slave Community: Plantation Life in the Old South* (New York, 1972) and Kenneth M. Stampp, *The Peculiar Institution: Slavery in the Antebellum South* (New York, [1956]). For Black life in the north, see Leon F. Litwack, *North of Slavery: The Negro in the Free States, 1790–1860* (Chicago, 1961) and Lorenzo J. Greene, *The Negro in Colonial New England, 1620–1776* (New York, 1942). On the origins of racism and race relations, see Winthrop P. Jordan, *White Over Black: American Attitudes Toward the Negro, 1550–1812* (Chapel Hill, N.C., 1968), pp. 116–22. See also Ira Berlin, *Slaves Without Masters: The Free Negro in the Antebellum South* (New York, 1974), for the situation of southern freedmen.

11. Christopher Fyfe, *History of Sierra Leone* (London, 1962); Hollis R. Lynch, *Edward W. Blyden (1832–1912), Pan-Negro Patriot* (London, 1966); Ellen Gibson Wilson, *The Loyal Blacks* (New York, [1976]).

12. *Frederick Douglass' Paper* (Rochester, N.Y.), April 1, 1852, p. 3.

13. *Elevator,* Nov. 29, 1867, p. 2; *Pacific Appeal,* July 12, 1862, p. 2.

14. *Pacific Appeal,* Nov. 8, 1862, p. 1, Nov. 29, 1862, p. 1, Dec. 13, 1862, pp. 1, 3, Dec. 27, 1862, p. 1, Nov. 29, 1862, p. 3, Aug. 30, 1862, p. 2, April 25, 1863, p. 1.

15. Ibid., March 7, 1863, p. 1, Aug. 30, 1862, p. 2, July 12, 1862, p. 2, July 19, 1862, p. 1, July 26, 1862, p. 1, Aug. 2, 1862, p. 1.

16. Ibid., Aug. 9, 1862, p. 1.

17. Ibid., June 7, 1862, p. 3.

18. F. W. Howay, "The Negro Immigration into Vancouver Island in 1858," *British Columbia Historical Quarterly* III (April, 1959), 101–13; *Pacific Appeal,* June 14, 1862, p. 2, April 18, 1863, p. 2, June 11, 1863, p. 2, Sept. 25, 1863, p. 3. On John Jamison Moore, see his *History of the A.M.E. Zion Church,* 2 vols. (York, Pa., 1884), pp. 367–73. See also *Pacific Appeal,* April 2, 1863, p. 3.

19. *Pacific Appeal,* Jan. 24, 1863, p. 2, Feb. 6, 1864, p. 2.

20. *Elevator,* April 2, 1869, p. 2; also, Aug. 30, 1867, pp. 2–3.

21. *Pacific Appeal,* Sept. 6, 1862, p. 2; *Elevator,* Oct. 30, 1868, p. 2, Sept. 25, 1868, p. 2.

22. *Elevator,* Sept. 22, 1865, p. 3.

23. *Pacific Appeal,* April 18, 1863, p. 2; *Elevator,* Aug. 4, 1865, p. 3, June 30, 1865, p. 3.

24. *Elevator,* April 24, 1868, p. 2, Dec. 25, 1868, p. 2.

25. *Elevator,* Oct. 24, 1874, p. 2; also, see New York *Weekly Anglo-African,* Nov. 5, 1859, p. 1; *Elevator,* March 13, 1868, p. 2; *Frederick Douglass' Paper,* April 13, 1855, p. 3.

26. Philadelphia *Christian Recorder,* Dec. 24, 1864, p. 206; *Frederick Douglass' Paper,* May 27, 1852, p. 1; *Pacific Appeal,* Jan. 30, 1864, p. 3; *Elevator,* Nov. 29, 1873, p. 3, Jan. 17, 1874, p. 2.

27. *Pacific Appeal,* June 14, 1862, p. 2; see also July 11, 1863, p. 2, Aug. 8, 1863, p. 3.

28. *Frederick Douglass' Paper,* May 27, 1852, p. 1; *Elevator,* Sept. 25, 1868, p. 2, April 24, 1868, p. 2, Sept. 25, 1868, p. 2. For discrimination in a mountain community, see *Elevator,* June 9, 1867, p. 2. On discrimination in San Francisco's hotels, see *Chronicle,* Sept. 28, 1897, p. 1; and San Francisco *Call,* Sept. 29, 1897, p. 4. Rudolph M. Lapp, "The Negro in Gold Rush California," *The Journal of Negro History* XIX (April 1964), 82 argues that the overland journey was especially grueling for Black travelers "because of their subordinate status." This

contention could be extended to include Afro-Americans who took other routes, as well.

29. United States Census Office, *Tenth Census, 1880: Population* (Washington, D.C., 1883), I: 538. Doris Marion Wright, "The Making of Cosmopolitan California: An Analysis of Immigration, 1848–1870," *California Historical Society Quarterly* XIX (Dec. 1940), 323–43 and XX (March 1941), 65–79. On the Chinese migration, see Gunther Barth, *Bitter Strength: A History of the Chinese in the United States, 1850–1870* (Cambridge, Mass., 1964), pp. 50–76. *Elevator,* Oct. 24, 1874, p. 2; Petition of Executive Committee of the Colored Citizens California State Union to General George Stoneman, Governor, Concerning the Appointment of William H. Blake to Notary Public, March 3, 1883, San Francisco, California State Archives, Sacramento, California; *Elevator,* June 19, 1868, p. 2, encourages the formation of an emigration association for Blacks. San Francisco *Vindicator,* Nov. 17, 1888, p. 2, mentions the end of a fraudulent migration scheme.

30. J. B. Sanderson to Catherine Sanderson, Feb. 27, 1857, Bancroft Library, University of California, Berkeley; Rudolph·M. Lapp, "Jeremiah B. Sanderson, Early California Negro Leader," *Journal of Negro History* LIII (Oct. 1968), 321–33; and William Wells Brown, *The Black Man, His Antecedents, His Genius, and His Achievements* (New York, 1969 ed.), pp. 91–92.

31. J. B. Sanderson to Catherine Sanderson, Feb. 27, 1857, Bancroft Library, University of California, Berkeley.

32. *Elevator,* Feb. 26, 1869, p. 2. Mifflin Gibbs landed nearly penniless after the Gold Rush. He explained he obtained accommodations, a job, and tools for his trade by dint of his perseverance and powers of persuasion: "Never disclose your poverty until the last gleam of hope has sunk beneath the horizon of your best effort, remembering that invincible determination holds the key to success." Gibbs, *Shadow and Light,* p. 42. In the 1920s a prospective southern migrant disregarded his wife's advice that he should purchase a round-trip ticket to California. Exhibiting the determination typical of westward-bound Blacks, he responded, "No, I'm going to sink or swim, live or die, but I am going to stay." Interview, E. A. Daly, Aug. 2, 1976.

33. *Elevator,* June 22, 1872, p. 1.

34. Ibid., May 8, 1868, p. 2.

35. Horace R. Cayton, "America's 10 Best Cities for Negroes," *Negro Digest* V (Oct. 1947), p. 4. Virginia Yans-McLaughlin, *Family and Community: Italian Immigrants in Buffalo, 1880–1930* (Ithaca, N.Y., 1977), ch. 3 discusses similar ways in which Italian kinship networks functioned, aiding migration and easing adjustment to the New World.

36. *Pacific Appeal,* July 18, 1863, p. 3. Having given copies to several whites, the correspondent reported: "They expressed great surprise at the amount of intelligence contained in its columns."

37. *Pacific Appeal,* Oct. 4, 1862, p. 1.

38. *Elevator,* Nov. 16, 1872, p. 3.

39. Ibid., Nov. 10, 1865, p. 3; San Francisco *Sentinel,* Sept. 10, 1890, p. 3, Sept. 20, 1890, p. 3.

40. *Call,* March 5, 1895, p. 7; for her life, see Alfreda M. Duster, ed., *Crusade for Justice: The Autobiography of Ida B. Wells* (Chicago, 1970); see the lectures advertised in *Pacific Appeal,* Feb. 6, 1864, p. 2; *Elevator,* Jan. 17, 1874, p. 2; *Sentinel,* Sept. 20, 1890, p. 3, for other topics; Adam Clayton Powell, *Against the Tide: An Autobiography by A. Clayton Powell, Sr.* (New York, 1938), p. 39; James Weldon Johnson, *Along This Way: The Autobiography of James Weldon Johnson* (New York, [1961]), pp. 207–8; *Chronicle,* Feb. 23, 1976, p. 6.

41. *Oakland Directory, 1872.* Original Schedule of the Ninth Census, 1870, California, San Francisco (hereafter cited as Manuscript Census, with the appropriate years); *Elevator,* March 22, 1873, p. 2; Studs Terkel, *Hard Times: An Oral History of the Great Depression*

(New York, [1970]), as quoted in Jervis Anderson, *A. Philip Randolph, a Biographical Portrait* (New York, [1973]), p. 160.

42. Cayton, "10 Best Cities."

43. *Pacific Appeal,* Oct. 31, 1863, p. 2; *Elevator,* Dec. 6, 1873, p. 3, May 18, 1872, p. 2, May 31, 1872, p. 3. Interview, Alfred Butler, July 29, 1976.

44. New York *Times,* Jan. 17, 1886, p. 10; *Chronicle,* Sept. 11, 1904, p. 20; San Francisco *Pacific Coast Appeal,* March 14, 1903, p. 4; *Chronicle,* Oct. 12, 1882, p. 3.

45. *Tenth Census, 1880: Population,* I: 416; *Twelfth Census, 1900: Population* (Washington, D.C., 1901), I: cxix; *Fifteenth Census, 1930: Population* (Washington, D.C., 1931), I: 18, II: 72. On the changes of the 1940s, see Charles S. Johnson, *The Negro War Worker in San Francisco, A Local Self-Survey* (San Francisco, 1944) and Edward Everett France, "Some Aspects of the Migration of the Negro to the San Francisco Bay Area Since 1940" (Ph.D. diss., University of California, Berkeley, 1962).

46. "Research suggests that selective processes were at work that brought a larger group of energetic and educated Negroes to California during the Gold Rush than might have been found in the Negro populations of the East and South." Lapp, "The Negro in Gold Rush California," p. 98. I believe these processes shaped the character of Black westerners throughout the nineteenth century. *Proceedings of the Second Annual Convention of the Colored Citizens of California, 1856* (San Francisco, 1856), p. 53. *Pacific Appeal,* Aug. 8, 1863, p. 2.

47. "The World in California," *Hutching's Illustrated California Magazine* I (July 1856–June 1857), 344.

48. Nat Love, *The Life and Adventures of Nat Love, Better Known in the Cattle Country as "Deadwood Dick" by Himself* (New York, 1968 ed.), p. 135. *Examiner,* Oct. 13, 1895, p. 17; "The World in California," p. 344.

49. *Elevator,* June 24, 1870, p. 1.

50. Charles Grier and Price M. Cobbs, *Black Rage* (New York, 1968); *Elevator,* Aug. 8, 1863, p. 3.

## *Chapter 6:* Neighbors

1. On northern residential patterns in the nineteenth century, see James Weldon Johnson, *Black Manhattan* (New York, 1968 ed.), pp. 58–59; and W. E. B. Du Bois, *The Philadelphia Negro* (New York, [1969 ed.]). On New York at the turn of the century, see Mary White Ovington, *Half A Man: The Status of the Negro in New York* (New York, 1911), pp. 18–26. On the midwest, see: Allan H. Spear, *Black Chicago: The Making of a Negro Ghetto, 1890–1920* (Chicago, 1967); David Vassar Taylor, "Pilgrim's Progress: Black St. Paul and the Making of an Urban Ghetto, 1870–1930" (Ph.D. diss., University of Minnesota, 1977); and David M. Katzman, *Before the Ghetto: Black Detroit in the Nineteenth Century* (Urbana, Ill., 1973). Kenneth L. Kusmer argues: "It seems doubtful that anything even remotely resembling a real black ghetto existed in American cities north or south, prior to the 1890s," *A Ghetto Takes Shape: Black Cleveland, 1870–1930* (Urbana, Ill., 1976), p. 12. See also Paul J. Lammermeir, "Cincinnati's Black Community: The Origins of a Ghetto, 1870–1880," in John H. Bracey, August Meier, and Elliot Rudwick, eds., *The Rise of the Ghetto* (Belmont, Calif., 1971). Historians of the south concur; for example, see: John W. Blassingame, *Black New Orleans: 1860–1880* (Chicago, 1973), p. 16; Ira Berlin, *Slaves Without Masters: The Free Negro in the Antebellum South* (New York, 1974), p. 253.

2. For the city's growth, see: John P. Young, *San Francisco: A History of the Pacific Coast Metropolis,* 2 vols. (San Francisco, [1912]); Roger W. Lotchin, *San Francisco, 1845–1856: From Hamlet to City* (New York, 1974), pp. 3–30; Bion J. Arnold, *Report on the Improvement and Development of the Transportation Facilities of San Francisco* (San

Francisco, 1913); Frank Soulé, John H. Gihon, and James Nisbet, *The Annals of San Francisco* (New York, 1855), map opposite p. 22; Margaret G. King, "The Growth of San Francisco, Illustrated by Shifts in the Density of Population" (M.A. thesis, University of California, Berkeley, 1928); and Martyn J. Bowden, "Dynamics of City Growth: An Historical Geography of the San Francisco Central District, 1850–1921" (Ph.D. diss., University of California, Berkeley, 1967).

3. Locations of Black residents were determined with the United States Census, beginning with the Eighth, in its published and manuscript versions. Henry G. Langley, comp., *The San Francisco Directory* (hereafter referred to, with the appropriate year, as *City Directory*) also gives addresses of Blacks and locations of institutions and businesses.

4. Richard H. Dillon, *Shanghaiing Days* (New York, [1961]); Benjamin Lloyd, *Lights and Shades of San Francisco* (San Francisco, 1876); William F. Rae, *Westward by Rail: The New Route to the East* (New York, 1871), p. 260; San Francisco *Chronicle,* March 17, 1889, p. 8, Feb. 7, 1904, p. 7; Herbert Asbury, *The Barbary Coast: An Informal History of the San Francisco Underworld* (New York, 1933), pp. 198–231; William M. Camp, *San Francisco, Port of Gold* (Garden City, N.Y., 1947), pp. 197–388; Young, *San Francisco,* II: 660–61; Andrew S. Hallidie, "Manufacturing in San Francisco," *The Overland Monthly* XI (June 1888), 637. Two useful views of the cityscape are: George H. Goddard, "Bird's Eye View of the City of San Francisco" (1868); and William R. Wheaton, "Index Map of the City of San Francisco" (1867); both are in the Bancroft Library, University of California, Berkeley.

5. [United States Census Bureau], Original Schedule of the Eighth Census, 1860, San Francisco, California (hereafter cited as Manuscript Census, with the appropriate year). *City Directory, 1860* gives the address of the Golden Gate Boarding House; San Francisco *Elevator,* June 30, 1865, p. 3; Delilah L. Beasley, *Negro Trail Blazers of California* (New York, [1969] ed.), p. 122; on Callender's boarders, Manuscript Census, 1880, and *Elevator,* March 17, 1877, p. 2; on Callender's career, San Francisco *Examiner,* June 16, 1889, p. 10; for problems of an old Black seaman, *Elevator,* Oct. 25, 1873, p. 2. San Francisco *Daily Alta California,* Nov. 29, 1889, p. 1.

6. San Francisco *Call,* Nov. 8, 1897, p. 32; Soulé, Gihon, and Nisbet, *Annals,* p. 472; Harold Langley, "The Negro in the Navy and the Merchant Marine," *Journal of Negro History* LII (Oct. 1967), 273–86; and Frederick Harrod, *Manning the New Navy* (Westport, Conn., 1978) discuss Blacks in the late nineteenth-century U.S. Navy. Asbury, *Barbary Coast,* pp. 104–5; for a romantic depiction of this environment in the 1920s, see the tale of the Jazz King in Oakland *Western Outlook,* Feb. 25, 1927, p. 7; Charles Keeler, *San Francisco and Thereabout* (San Francisco, 1902), pp. 14–15 gives a similar portrait.

7. Dillon, *Shanghaiing Days,* p. 180; *Daily Alta California,* Nov. 29, 1888, p. 1, Dec. 15, 1886, p. 1; Young, *San Francisco,* II: 623; Edwin S. Morby, trans. and ed., *San Francisco in the Seventies: The City As Viewed by a Mexican Political Exile,* by Guillermo Prieto (San Francisco, 1938), p. 75; Walton Bean, *California: An Interpretive History* (San Francisco, [1968]), pp. 287–88. Interview, Aurelious Alberga, July 27, 1976.

8. Bean, *California,* pp. 287–88; Arnold, *Report,* p. xvii.

9. Horace R. Cayton, *Long Old Road* (Seattle, [1967]), pp. 124–26. Aurelious P. Alberga, J. C. Rivers and John Taylor ran bootblack stands near the terminal building; San Francisco *Western Appeal,* April 1, 1927, p. 3; *City Directory, 1900; Western Appeal,* May 3, 1922, p. 1.

10. Interview, Royal Towns, Aug. 30, 1973.

11. *Call,* Nov. 8, 1897, p. 32; Soulé, Gihon, and Nisbet, *Annals,* p. 472; Asbury, *Barbary Coast,* pp. 104–5; Workers of the Writers' Program of the Works Project Administration in Northern California, *San Francisco: The Bay and its Cities* (New York, 1947), pp. 214–16.

12. San Francisco *Vindicator,* March 16, 1887, p. 1, June 11, 1887, p. 2; *Call,* July 10, 1900, p. 12, April 7, 1900, p. 7.

13. *Vindicator*, May 16, 1887, p. 1; Workers of the Writers' Program, *San Francisco*, pp. 106–7; Clifton Rather, *Here's How: An Autobiography* (Oakland, 1968–70), pp. 21–23; Asbury, *Barbary Coast*, pp. 105, 130, 235, 255; Sally Stanford, *The Lady of the House: The Autobiography of Sally Stanford* (New York, 1966), pp. 46–47, 66–69; *Western Appeal*, Jan. 13, 1928, p. 8, tells of the dispersal of resorts after the closing of vice districts. Elizabeth Anne Brown, "The Enforcement of Prohibition in San Francisco, California" (M.A. thesis, University of California, Berkeley, 1948), pp. 20, 22, 31–39; San Francisco *Spokesman*, Sept. 23, 1932, p. 1 tells of a Black social "club" in the Western Addition.

14. Manuscript Census, 1880.

15. Asbury, *Barbary Coast*, p. 130; *Alta California*, Jan. 30, 1873, p. 1; San Francisco *Evening Bulletin*, Jan. 30, 1873, p. 3; *Chronicle*, Jan. 30, 1873, p. 3, Oct. 22, 1875, p. 3. (*Daily Alta California*, Jan. 31, 1873, p. 1 gives details of Tuers's trials.) Contrast this case with that reported in the *Daily Alta California*, Sept. 6, 1888, p. 2.

16. *Elevator*, Dec. 29, 1865, p. 2, Jan. 7, 1874, p. 3, Oct. 24, 1874, p. 2.

17. San Francisco *Pacific Appeal*, March 5, 1864, p. 4, Jan. 7, 1871, p. 2; *City Directory, 1860*, p. 152; *Elevator*, Oct. 18, 1871, p. 2.

18. *Elevator*, June 11, 1898, p. 3, Oct. 18, 1890, p. 3, June 16, 1892, p. 3.

19. Ibid., June 11, 1898, p. 3; *City Directory, 1900* and *1970*; Marshall and Jean Stearns, *Jazz Dance: The Story of American Vernacular Dance* (New York, [1968]), p. 128; *Western Appeal*, Oct. 19, 1921; Oakland *Pacific Times*, July 19, 1912, p. 2; Samuel Dickson, *San Francisco Kaleidoscope* (Stanford, Calif., 1949), pp. 254–55; *Examiner*, Dec. 26, 1921, p. 1.

20. This world is depicted in: Ann Charters, *Nobody: The Story of "Bert" Williams* (London, [1970]); Rudi Blesh and Harriet Janis, *They All Played Ragtime* (New York, 1971 ed.); Alan Lomax, *Mister Jelly Roll: The Fortunes of Jelly Roll Morton, New Orleans Creole and "Inventor of Jazz"* (New York, [1950]); James Weldon Johnson, *Along This Way* (New York, [1961] ed.), and Johnson, *Black Manhattan*.

21. Quote is from Oscar Lewis, ed., *This Was San Francisco* (New York, 1962), pp. 174–75. Bowden, *Dynamics*, p. 57; Samuel Williams, "The City of the Golden Gate," *Scribners' Monthly* X (July 1875), 270; the Manuscript Censuses of 1880 and 1900 were helpful for analyzing locations of different citizens and groups because they give street addresses. Lloyd, *Lights and Shades*, p. 79, and the account of Chinatown, is valuable; on the Latin Quarter, see *Call*, March 6, 1895, p. 4.

22. Lotchin, *San Francisco*, pp. 100–135 is a good discussion of ethnicity in San Francisco.

23. Manuscript Census, 1880.

24. Ibid. Cloverdale *Reveille*, April 8, 1882, p. 2; Roberto Daughters brought this article to my attention.

25. *Spokesman*, Sept. 20, 1934, p. 1; James Abajian informed me of Jean Ng. Also ibid., Jan. 20, 1933, p. 1.

26. Interviews, Ethel Terrell, April 20, 1973, Claudia Cheltenham, April 17, 1973. Mrs. Cheltenham could give no reason for being presumed Spanish; her granddaughter, Jewel Cooper, pointed out that it would have been easy for her to assume a Spanish identity, as the aged informant spent several years in Panama as a young girl and knew Spanish.

27. Manuscript Census, 1880.

28. Sanborn Fire Insurance Maps, Department of Geography, California State University, Northridge, California.

29. *City Directory, 1865*, p. 599; *City Directory, 1872*, pp. 870, 875–76. *Elevator*, March 18, 1870, p. 2, Nov. 29, 1873, p. 2, Dec. 27, 1863, p. 2, May 2, 1885, p. 3, June 18, 1892, p. 3, June 11, 1898, p. 3; San Francisco *Pacific Coast Appeal*, May 3, 1902, p. 8. See King, "Growth of San Francisco"; Bowden, "Dynamics"; Arnold, *Report;* and Judd Lewis Kahn,

"Imperial San Francisco: History of a Vision" (Ph.D. diss., University of California, 1971) on the rebuilding of the metropolis. Charles S. Johnson, *The Negro War Worker in San Francisco; A Local Self-Survey* (San Francisco, 1944), p. 3.

30. Manuscript Census.

31. *Chronicle,* Feb. 7, 1904, p. 7.

32. Johnson, *Negro War Worker,* p. 3; *Spokesman,* July 6, 1933, p. 6; Maya Angelou, *I Know Why the Caged Bird Sings* (New York, 1971 ed.) describes the city in the 1940s (Patricia Myers Davidson informed me of this); *Chronicle,* Sept. 19, 1945, p. 13. The *City Directory, 1860* and *1870,* the Manuscript Censuses of 1880 and 1900, and Charles F. Tilghman, comp., *Colored Directory of the Leading Cities of Northern California, 1916–1917* (Oakland, 1916) all indicated widespread distribution of Afro-Americans in San Francisco and the East Bay.

33. Interview, Royal Towns, Aug. 30, 1973. Towns's father spoke Spanish and some Chinese.

34. Gunther Barth, "Metropolism and Urban Elites in the Far West," in Frederic Cople Jaher, ed., *The Age of Industrialism in America: Essays in Social Structure and Cultural Values* (New York, 1968), pp. 158–87; Gilbert Osofsky, "The Enduring Ghetto," *Journal of American History* LV (Sept. 1968), 243; Allan Spear, "The Origins of the Urban Ghetto, 1870–1915," in Nathan I. Huggins, et al., eds., *Key Issues in the Afro-American Experience,* 2 vols. (New York, [1971]), II: 153–56.

35. Young, *San Francisco,* II: 618 (on the growth of Oakland) and II: 939 (on its manufacturing increase). Arnold, *Report,* pp. xvii, 13; Young, *San Francisco,* II: 575–76; Edgar M. Kahn, *Cable Car Days in San Francisco* (Stanford, Calif., [1944]), pp. 27–70.

36. Young, *San Francisco,* II: 862, 864; Arnold, *Report,* table 3 and plate 5 for data on the shift of the San Francisco population; also King, "Growth of San Francisco," pp. 119–23, 142–45.

37. United States Census Office, *Fifteenth Census, 1930: Population* (Washington, D.C., 1931), I: 165, II: 72 for the number of Blacks in Oakland in 1930 and in previous decades; *Fourteenth Census, 1920: Population,* III: 127 indicates the move of Black folk to the Western Addition and shows that few lived in the city center.

38. Young, *San Francisco,* II: 618; *Tenth Census, 1880: Population* (Washington, D.C., 1883), I: 416; *Fifteenth Census,* II: 72; *Sixteenth Census, 1940: Population* (Washington, D.C., 1943), part 1, pp. 599, 637, 657. Arnold, *Report,* plate 5.

39. In *Chronicle,* June 6, 1894, p. 5, a Black minister mentions union discrimination. Beasley, *Negro Trail Blazers,* p. 159.

40. *Chronicle,* June 16, 1947, p. 10.

41. *Daily Alta California,* Oct. 21, 1889, p. 8; *Spokesman,* March 19, 1932, p. 3; Oakland *Sunshine,* Dec. 21, 1907, p. 2; interview, Claudia Cheltenham, April 17, 1973.

42. *Fifteenth Census,* VI: 61; higher rents were charged in San Francisco after 1906; see Young, *San Francisco,* II: 864; *Chronicle,* Feb. 7, 1904, p. 3; on Black Oaklanders, see "A Successful Business Venture," *The Colored American Magazine* XIII (Dec. 1907), 269–72. See the pictures of Bay Area homes throughout Tilghman, *Directory.*

43. *Chronicle,* Nov. 17, 1947, p. 24, June 16, 1947, p. 10. See also ibid., Sept. 19, 1945, p. 13, in which a National Urban League spokesman compares San Francisco's Black district of the 1940s to Harlem a generation earlier: "San Francisco's Negro district is today right where the New York and Chicago districts were forty years ago." Thomas Lee Philpott, *The Slum and the Ghetto: Neighborhood Deterioration and Middle-Class Reform, Chicago, 1880–1930* (New York, 1978) is an excellent comparative analysis of the neighborhoods and housing of Blacks and white ethnic groups.

44. Interview, Ed Johnson, Aug. 14, 1973. See also Cayton, *Long Old Road,* pp. 1–40, for an account of his childhood in the Pacific Northwest; and Elmer R. Rusco, *"Good Time*

*Coming?": Black Nevadans in the Nineteenth Century* (Westport, Conn., [1975]). Los
Angeles's Black population was also distributed before the 1920s; see Lawrence B. de Graaf,
"The City of Black Angels: Emergence of the Los Angeles Ghetto, 1890–1930," *Pacific
Historical Review* XXXIX (Aug. 1970), 333.

45. John Daniels, *In Freedom's Birthplace: A Study of the Boston Negroes* (Boston,
1914), pp. 150, 459–60. Sam B. Warner, Jr., *Streetcar Suburbs: The Process of Growth in
Boston, 1870–1900* (New York, 1971).

## Chapter 7: Leaders

1. Eugene Berwanger, *The Frontier Against Slavery: Western Anti-Negro Prejudice and
the Slavery Extension Controversy* (Urbana, Ill., 1967), p. 60; Leonard Pitt, *The Decline of
the Californios: A Social History of the Spanish-Speaking Californians, 1846–1890*
(Berkeley, 1966); Clyde Duniway, "Slavery in California After 1848," *Annual Report of the
American Historical Association for the Year 1905,* I (Washington, D.C., 1906), 241–48;
James Fisher, "The Struggle for Negro Testimony in California, 1851–1863," *Southern
California Quarterly* LI (Dec. 1969), 313–24; Rudolph M. Lapp, *Blacks in Gold Rush
California* (New Haven, Conn., 1977), pp. 126–58, 210–38; Philip M. Montesano, "The San
Francisco Black Community, 1849–1890: The Quest for 'Equality Before the Law'" (Ph.D.
diss., University of California, Santa Barbara, 1974); Gerald Stanley, "Racism and the Early
Republican Party: The 1856 Presidential Election in California," *Pacific Historical Review*
XLIII (May 1974), 171–87; Charles Wollenburg, ed., *Ethnic Conflict in California History*
(Los Angeles, 1970); Wollenburg, *All Deliberate Speed: Segregation and Exclusion in
California Schools* (Berkeley, 1976).

William A. Leidesdorff, a West Indian of African descent, came to Yerba Buena in the
1840s and enjoyed the non-racist climate. He prospered and became a member of the city
council. Afro-Americans have claimed him as a member of their group, even though he did
not represent himself as a Black person in California. Frank Soulé, John H. Gihon, and James
Nisbet, *The Annals of San Francisco* (New York, 1855), p. 201; Delilah L. Beasley, *The Negro
Trail Blazers of California* (New York, [1969]), pp. 107–9.

2. Duniway, "Slavery in California"; Fisher, "Struggle for Negro Testimony"; Paul
Finkelman, "Slavery and Law in California" (unpublished essay in the author's possession);
on intermarriage, San Francisco *Spokesman,* April 30, 1932, p. 3.

3. J. D. Brotherwick, *Three Years in California* (London, 1867), p. 163; cited in
Berwanger, *Frontier Against Slavery,* p. 61; see Chapters 3 and 4.

4. San Francisco *Pacific Appeal,* Jan. 15, 1876, p. 1; San Francisco *Call,* April 7, 1897, p.
11, Sept. 29, 1897, p. 4; San Francisco *Chronicle,* Jan. 19, 1876, p. 2; Herbert Aptheker, *A
Documentary History of the Negro,* I (New York, 1967 ed.), 373–74; Oakland *Western
Outlook,* March 6, 1915, p. 2, March 13, 1915, p. 2.

5. *Call,* Sept. 29, 1897, p. 4, Sept. 28, 1897, p. 1.

6. *Call,* Sept. 28, 1897, p. 1, Sept. 29, 1897, p. 4; despite Jackson's claims, the San
Francisco *Vindicator,* Nov. 17, 1888, p. 2, mentioned an incident in which he experienced
discrimination; *Call,* Aug. 1, 1897, p. 16.

7. Alexander Saxton, *The Indispensable Enemy: Labor and the Anti-Chinese Movement
in California* (Berkeley, 1971); Gunther Barth, *Bitter Strength, A History of the Chinese in the
United States, 1850–1870* (Cambridge, Mass., 1964); and Roger Daniels, *The Politics of
Prejudice: The Anti-Japanese Movement in California, and the Struggle for Japanese
Exclusion* (Berkeley, 1962).

8. James Weldon Johnson, *Along This Way: The Autobiography of James Weldon*

*Johnson* (New York, 1968 ed.), pp. 207–8; Gunnar Myrdal, *An American Dilemma: The Negro Problem and Modern Democracy* (New York, [1944]), p. 186, used Johnson's views to publicize the favorable racial climate of California.

9. Incidents on streetcars are reported in the San Francisco *Daily Alta California*, Oct. 18, 1866, p. 1, involving Mary Ellen "Mammy" Pleasant; in the *Pacific Appeal*, Nov. 21, 1863, p. 2; and in the San Francisco *Elevator*, Feb. 18, 1870, p. 2. Beasley, *Negro Trail Blazers*, p. 65; *Elevator*, May 14, 1869, p. 2; *Western Outlook*, March 6, 1915, p. 2; and San Francisco *Sun*, June 11, 1948, p. 4, refer to other kinds of discrimination.

10. For discussions of Black institutions in two other cities, see Daniel Perlman, "Organizations of the Free Negro in New York City, 1800–1860," *The Journal of Negro History* LVI (July 1971), 181–97, and John Blassingame, *Black New Orleans: 1860–1880* (Chicago, 1973).

11. *Pacific Appeal*, Sept. 20, 1862, p. 2.

12. Ibid., June 7, 1862, p. 2; August Meier, *Negro Thought in America, 1880–1915: Racial Ideologies in the Age of Booker T. Washington* (Ann Arbor, Mich., 1963) traces developments in Black social thought following Reconstruction.

13. *Pacific Appeal*, June 7, 1862, p. 2.

14. *Elevator*, June 10, 1870, p. 2. Until modern times, California law permitted separate but equal educational facilities; Wollenburg, *All Deliberate Speed*, pp. 26–27, 179; much of the scholarly literature focuses on nineteenth-century antislavery and civil rights struggles; see Chapter 7, note 1.

15. *Pacific Appeal*, June 7, 1862, p. 2.

16. Ibid. On the founding of the *Mirror*, see *Proceedings of the Second Annual Convention of the Colored Citizens of the State of California*, December 10, 1856 (San Francisco, 1855).

17. *Pacific Appeal*, Aug. 29, 1863, p. 2, June 6, 1863, p. 3, June 20, 1863, p. 3, May 23, 1863, p. 3.

18. *Proceedings of the First State Convention of the Colored Citizens of the State of California* (San Francisco, 1855); to view the conventions in historical perspective, see Howard Holman Bell, ed., *Minutes of the Proceedings of the National Negro Conventions, 1830–1864* (New York, 1969 ed.), and *A Survey of the Negro Convention Movement, 1830–1861* (New York, 1969 ed.); and Lapp, *Blacks in Gold Rush California*, pp. 186–209; *Pacific Appeal*, Aug. 1, 1863, pp. 2–3; *Elevator*, Sept. 11, 1868, p. 2, Oct. 16, 1868, p. 2, and, on Yates, Nov. 27, 1868, p. 3.

19. *Elevator*, Sept. 11, 1868, p. 2, Oct. 16, 1868, p. 2.

20. *Elevator*, Sept. 11, 1868, p. 2.

21. *Elevator*, Nov. 3, 1865, p. 2, April 7, 1865, p. 1, Dec. 1, 1865, p. 2, June 25, 1867, p. 3; *Pacific Appeal*, Aug. 31, 1867, p. 3; African Methodist Episcopal Church, *A.M.E. Church Proceedings* (San Francisco, 1863), p. 24.

22. *Pacific Appeal*, May 30, 1863, pp. 2–3, Sept. 2, 1863, p. 1. Sept. 19, 1863, p. 3; Henry G. Langley, comp., *The San Francisco Directory, 1865* (hereafter referred to as *City Directory*, with the appropriate year); *Elevator*, Nov. 3, 1865, p. 2, March 30, 1866, p. 2, June 17, 1870, p. 2. James R. Starkey, from Newbern, North Carolina, obtained the funds for his freedom by writing northern abolitionists; Carter G. Woodson, *The Mind of the Negro as Reflected in Letters Written During the Crisis* (Washington, D.C., 1926), pp. 76–82, reprints Starkey's letters. San Francisco *Pacific Coast Appeal*, April 23, 1904, p. 2; *Chronicle*, Feb. 7, 1904, p. 7 discusses Theophilus B. Morton and J. C. Rivers, though not by name; also, see the Oakland *Independent*, Dec. 14, 1929, p. 1.

23. *Elevator*, Nov. 3, 1865, p. 2, June 25, 1863, p. 3; *Pacific Appeal*, June 20, 1863, p. 3; Martin Robison Delany, *The Condition, Elevation, Emigration, and Destiny of the Colored People of the United States* (New York, 1968 ed.), p. 104.

24. New York *Weekly Anglo-African,* Nov. 26, 1859, p. 1; *Pacific Appeal,* April 12, 1862, p. 2; *Elevator,* June 25, 1869, p. 3, June 20, 1874, p. 3, June 27, 1874, p. 2; Beasley, *Negro Trail Blazers,* pp. 134, 146, 190–91, 194–97; *Chronicle,* Jan. 18, 1922, p. 14.

25. The classic critique of Black middle-class life is, of course, E. Franklin Frazier, *Black Bourgeoisie* (Glencoe, Ill., 1957). James M. McPherson, *The Abolitionist Legacy: From Reconstruction to the NAACP* (Princeton, [1975]) discusses the postbellum activities of these humanitarians, including some Black reformers, but does not mention San Franciscans.

26. Richard Robert Wright, *The Bishops of the African Methodist Episcopal Church* (Nashville, Tenn., 1963), pp. 350–52; *Pacific Appeal,* June 6, 1863, p. 3.

27. Wright, *Bishops,* pp. 350–52, 551, quoted in Larry George Murphy, "Equality Before the Law: The Struggle of Nineteenth-Century Black Californians for Social and Political Justice" (Ph.D. diss., Graduate Theological Union, 1973), p. 67; *Christian Recorder* (Philadelphia), Jan. 21, 1864, p. 10, Sept. 24, 1864, p. 153; *Pacific Appeal,* June 6, 1863, p. 3. The *Weekly Anglo-African,* Jan. 14, 1860, p. 3, claimed Ward had "but few equals in the A.M.E. pulpit." See *Elevator,* Sept. 11, 1868, p. 2, for the steamboat passenger's letter.

28. *Weekly Anglo-African,* Jan. 14, 1860, p. 3; Wright, *Bishops,* pp. 350–52; *Pacific Appeal,* June 6, 1863, p. 3.

29. Sue Bailey Thurman, *Pioneers of Negro Origin in California* (San Francisco, 1949); David Henry Bradley, Sr., *A History of the A.M.E. Zion Church,* 2 vols. (Nashville, Tenn., [1956 and 1957]), I: 162–67, II: 38; on John Jamison Moore, see Moore's *History of the A.M.E. Zion Church* (York, Pa., 1884), pp. 367–73; Beasley, *Negro Trail Blazers,* p. 160; *City Directory, 1862,* p. 599 and *1865,* p. 552; *Christian Recorder,* Jan. 21, 1864, p. 10. A copy of the *Lunar Visitor* (San Francisco), I (Feb. 1862) is in the Bancroft Library, University of California, Berkeley.

30. Alexander Walters, *My Life and Work* (New York, [1917]), pp. 45–49. Walters claimed: "The three years I spent in San Francisco were the happiest and most devoted of all my life." He there met Mary E. Pleasants, who donated two hundred dollars for him to attend a church conference in New York City in 1884 (p. 46).

31. *Call,* April 27, 1889, p. 5; and New York *Age,* May 18, 1889, p. 41; see also *Weekly Anglo-African,* June 23, 1860, p. 2, and July 7, 1860, p. 1; Delany, *Condition,* pp. 102–4; Irving Garland Penn, *The Afro-American Press and Its Editors* (Springfield, Mass., 1891), p. 91–99; Beasley, *Negro Trail Blazers,* pp. 252–53; Aptheker, *Documentary History,* 1: 99, 109, 133, 163–64, 238, 235, 11: 624, 651; for an account of Bell's character, *Elevator,* July 3, 1868, p. 2; Dec. 21, 1872, p. 2, Dec. 29, 1872, p. 2 for a possible recounting of Bell's childhood. Benjamin Quarles, *Black Abolitionists* (New York, [1969]), pp. 20, 31, 95, 106–7, 123, 171; Howard Holman Bell, "The Negro Convention Movement, 1830–1860, New Perspectives," *Negro History Bulletin* XIV (Feb. 1951), 103–5; Bell, "National Negro Conventions of the Middle 1840s: Moral Suasion vs. Political Action," *The Journal of Negro History* XLII (Oct. 1957), 247–60; Philip M. Montesano, "Philip Alexander Bell, San Francisco Black Community Politician of the 1860s" (Typed manuscript, Special Collections, San Francisco Public Library); William Wells Brown, *The Rising Sun, or The Antecedents and Advancement of the Colored Race* (Boston, 1876), pp. 470–72; Sally Garey, "Some Aspects of Mid-Nineteenth Century Black Uplift: Philip A. Bell and the San Francisco *Elevator*" (Seminar paper, University of California, Berkeley, 1967) introduced me to the journalist and his newspapers.

32. Aptheker, *Documentary History,* I: 109, 133, 163, 164, 238; *Age,* May 11, 1889, p. 4, May 18, 1889, p. 1; *Call,* April 27, 1889, p. 5; *Elevator,* July 14, 1865, p. 2, Dec. 21, 1872, p. 2, Dec. 29, 1872, p. 2; Quarles, *Black Abolitionists,* p. 20; Bell, "Negro Conventions," p. 258; Delany, *Condition,* pp. 102–3.

33. Bell, "Negro Conventions," pp. 257–60; *Age,* May 11, 1889, p. 4, May 18, 1889, p. 1; see Martin R. Delany's depiction of Bell in *Blake, or The Huts of America* (Boston, [1970]), pp. 157, 188, 318–19.

34. *Weekly Anglo-African,* June 23, 1860, p. 2, July 7, 1860, p. 1; on the famous case of the California slave, Rudolph M. Lapp, *Archy Lee, A California Fugitive Slave* (San Francisco, 1969); *Elevator,* May 6, 1879, p. 3; *Alta California,* Dec. 4, 1879, p. 1, cited in Montesano, "Philip Alexander Bell," p. 17.

35. George P. Rowell and Co., *American Newspaper Directory* (New York, 1869) gives circulations of 800 each for the *Pacific Appeal* and the *Elevator.* The San Francisco Executive Committee claimed it cost $150 per month to support a "first-class weekly paper" like the *Mirror of the Times; Elevator,* May 26, 1865, p. 3; *Pacific Appeal,* March 6, 1876, on the hardships Bell endured in his old age; *Call,* April 27, 1889, p. 5.

36. Frederick Douglass, *Life and Times of Frederick Douglass* (Hartford, Conn., 1881); *The Colored American, Pacific Appeal,* and *Elevator* are available for the interested reader. William M. Trotter, editor of the Boston *Guardian* and opponent of Booker T. Washington, also suffered a tragic end; see Stephen R. Fox, *The Guardian of Boston: William Monroe Trotter* (New York, 1971).

37. Francis N. Lortie, Jr., "San Francisco's Black Community, 1870–1890: Dilemma in the Struggle for Equality" (M.A. thesis, San Francisco State College, 1970), pp. 32–39; *Elevator,* Sept. 8, 1888, p. 2; Beasley, *Negro Trail Blazers,* pp. 253–56, 260–61; *Pacific Coast Appeal,* Dec. 5, 1903, p. 2.

38. Beasley, *Negro Trail Blazers,* p. 253; San Francisco *Examiner,* June 16, 1889, p. 10; William J. Simmons, *Men of Mark* (Chicago, 1970 ed.), pp. 711–12; Emma Lou Thornbrough, "American Negro Newspapers, 1880–1914," *Business History Review* XL (Winter 1966), 467–90 analyzes the successes and failures of Black journals. Only a few issues of the *Vindicator* and the *Sentinel* remain.

39. Quoted in Robert C. Francis, "A History of Negro Business in the San Francisco Bay Region" (M.A. thesis, University of California, Berkeley, 1928), pp. 35–36. Interview, E. A. Daly, Aug. 2, 1976; Oakland *California Voice,* March 4, 1927, p. 2.

40. San Francisco *Western Appeal,* Aug. 20, 1926, p. 4; *Independent,* Dec. 14, 1929, p. 11; Oakland *Tribune,* Oct. 14, 1934.

41. *Pacific Appeal,* June 7, 1862, p. 2, April 5, 1862, p. 2; *Elevator,* Aug. 18, 1865, p. 2, Nov. 10, 1865, p. 3, Nov. 15, 1873, pp. 2–3; *Chronicle,* Sept. 1, 1881, p. 3, Oct. 12, 1882, p. 3; *Call,* Oct. 11, 1882, p. 3.

42. *Pacific Appeal,* March 7, 1863, p. 4, Sept. 20, 1862, p. 4; *Daily Alta California,* Sept. 17, 1889, p. 4; *Chronicle,* Oct. 29, 1889, pp. 7–8; Articles of Incorporation of the Afro-American State League of California, Office of the Secretary of State, California State Archives; T. B. Morton, *Vindication of Honorable M. M. Estee. Address delivered by T. B. Morton, president of the Afro-American League of San Francisco at its regular Monthly meeting, July 2, 1894* (San Francisco, 1894); *Chronicle,* Jan. 9, 1903, p. 9, Aug. 7, 1903, p. 7, Jan. 12, 1903, p. 10, Sept. 17, 1904, p. 5; *Western Outlook,* Dec. 10, 1927, p. 1, June 11, 1927, p. 1. See also Emma Lou Thornbrough, "The National Afro-American League, 1887–1908," *The Journal of Southern History* XVII (Nov. 1961), 494–512.

43. Articles of Incorporation of the Afro-American State League of California, Office of the Secretary of State, California State Archives.

44. *Pacific Appeal,* June 21, 1862, p. 3; *Elevator,* Nov. 10, 1865, p. 3, Nov. 17, 1865, p. 3; April 22, 1870, p. 3; *Call,* July 3, 1898, p. 71.

45. W. E. B. Du Bois, *The Negro Church* (Atlanta, Ga., 1903); E. Franklin Frazier, *The Negro Family in the United States* (Chicago, 1966 rev. and abridged ed.); Melvin D. Williams, *Community in a Black Pentecostal Church: An Anthropological Study* (Pittsburgh, 1974) is an excellent analysis of the role of the church in the life of poor and working-class Black urbanites.

46. *Pacific Appeal,* May 5, 1862, p. 1, June 6, 1863, p. 3; *Frederick Douglass' Paper*

NOTES203

(Rochester, N.Y.), Sept. 22, 1854, p. 4; *City Directory, 1862*, p. 552; *1865*, p. 599; *Christian Recorder*, Aug. 29, 1863, p. 137; *Weekly Anglo-African*, Nov. 19, 1859, p. 1.

47. *Christian Recorder*, Sept. 24, 1864, p. 153, Jan. 21, 1864, p. 10; *Pacific Appeal*, Nov. 7, 1863, p. 3, March 5, 1864, p. 3; *Elevator*, April 7, 1865, p. 2; *City Directory, 1865*, p. 599.

48. *City Directory, 1872*, pp. 875–76; *Elevator*, April 18, 1874, p. 2.

49. *Christian Recorder*, Sept. 24, 1864, p. 153; *City Directory, 1872*, p. 876; *Elevator*, Sept. 17, 1869, p. 2. Bishop John Jamison Moore described the San Francisco A.M.E. Zion Church in 1884 as "worth fifty thousand dollars, the colored people in this country having none which excell it." Moore, *History*, p. 370.

50. *City Directory, 1865*, p. 599; *Elevator*, March 18, 1869, p. 2, April 25, 1874, p. 2.

51. A.M.E. Church, *A.M.E. Church Proceedings, 1904*, tables following p. 34; for the Oakland churches of the 1930s, see *Spokesman*, Feb. 16, 1933, p. 4. Third Baptist Church, *Through His Power*, at the California Historical Society.

52. *Pacific Appeal*, May 24, 1862, p. 2, June 7, 1862, p. 2, April 5, 1862, p. 2; Beasley, *Negro Trail Blazers*. Articles and histories of special interest for Negroes were also published, as well as articles on Mohammed the prophet, the customs of Abyssinians, the underground railroad in New York, and the history of the Negro race; *Elevator*, Jan. 18, 1873, p. 2, March 2, 1866, p. 1, March 9, 1866, p. 2, March 12, 1869, p. 1; *Pacific Appeal*, Nov. 18, 25, 1871, p. 1.

53. *Daily Alta California*, Nov. 29, 1889, p. 8; *Elevator*, Jan. 5, 1866, p. 2. Edwin S. Redkey, *Black Exodus: Black Nationalist and Back to Africa Movements, 1890–1910* (New Haven, Conn., 1969) discusses Negroes and Africa at the turn of the century.

54. *Elevator*, July 7, 1865, p. 2, May 14, 1869, p. 2; *Pacific Appeal*, July 6, 1872, p. 2; *Pacific Coast Appeal*, May 3, 1902, pp. 4–5; *Call*, June 6, 1894, p. 3; *Elevator*, Jan. 8, 1869, p. 3, July 3, 1886, p. 2; *Pacific Appeal*, Dec. 12, 1863, p. 4, Aug. 15, 1863, p. 1, Feb. 27, 1864, p. 2; *Western Outlook*, Jan. 8, 1927, p. 2; *Call*, Sept. 15, 1896, p. 4; see the use of the expression "of African descent" in *Elevator*, Nov. 29, 1873, p. 2; and another use of "African" for American Blacks in *Pacific Appeal*, Sept. 6, 1862. Of course the word is also used in the name of the African Methodist Episcopal Churches; *California Voice*, Dec. 18, 1925, p. 2.

55. *Vindicator*, July 30, 1887, p. 1; *Daily Alta California*, Sept. 17, 1889, p. 4.

56. John A. Barber was elected Most Worshipful Grand Master of the Grand Lodge of F. and A.A.Y. Masons for the State of California, *Elevator*, July 7, 1865, p. 3; and *Examiner*, June 16, 1889, p. 10; *Pacific Appeal*, Nov. 5, 1870, p. 2.

57. *Pacific Appeal*, Sept. 19, 1863, p. 4, Dec. 26, 1863, p. 4; *Christian Recorder*, Sept. 24, 1864, p. 153, Oct. 22, 1864; *Age*, Dec. 14, 1890, p. 4.

58. *Elevator*, March 25, 1870, p. 2; Stockton *Evening Mail*, May 9, 1892, p. 5; I would like to thank Professor Howard Dodson for bringing the Stockton article to my attention.

59. *Chronicle*, Feb. 7, 1904, p. 7. Clipping in Afro-American file of George C. Pardee Papers, Bancroft Library, University of California, Berkeley.

60. *Elevator*, Nov. 24, 1865, p. 2.

### Chapter 8: Cosmopolitans

1. John Blassingame, *Black New Orleans, 1860–1880* (Chicago, [1973]), pp. 174–75; Barbara Ann Richardson, "A History of Blacks in Jacksonville, Florida, 1860–1895: A Socio-Economic and Political Study" (Ph.D. diss., Carnegie-Mellon University, 1975), p. 99; George M. Fredrickson, *The Black Image in the White Mind: The Debate on Afro-American Character and Destiny, 1817–1914* (New York, 1971), ch. 8–10; and Thomas F. Gossett, *Race: The History of an Idea in America* (Dallas, 1963), ch. 4, 7, 8, 11, 14, treat race theories at the turn of the last century. The classic examples of Negrophobic literature are Thomas Dixon, *The Leopard's Spots: A Romance of the White Man's Burden* (New York, 1902), and *The*

*Clansman: An Historical Romance of the Ku Klux Klan* (New York, 1905). D. W. Griffith based his film *The Birth of a Nation* on *The Clansman*.

2. Frank Soulé, John H. Gihon, and James Nisbet, *The Annals of San Francisco* (New York, 1855), pp. 257–58; Amelia Neville, *The Fantastic City: Memoirs of the Social and Romantic Life of Old San Francisco* (Boston, 1932), pp. 179–80; Evelyn Wells, *Champagne Days of San Francisco* (New York, 1947), pp. 117, 173–74.

3. Julia Cooley Altrocchi, *The Spectacular San Franciscans* (New York, 1949), p. 69; Edwin S. Morby, trans. and ed., *San Francisco in the Seventies: The City As Viewed By A Mexican Political Exile*, by Guillermo Prieto (San Francisco, 1938), sketch opposite p. 70; San Francisco *Call*, Jan. 16, 1887, p. 1; Wells, *Champagne Days*, p. 112; also, San Francisco *Examiner*, Nov. 8, 1896, p. 29, for mention of a Negro bard in the article "Round the World Via Cable Car," which gave a romantic view of the many representatives of the world in San Francisco.

4. *Call*, March 13, 1895, p. 5; see also Morby, *San Francisco*, p. 112.

5. *Call*, May 7, 1889, p. 17, Dec. 29, 1901, p. 2; Wells, *Champagne Days*, pp. 173–74; *The Overland Monthly* XV (Sept. 1875), p. 299. San Francisco *Chronicle*, Nov. 2, 1904, p. 13; San Francisco *Spokesman*, March 26, 1932, p. 1.

6. *Chronicle*, June 6, 1894, p. 5; *Call*, June 6, 1894, p. 3.

7. Clipping in John Daggett Scrapbook, I: 100 in California State Archives, Sacramento, California. The reference to high life is from Robert Austin Warner, *New Haven Negroes: A Social History* (New Haven, Conn., 1940), p. 218; see also ibid, pp. 255–56; Hinton Rowan Helper, *Land of Gold: Reality versus Fiction* (Baltimore, 1855), p. 275; Soulé, Gihon, and Nisbet, *Annals*, p. 472; for unflattering descriptions, *Call*, Nov. 8, 1897, p. 32.

8. Robert Toll, *Blacking Up: The Minstrel Show in Nineteenth-Century America* (New York, 1974); and Carl Wittke, *Tambo and Bones: A History of the American Minstrel Stage* (Durham, N.C., 1930), are good introductions to minstrelsy. Nathan I. Huggins, *Harlem Renaissance* (New York, 1971), ch. 6, provides an excellent understanding of minstrelsy's functions and offers a superb discussion of the psychological undercurrents in this and other popular forms of entertainment; San Francisco *Pacific Appeal*, May 24, 1862, p. 2; New York *Weekly Anglo-African*, Nov. 5, 1859, p. 1.

9. *Call*, Nov. 4, 1908, p. 7; Oakland *Western American*, June 8, 1929, p. 1, June 22, 1921, p. 4.

10. *Chronicle*, Aug. 5, 1914, p. 7.

11. San Francisco *Pacific Coast Appeal*, Nov. 26, 1904, p. 2; Oakland *Western Outlook*, Jan. 23, 1915, p. 1.

12. John P. Young, *San Francisco: A History of the Pacific Coast Metropolis*, 2 vols. (San Francisco, 1912), II: 595, quoted from James Bryce, *American Commonwealth*. Typical social events of the Civil War years included an Old Folks Supper in which a string and brass band played "favorite operatic airs, fashionable waltzes, polkas, [and] marches," and dances featuring polkas, mazourkas, and schottisches—derived from European sources; occasionally the suppers were attended by Black women in eighteenth-century costumes and men in "citizen's dress" of the revolutionary era; San Francisco *Elevator*, April 2, 1869, p. 2, June 1, 1872, p. 3; *Pacific Appeal*, Oct. 17, 1873, p. 4, Oct. 25, 1863, p. 2; *Elevator*, June 1, 1872, p. 3.

13. Altrocchi, *Spectacular San Franciscans*, pp. 179–80; Foster Rhea Dulles, *A History of Recreation: America Learns to Play* (New York, 1965 ed.), pp. 182, 193–94; *Pacific Appeal*, Sept. 30, 1871, p. 3, Sept. 2, 1871, p. 3.

14. *Pacific Appeal*, Sept. 30, 1871, p. 3.

15. Ibid., August 26, 1871, p. 3.

16. *Elevator*, Oct. 16, 1868, pp. 2–3; Delilah L. Beasley, *The Negro Trail Blazers of California* (New York, [1969]) gives the ancestry of some Black Californians; *Pacific Appeal*, Aug. 1, 1863, pp. 2–3, June 6, 1863, p. 3.

17. *Elevator*, Dec. 21, 1872, as quoted in Sally Garey, "Some Aspects of Mid-Nineteenth Century Black Uplift: Philip A. Bell and the San Francisco *Elevator*" (seminar paper, University of California, Berkeley, 1967), p. 4; *Pacific Appeal*, April 19, 1862, p. 2.

18. *Call*, Aug. 2, 1864, p. 2, as quoted in Edgar M. Branch, ed., *Clemens of the Call: Mark Twain in San Francisco* (Berkeley, [1969]), pp. 56–57; *Elevator*, May 2, 1874, p. 2.

19. Fannie Barrier Williams, "Perils of the White Negro," *The Colored American Magazine* XIII (Dec. 1907), pp. 21–23. Interviews, Dr. Earl Lenear, Jan. 11, 1973, Royal Towns, Aug. 30, 1973.

20. "The World in California," *Hutchings' Illustrated California Magazine* I (July 1856–June 1857), 387; quoted in *Elevator*, Oct. 27, 1865, p. 2; Charles Keeler, *San Francisco and Thereabout* (San Francisco, 1902), pp. 14–15.

21. *Pacific Appeal*, April 5, 1862, p. 2; Beasley, *Negro Trail Blazers*, p. 54.

22. Ann Charters, *Nobody: The Story of "Bert" Williams* (London, 1970), pp. 18, 25. For other instances of residents switching their racial identity, see San Francisco *Daily Alta California*, Nov. 5, 1888, p. 4, and *Western American*, Dec. 2, 1927, p. 1, in which policemen don blackface; Oakland *Sunshine*, Dec. 7, 1918, p. 2, in which an "Indian" cohabiting with a white woman in Oakland became a Negro after her death—presumably it was safer for an Indian to live with a white woman than for a Black; in *Spokesman*, May 17, 1934, p. 1, an apparently white waiter, accused of discriminating against a Black patron, claimed he himself was of North African descent and consequently could not possibly be prejudiced against Blacks.

23. W. E. B. Du Bois, *Souls of Black Folk*, in John Hope Franklin, ed., *Three Negro Classics* (New York, 1968 ed.), pp. 214–15. Du Bois contrasted older urban dwellers with newcomers from the south, helping me to understand how exclusive social functions perpetuated differences among Blacks; see W. E. B. Du Bois, *The Black North in 1901: A Social Study* (New York, 1969 ed.), p. 39.

24. *Frederick Douglass' Paper* (Rochester, N.Y.), April 1, 1852, p. 3.

25. *Weekly Anglo-African*, March 3, 1860, p. 3.

26. *Pacific Appeal*, Sept. 28, 1867, p. 2.

27. *Pacific Appeal*, Jan. 20, 1876, p. 1, May 6, 1876, p. 2.

28. *Elevator*, Oct. 31, 1874, p. 3, Dec. 29, 1871, pp. 2–3.

29. *Western Outlook*, Jan. 9, 1915, p. 2; *Western Appeal*, Nov. 16, 1921, p. 1, March 8, 1922, p. 2; Oakland *California Voice*, March 4, 1927, p. 1; see the wedding of David Ruggles, *Western Outlook*, Jan. 2, 1915, p. 3, which seems to have had all the trappings of a major society affair.

30. *California Voice*, March 4, 1927, p. 1; San Francisco *Western Appeal*, Feb. 25, 1927, p. 5.

31. San Francisco *Sentinel*, Dec. 6, 1890, p. 2.

32. *Pacific Appeal*, May 9, 1863, p. 2.

33. John Alexander Somerville, *Man of Color: An Autobiography* (Los Angeles, 1949), pp. 49–55.

34. *Call*, July 5, 1898, p. 6.

35. *Elevator*, Dec. 27, 1867, p. 3, Jan. 3, 1868, pp. 2–3.

36. *Pacific Coast Appeal*, May 3, 1902, p. 4; Beasley, *Negro Trail Blazers*, p. 280; Henry G. Langley, comp., *The San Francisco Directory, 1869*, p. 450 (hereafter cited as *City Directory*, with the appropriate year); *City Directory, 1872*, p. 913; *Elevator*, June 25, 1869, p. 3, Jan. 1, 1869, p. 2, June 25, 1869, p. 3.

37. *Elevator*, Jan. 5, 1866, p. 3. During or after the World War I years Oscar Hudson, the Black lawyer and consul for Liberia, organized a drum corps of approximately two dozen Black youths. A photograph of Mr. and Mrs. Hudson and the youngsters can be found in the East Bay Negro Historical Society, Oakland.

38. *Elevator,* May 16, 1874, p. 3, May 30, 1874, p. 3.

39. Ibid., May 4, 1872, p. 3.

40. *Western Appeal,* Dec. 21, 1921, p. 4; on Black soldiers, see: William H. Leckie, *The Buffalo Soldiers, A Narrative of the Negro Cavalry in the West* (Norman, Okla., 1967); Arlen L. Fowler, *The Black Infantry in the West, 1869–1901* (Westport, Conn., 1971); Joseph T. Wilson, *The Black Phalanx: A History of the Negro Soldiers of the United States in the Wars of 1775–1812 and 1861–65* (New York, 1868 ed.); Theophilus G. Steward, *The Colored Regulars in the United States Army* (Philadelphia, 1904); Willard B. Gatewood, Jr., *"Smoked Yankees" and the Struggle for Empire: Letters From Negro Soldiers* (Chicago, [1971]); and William Wells Brown, *The Negro in the American Rebellion* (Boston, 1867).

41. *Call,* April 8, 1899, p. 7. See *Chronicle,* Nov. 24, 1903, p. 13, Dec. 2, 1903, p. 8, for brief accounts of fights between Black soldiers and whites.

42. *Call,* April 8, 1899, p. 7.

43. *Call,* June 23, 1899, p. 7, June 24, 1899, p. 12.

44. William Muraskin, *Middle-Class Blacks in a White Society: Prince Hall Freemasonry in America* (Berkeley, 1975).

45. See the portraits in: Beasley, *Negro Trail Blazers;* the Black newspapers (after 1900); the Bancroft Library, University of California, Berkeley; the California Historical Society Library; and the East Bay Negro Historical Society. A number of families, such as those of Walter L. Gibson and Royal E. Towns, also have quite a few nineteenth-century photographs.

46. *Elevator,* Aug. 9, 1873, p. 2; see Aug. 30, 1873, p. 2 on Edmonia Lewis; Oakland *Independent,* Dec. 14, 1929, p.4; *California Voice,* March 4, 1927, p. 1; *Pacific Appeal,* March 28, 1863, p. 4; *Elevator,* Oct. 19, 1872, p. 3. See the cruel stereotyping of Blacks on ragtime music sheets reproduced in William J. Schafer and Johannes Riedel, *The Art of Ragtime: Form and Meaning of An Original Black American Art* (Baton Rouge, La., [1973]). *Pacific Coast Appeal,* Feb. 13, 1904, p. 1, March 5, 1904, pp. 1, 2; *Western Outlook,* Jan. 23, 1915, p. 3, Feb. 13, 1915, p. 3; *City Directory, 1895, 1904, 1905.*

47. *City Directory, 1862; Pacific Appeal,* Sept. 13, 1862, pp. 2, 4, Nov. 8, 1862, p. 3; *Elevator,* May 12, 1865, p. 3; see the comments of J. G. Wilson and J. H. Townsend on the rules of gentlemen, *Proceedings of the First State Convention of the Colored Citizens of the State of California, 1855* (Sacramento, 1855), p. 4.

48. *Sentinel,* Sept. 20, 1890, p. 2, on the need for Blacks to become citizens of the world.

49. *Sentinel,* Dec. 13, 1890, p. 2; *Elevator,* Nov. 8, 1867, p. 2.

50. *Elevator,* Aug. 9, 1873, p. 2, Dec. 13, 1890, p. 2.

51. *Call,* March 22, 1900, p. 4; see also Nov. 4, 1897, p. 4, March 7, 1898, p. 12, Nov. 13, 1889, p. 1, Sept. 22, 1897, p. 12, and March 17, 1900, p. 1; interview, Aurelious P. Alberga, July 27, 1976. Professor Barry Higman, Department of History, University of the West Indies, Mona, Jamaica kindly provided information on Jackson's early life and career in Australia.

52. *Examiner,* Nov. 11, 1889, p. 1; *Call,* March 17, 1898, p. 5, May 22, 1891, p. 8; *Chronicle,* Dec. 6, 1903, p. 30, Dec. 11, 1903, p. 4; John Rickard Betts, *America's Sporting Heritage: 1850–1950* (Reading, Mass., [1974]) on the development of sports in the U.S.

53. *Call,* Sept. 22, 1897, p. 12, March 10, 1894, p. 1, March 22, 1900, p. 4, March 7, 1898, p. 12; Nat Fleischer, *Black Dynamite: The Story of the Negro in the Prize Ring from 1782 to 1938,* vol. 1 (New York, [1938]), pp. 123–72.

54. *Call,* Nov. 3, 1896, p. 14.

55. *Chronicle,* Dec. 10, 1903, p. 4; see also Dec. 6, 1903, p. 30. *Call,* June 9, 1900, pp. 5, 11. Finis Farr, *Black Champion: The Life and Times of Jack Johnson* (Greenwich, Conn. [1969 ed.]), p. 184, on the boxer praised by *Ring* magazine editor Nat Fleischer, who "after years devoted to the study of heavyweight fighters" could, without hesitation, name Jack Johnson as "the greatest of them all."

56. *Call,* March 22, 1891, p. 8 on the Jackson-Corbett fight; March 22, 1900, p. 4.

57. *Call,* March 17, 1898, p. 5; on his ill health in Australia, April 17, 1901, p. 1; on the color line, *Examiner,* Nov. 13, 1889, p. 1; *Call,* Sept. 28, 1897, p. 1.

58. Aurelious Alberga, born in San Francisco in 1884, boxed for a period in his youth; he also claimed he knew Peter Jackson and spoke very highly of him. Alfred Butler and Royal Towns, both Bay Area natives, also admired Jackson and Jack Johnson when they were youngsters. See Lawrence Levine's discussion of Johnson as a hero in *Black Culture and Black Consciousness* (New York, 1977), pp. 430–33.

59. *Pacific Appeal,* May 23, 1863, p. 1–2.

60. Stanley M. Elkins, *Slavery: A Problem in American Institutional and Intellectual Life* (New York, [1963] ed.) presents a classic statement of the belief that plantation slavery turned most Afro-Americans into docile and child-like creatures. Recent scholarship, such as John Blassingame, *The Slave Community: Plantation Life in the Antebellum South* (New York, 1972); Eugene Genovese, *Roll, Jordan, Roll: The World the Slaves Made* (New York, 1974); and Levine, *Black Culture,* disputes this interpretation.

## *Chapter 9:* Rounders

1. Abraham Lincoln Dennis, son of the pioneer George Washington Dennis, was proprietor of the Vestibule Cafe at the turn of the century; San Francisco *Pacific Coast Appeal,* Dec. 19, 1903, p. 4; San Francisco *Spokesman,* Feb. 16, 1933, p. 6, Feb. 23, 1933, p. 2.

2. Oakland *Western Outlook,* Jan. 2, 1915, p. 3. On the night life, see: Herbert Asbury, *The Barbary Coast: An Informal History of the San Francisco Underworld* (New York, 1933); Evelyn Wells, *Champagne Days of San Francisco* (New York, 1947); Ann Charters, *Nobody: The Story of "Bert" Williams* (New York, 1970), pp. 20–25; Sally Stanford, *The Lady of the House: The Autobiography of Sally Stanford* (New York, 1966).

3. *Spokesman,* May 25, 1933, p. 6.

4. [Noah Brooks], "Restaurant Life in San Francisco," *The Overland Monthly* I (Nov. 1868), 467.

5. Harriet Lane Levy, *920 O'Farrell Street* (Garden City, N.Y., 1947), and Wells, *Champagne Days* provide a look at late nineteenth-century customs, attitudes, and morals in San Francisco. San Francisco *Examiner,* Sept. 12, 1913, p. 20, and Sept. 15, 1913, p. 2, discusses recreation and morality. Workers of the Writers' Program of the Works Project Administration in Northern California, *San Francisco: the Bay and Its Cities* (New York, 1947), p. 107. Amelia Neville, *The Fantastic City: Memoirs of the Social and Romantic Life of Old San Francisco* (Boston, 1932), p. 210.

6. *Examiner,* Jan. 14, 1917, p. 4.

7. Stanford, *Lady,* p. 66; Elizabeth A. Brown, "The Enforcement of Prohibition in San Francisco" (M.A. thesis, University of California, Berkeley, 1948), pp. 20, 22; John P. Young, *San Francisco: A History of the Pacific Coast Metropolis,* 2 vols. (San Francisco, [1912]), II: 62; *Examiner,* Sept. 12, 1913, p. 20, Jan. 15, 1917, p. 1, Jan. 20, 1917, p. 1.

8. *Examiner,* Jan. 20, 1917, p. 1; Stanford, *Lady,* pp. 46–47; Liston F. Sabran, "Mayor James Rolph, Jr. and the End of the Barbary Coast" (M.A. thesis, San Francisco State University, 1961).

9. San Francisco *Western Appeal,* Feb. 18, 1922, p. 1, Feb. 25, 1927, p. 5.

10. New York *Weekly Anglo-African,* Nov. 5, 1859, p. 1; San Francisco *Elevator,* Nov. 1, 1869, p. 2; San Francisco *Pacific Appeal,* May 24, 1862, p. 2.

11. *Elevator,* Feb. 7, 1868, p. 2, Aug. 16, 1873, p. 2; *Pacific Appeal,* Nov. 5, 1870, p. 2; *Christian Recorder* (Philadelphia), March 11, 1864, p. 38; Oakland *Western American,* Jan. 4, 1929, p. 1.

12. *Pacific Appeal,* Jan. 2, 1864, p. 2; *Elevator,* July 7, 1868, p. 2; Edgar M. Branch, ed., *Clemens of the Call: Mark Twain in San Francisco* (Berkeley, 1969), pp. 56–57.

13. *Elevator,* July 7, 1868, p. 2, April 28, 1865, p. 4; *Western Outlook,* April 10, 1915, p. 2; Oakland *Sunshine,* June 12, 1915, p. 2; Oakland *California Voice,* Aug. 6, 1926, p. 12.

14. *Pacific Appeal,* Nov. 5, 1870, p. 2; *Western Appeal,* Feb. 25, 1927, p. 2, April 1, 1927, p. 3; *Western Outlook,* March 17, 1928, p. 4; *Western Appeal,* March 8, 1922, p. 1.

15. *Elevator,* July 5, 1867, p. 4, Jan. 15, 1869, pp. 2–3, Oct. 18, 1890, p. 3, July 3, 1886, p. 3, June 11, 1898, p. 3; Henry G. Langley, comp., *The San Francisco Directory, 1907* (hereafter cited as *City Directory,* with the appropriate year), entry for Louis V. Purcell.

16. Workers of the Writers' Program, *San Francisco,* p. 216; Marshall and Jean Stearns, *Jazz Dance: the Story of American Vernacular Dance* (New York, 1968), p. 128; Asbury, *Barbary Coast,* pp. 292–93.

17. Los Angeles *Eagle,* July 24, 1915, p. 3; *Western Outlook,* Jan. 9, 1915, pp. 2–3; *Western Appeal,* Nov. 12, 1921, p. 2.

18. *Western Appeal,* Feb. 1, 1922, p. 4; *Sunshine,* March 20, 1915, p. 1; Arnold Genthe, *As I Remember* (New York, [1936]), pp. 175–76.

19. *Western Outlook,* Nov. 28, 1914, p. 2.

20. Ibid., Dec. 12, 1914, p. 2, Feb. 20, 1915, p. 3; on the Clef Club, Tom Fletcher, *The Tom Fletcher Story: 100 Years of the Negro in Show Business* (New York, 1954), p. 201.

21. San Francisco *Chronicle* and *Examiner,* weeks beginning Nov. 18 and Dec. 19, 1921; the Federal Records Center in San Bruno, California has material on the case, but no court transcript exists. Samuel Dickson, *San Francisco Kaleidoscope* (Stanford, Calif., 1949), pp. 254–55.

22. King Oliver and his band played at the Second Annual Grand Ball of the West Indian Cricket Club of San Francisco in 1922; *Western Outlook,* March 25, 1922, p. 2, Nov. 28, 1914, p. 2; Arna Bontemps, ed., *Father of the Blues: An Autobiography by W. C. Handy* (New York, 1970 ed.); Fletcher, *Tom Fletcher Story;* and James Weldon Johnson, *Black Manhattan* (New York, 1968) offer insiders' accounts of the evolution of Black entertainment in the late nineteenth and early twentieth centuries. Charters, *Nobody;* Rudi Blesh and Harriet Janis, *They All Played Ragtime* (New York, 1971 ed.); William J. Schafer and Johannes Riedel, *The Art of Ragtime: Form and Meaning of An Original Black American Art* (Baton Rouge, La., [1973]); and Stearns, *Jazz Dance* are valuable. Eileen Southern, *The Music of Black Americans: A History* (New York, [1971]) is a good overview of the development of Black music.

23. Southern, *Music,* pp. 105–48.

24. Ibid., pp. 112–14; *Frederick Douglass' Paper* (Rochester, N.Y.), April 13, 1855, p. 3.

25. Quoted in the *Elevator,* Dec. 4, 1868, p. 3.

26. Stockton *Evening Mail,* May 11, 1892, p. 1. I would like to thank Howard Dodson for bringing this article to my attention.

27. Tom Stoddard, author of a number of articles on Black musicians in the Bay Area before 1920, was kind enough to permit me to read his manuscript on this topic. He influenced my thinking in this section. Interviews with Ethel Terrell, a vaudeville musician who settled in San Francisco in the 1920s, and Freddie McWilliams also served as a basis for my ideas.

28. Charters, *Nobody,* p. 18; Blesh and Janis, *Ragtime,* p. 139. Peter Tamony, "Jazz: The Word, and Its Extension to Music," *Americanisms: Content and Continuum* XXIII (Dec. 1968), p. 13. See San Francisco *Call-Bulletin,* March 6, 1913, p. 16, for the term's first appearance in print, and ibid., Sept. 3, 1938, p. 3, for the quote concerning Purcell's.

29. *Examiner,* Jan. 17, 1917, p. 5. Although he may not have been particularly knowledgeable of Black music, George Schuyler, the Black journalist who passed through San Francisco as a young soldier in about 1912, heard ragtime and jazz when he visited the

Barbary Coast. This was before the general public knew of jazz. George Schuyler, *Black and Conservative: The Autobiography of George S. Schuyler* (New Rochelle, N.Y., [1966]), p. 49.

30. Ortiz M. Walton, *Music: Black, White, and Blue* (New York, 1972), pp. 46–59.

31. Charles Keeler, *San Francisco and Thereabout* (San Francisco, 1902), p. 54; Wells, *Champagne Days,* has a useful chapter entitled "Seeing the Elephant."

32. *Western Outlook,* Jan. 2, 1915, pp. 2–3.

33. Genthe, *As I Remember,* pp. 175–76; *Examiner,* Sept. 30, 1913, p. 1; Fred Brandt and Andrew Y. Wood, *Fascinating San Francisco* (San Francisco, 1924), p. 26; Wells, *Champagne Days,* p. 125; *California Voice,* Oct. 1, 1921, p. 4; *Western Appeal,* March 8, 1922, p. 1.

34. *Chronicle,* Dec. 27, 1921, p. 1, Jan. 2, 1922, p. 6; *Examiner,* Sept. 30, 1913, p. 1, Dec. 26, 1921, p. 1; *Western American,* June 25, 1926, p. 7.

35. *Examiner,* Jan. 22, 1917, pp. 3, 7, Jan. 26, 1917, p. 5, Jan. 14, 1917, p. 4.

36. Ibid., beginning Sept. 13, 1913 and Jan. 14, 1917, p. 4.

37. *Spokesman,* Nov. 17, 1932, p. 1. James Weldon Johnson noted the race issue's sexual dimension in his autobiography; see *Along This Way: The Autobiography of James Weldon Johnson* (New York, [1968 ed.]), p. 170.

38. Joseph R. Gusfield, "Prohibition: The Impact of Political Utopianism," in Richard M. Abrams and Lawrence Levine, *The Shaping of Twentieth Century America* (Boston, 2nd ed. [1971]), pp. 309–41. Also, Stanley Coben, "A Study in Nativism: The American Red Scare of 1919–20," in ibid., pp. 289–306.

39. *Examiner,* Dec. 26, 1921, p. 1, Dec. 28, 1921, p. 3, Dec. 29, 1921, p. 13; *Western Appeal,* undated, but may be Jan. 4, 1912, p. 20.

40. *Examiner,* Oct. 1, 1913, p. 1

41. *Examiner,* Feb. 15, 1917, p. 3. A coalition of reform groups successfully kept the Jack Johnson–Jim Jeffries heavyweight championship fight out of San Francisco; state and local politicians feared such a match would prevent the city from hosting the Panama-Pacific Exhibition (boxing was illegal in California). See Finis Farr, *Black Champion: The Life and Times of Jack Johnson* (Greenwich, Conn., [1969]), pp. 68–71.

42. *Examiner,* Dec. 26, 1921, p. 1, Dec. 15, 1917, p. 10, Dec. 23, 1921, p. 17; *Western Appeal,* Aug. 17, 1921, p. 1, Dec. 21, 1921, p. 24; *Examiner,* Dec. 29, 1921, p. 13, Feb. 6, 1922, p. 13; *Chronicle,* Dec. 27, 1921, p. 1, Dec. 28, 1921, p. 3, Dec. 30, 1921, p. 3.

43. *Western American,* Jan. 13, 1928, p. 8.

44. *Examiner,* Sept. 15, 1913, p. 2, Sept. 12, 1913, p. 20.

45. Editorial in *Examiner,* Jan. 13, 1917, p. 6.

46. *Western Appeal,* April 8, 1922, p. 1. On discrimination in a Bay Area "Y," interview, Ida Jackson, Jan. 19, 1972, Oakland Museum.

47. "Inside Facts," an article in the Pamphlet Box on Negroes in the Bancroft Library, University of California, Berkeley; on the founding of the community center, see: *Examiner,* April 19, 1920, p. 11; *Chronicle,* Oct. 6, 1941, p. 11; "Fifty Years in Action," Booker T. Washington Community Center *Fiftieth Anniversary Program, 1920–1970,* which was kindly sent to me by Mrs. Emma J. Scott Jones. Booker T. Washington Community Center, Annual Reports, 1926, p. 2, Bancroft Library, University of California, Berkeley.

48. "Inside Facts," Pamphlet Box, Bancroft Library, University of California, Berkeley.

49. See Community Center, Annual Reports, Bancroft Library, University of California, Berkeley.

50. Southern, *Music,* pp. 265–67. Nathan I. Huggins, *Harlem Renaissance* (New York, 1971), ch. 6.

51. Huggins, *Harlem,* ch. 6.

52. See Johnson, *Along This Way,* p. 87.

53. Alan Lomax, *Mister Jelly Roll: The Fortunes of Jelly Roll Morton, New Orleans Creole and "Inventor of Jazz"* (New York, [1950]), pp. 167–69. *Chronicle,* week beginning Dec. 21, 1921, p. 24.

54. Mary Goodrich, *The Palace Hotel* (San Francisco, 1930), p. 34.

55. Huggins, *Harlem,* ch. 6, brilliantly analyzes the similarities between ministrelsy and cabaret life.

56. *Spokesman,* March 26, 1932, p. 1, May 21, 1932, p. 1.

*Chapter 10:* Newcomers

1. Interview, Ethel Terrell, April 20, 1973.

2. Interview, Martel Meneweather, June 13, 1975.

3. On housing discrimination, San Francisco *Spokesman,* March 19, 1932, p. 3. On the influx of white southerners and racial confrontations, see: interview, E. A. Daly, Earl Warren Oral History Project, University of California, Berkeley, p. 10; interview, Byron Rumford, Earl Warren Oral History Project, pp. 19, 21–22.

4. Interview, Urania Cummings, Aug. 4, 1976.

5. Ibid.

6. Margaret Johnson, "The Negroes in West Berkeley," *Immigration and Race Problems* (1949–53), pp. 874, 869, 871; interview, Urania Cummings, Aug. 4, 1976.

7. Interview, Eleanor Carroll Watkins, July 30, 1976. If the last few words seem to weaken the statement, some clarification should be made. Although she lived on the Pacific slope her entire life, Mrs. Watkins became acquainted with eastern ways from her mother, who came from Annapolis, Maryland. Her mother never forgot the traditions, the class and social consciousness, and the refinement of certain types of east-coast urban life. So Mrs. Watkins understood this phase of eastern society from her mother's attitudes, from the contrasting west-coast life, and from conversations with easterners.

8. Interviews, C. L. Dellums and Ida Jackson, Earl Warren Oral History Project, University of California, Berkeley; interviews, Tarea Hall Pittman and Alvin D. Nurse, Oakland Museum; interviews, Martel Meneweather, June 13, 1975, E. A. Daly, Aug. 3, 1976; conversation with Lillian Dixon, April 3, 1975.

9. Charles S. Johnson, *The Negro War Worker in San Francisco: A Local Self-Survey* (San Francisco, 1944), pp. 4, 5, 79–81.

10. Interview, Matt Crawford, Aug. 3, 1976.

11. Davis McEntire and Julia R. Tarnopol, "Postwar Status of Negro Workers in San Francisco Area," *Monthly Labor Review* LXX (June 1950), 612, and Johnson, *Negro War Worker,* p. 3, give some contemporary estimates of population growth. See also: San Francisco *Chronicle,* May 3, 1948, p. 13; United States Bureau of the Census, *Sixteenth Census, 1940: Population* (Washington, D.C., 1943), part 1, pp. 599, 637, 657; *Negro Population in Selected Places and Selected Counties, Supplementary Report* (Washington, D.C., June 1971), p. 5 for the growth of the Black population in the Bay Area between 1940 and 1970. Interview, John Watkins, Aug. 13, 1976.

12. Interview, Matt Crawford, Aug. 3, 1976.

13. Ibid. Interview, Alvin D. Nurse, Feb. 2, 1972, Oakland Museum.

14. Barbara Sawyer, "Negroes in West Oakland," *Immigration and Race Problems* (1949–53), p. 850 contends that in wartime, Bay Area wages rose to as much as $100 per week, compared to $20–$25 per week in the south and in the Bay Area before the war; Johnson, *Negro War Worker,* p. 84.

15. The project was "financed by a San Francisco citizen, administered by the Y.W.C.A., and carried out in connection with the Race Relations Program of the American Missionary

Association, Dr. Charles S. Johnson, Director, and the Julius Rosenwald Fund." A copy of the report is in the Bancroft Library, University of California, Berkeley.

16. Johnson, *Negro War Worker,* pp. 16–17.

17. Ibid., pp. 61–64.

18. Ibid., p. 63.

19. Ibid., p. 80.

20. Ibid., p. 14.

21. Johnson, *Negro War Worker,* pp. 3–4.

22. Johnson, *Negro War Worker,* pp. 8, 15; McEntire and Tarnopol, "Postwar Status," p. 613.

23. Johnson, *Negro War Worker,* p. 8.

24. Joseph Boskin, ed., *Urban Racial Violence in the Twentieth Century* (Beverly Hills, 1976 ed.); Chester Himes, "Zoot Riots are Race Riots," *Black on Black, Baby Sister, and Selected Writings* (Garden City, N.J., 1973), pp. 220–26.

25. Johnson, *Negro War Worker,* p. 32.

26. Ibid., p. 29. Thomas Lee Philpott, *The Slum and the Ghetto: Neighborhood Deterioration and Middle-Class Reform, Chicago, 1880–1930* (New York, 1978), pp. 162–200, 407–10, is an excellent analysis of how whites used restrictive convenants and violent means to segregate Blacks.

27. On the development of the Fillmore district, see Margaret G. King, "The Growth of San Francisco Illustrated by Shifts in the Density of Population" (M.A. thesis, University of California, Berkeley, 1928), p. 138; also, *Spokesman,* July 6, 1933, p. 6

28. Johnson, *Negro War Worker,* pp. 20–21.

29. Ibid., p. 21.

30. Ibid., p. 22.

31. Ibid., p. 23.

32. Ibid.

33. Ibid., p. 24.

34. Ibid., pp. 24, 27.

35. On the question of property depreciation following Negro occupancy, an official of a Fillmore District merchants' group said: "There has been no depreciation in the Fillmore property; first because its value was already down, and second, because it is impossible to estimate the true effect of the Negro migrations to the district. . . . Even in cases where merchants have scruples against Negro trade, they admit their volume of business and profit has increased." The head of an improvement club stated: "Where not affected by industrial expansion, most property depreciation is due to the inability or neglect of some owners to keep their property in good condition"; ibid., p. 31.

36. Ibid., pp. 92–93.

37. Ibid.

38. Interview, Aurelious Alberga, July 27, 1976.

39. Interview, Freddie McWilliams, Aug. 9, 1976.

40. Interview, John Watkins, Aug. 13, 1976.

41. Interviews, Freddie McWilliams, Aug. 9, 1976, and Vivian Osborn Marsh, Aug. 16, 1976.

42. Interview, Eugene Lasartemay, July 23, 1976.

43. Interview, Urania Cummings, Aug. 4, 1976.

44. This opinion is expressed in the interviews of the Earl Warren Oral History Project, University of California, Berkeley.

45. Interview, Martel Meneweather, June 13, 1975.

46. Ibid.

47. Interviews, Matt Crawford, Aug. 3, 1976, Eugene Lasartemay, July 23, 1976, and Martel Meneweather, June 13, 1975.

48. Interviews, E. A. Daly, Aug. 2, 1976, and Vivian Osborn Marsh, Aug. 16, 1976.

49. Interview, John Watkins, Aug. 13, 1976.

50. Interview, Eleanor Carroll Watkins, July 30, 1976; the Oakland Museum interviews with Black Oaklanders document the struggles.

51. Interview, Eleanor Carroll Watkins, July 30, 1976.

# Bibliographical Essay

A variety of primary sources are useful for scholars interested in the topic of Black urbanites in San Francisco and on the Pacific slope. The United States Bureau of the Census collected demographic information which can be culled from the Manuscript Census; the federal census documents of 1860, 1870, 1880, and 1900, in addition to a state enumeration for 1852, are available. Scholars can compile this data and perform the complicated analyses used by cliometricians for other topics. Some simpler tabulations of the kind I made have also been undertaken by: James A. Fisher, "The California Negro—1860—An Analysis of State Census Returns," in San Francisco African-American Historical and Cultural Society, Inc., Blacks in the West, No. 1 Manuscript Series, 1976; Ernest V. Siracusa, Jr., "Black 49'ers: The Negro in the California Gold Rush, 1848–1861" (typed essay on microfilm, June 1969, Bancroft Library, University of California, Berkeley); and Philip M. Montesano, "The San Francisco Black Community, 1849–1890: The Quest for 'Equality Before the Law'" (Ph.D. diss., University of California, Santa Barbara, 1974). California's state censuses have little value except for comparisons at the state level.

Some few documents and petitions of Black San Franciscans are preserved in the offices of the Governor and the Secretary of the State of California. These include articles of incorporation of Black enterprises and race organizations and letters concerning appointments of notaries public. If researchers do not have a specific name or organization and year, however, their task is formidable, depending on whether the records have been indexed by race.

Government reports rarely mention Afro-Americans and thus shed little light on their condition. Annual reports of the San Francisco school board provide information on Black schools during the mid-nineteenth century. *The San Francisco Directory* lists names, occupations, and addresses of some heads of households; the designation "colored" disappears after 1876, limiting the *Directory's* utility. It does include brief histories of and data on Black churches and Masonic lodges, as well as the names of the officers of each.

Librarians have only begun to process the material on Afro-Americans in the letters and manuscripts of famous and well-to-do whites. Afro-Americans were not on the minds of the Sharons, the Crockers, and the Huntingtons, so we should not be surprised if the most careful gleaning of their records turns up very little for those interested in Afro-American history.

But Afro-Americans themselves left a number of unpublished and published records. There are very few letters, with the exception of those among the Charlotte Brown Papers in the California Historical Society Library and the Jeremiah B. Sanderson Papers in the Bancroft Library, University of California, Berkeley. Also useful are *The Proceedings of the State Conventions of the Colored Citizens of the State of California* and the *Proceedings* or *Official Minutes of the California Conference of the African Methodist Episcopal Church.* The former, which has been recently republished, is useful for understanding politics and civil rights in the mid-nineteenth century. It also contains valuable statistics, as well as records of debates. The *Official Minutes* contains statistical data on the size and wealth of the churches, particularly at the turn of the century. Annual Records of the Booker T. Washington Community Service Center, 1926–1931 are the most detailed of all records of Black institutions. As Afro-American history gets the attention it deserves, more valuable materials will undoubtedly be made available to libraries, but at present only a few documents, constitutions, by-laws, and programs of Afro-American societies are accessible.

A number of dissertations and theses afford an understanding of the scene in San Francisco and the far west. The growth of the physical setting, and the politics affecting the city's expansion, are discussed in Martyn J. Bowden, "Dynamics of City Growth: An Historical Geography of the San Francisco Central District, 1850–1931" (Ph.D. diss., University of California, Berkeley, 1967) and Margaret G. King, "The Growth of San Francisco Illustrated by Shifts in the Density of Population" (M.A. thesis, University of California, Berkeley, 1928). Judd Lewis Kahn, "Imperial San Francisco: History of a Vision" (Ph.D. diss., University of California, Berkeley, 1971) focuses on the rebuilding of the city after 1906.

Several theses and dissertations analyze labor relations, prohibition, and other topics. Edward Paul Eaves, "A History of the Cooks' and Waiters' Union of San Francisco" (M.A. thesis, University of California, Berkeley, 1930) provides the background for understanding the Palace Hotel change-over, but does not discuss the Afro-Americans who were replaced. Robert Coleman Francis, "A History of Labor on the San Francisco Waterfront" (Ph.D. diss., University of California, Berkeley, 1934) treats an area of San Francisco's economic life from which Negroes were excluded, except as strikebreakers, until 1934. Neil Larry Shumsky, "Tar Flat and Nob Hill: A Social History of Industrial San Francisco During the 1870s" (Ph.D. diss., University of California, Berkeley, 1972) permits an understanding of the city's economic development and its effects on various classes in the nineteenth century.

Vice and ethnic districts are treated in Elizabeth Anne Brown, "The Enforcement of Prohibition in San Francisco, California" (M.A. thesis, University of California, Berkeley, 1948); Liston F. Sabran, "Mayor James Rolph, Jr. and the End of the Barbary Coast" (M.A. thesis, San Francisco State University, 1961); and Helen Virginia Cather, "The History of San Francisco's Chinatown" (M.A. thesis, University of California, Berkeley, 1932).

Several theses and a few dissertations analyze Afro-American topics. The oldest are Berlinda Davison, "Educational Status of the Negro in the San Francisco Bay Region" (M.A. thesis, University of California, Berkeley, 1921), and Robert Coleman Francis, "A Survey of Negro Business in the San Francisco Bay Region"

(M.A. thesis, University of California, Berkeley, 1928). Another early study is A. Odell Thurman, "The Negro in California Before 1890" (M.A. thesis, College of the Pacific, Stockton, 1945). Several dissertations and theses focus on migration and social history. Edward Everett France, "Some Aspects of the Migration of the Negro to the San Francisco Bay Area Since 1940" (Ph.D. diss., University of California, Berkeley, 1962), and Lawrence Brooks de Graaf, "Negro Migration to Los Angeles, 1930 to 1950" (Ph.D. diss., University of California, Los Angeles, 1962) enable the reader to compare the Blacks of the two cities. Unfortunately, the University of California at Los Angeles does not have the copy of de Graaf's dissertation. James A. Fisher, "A Social History of the Negro in California, 1860–1890" (M.A. thesis, Sacramento State University, 1966) foreshadows the interest in civil rights that produced a number of graduate studies in the 1960s.

Sheila M. Skjeie, "California and the Fifteenth Amendment: A Study of Racism" (Ph.D. diss., Sacramento State University, Sacramento, 1973) analyzes California's belated adoption of the Fifteenth Amendment. A seminar paper by Sally Garey, "Some Aspects of Mid-Nineteenth Century Black Uplift: Philip A. Bell and the San Francisco *Elevator*" (University of California, Berkeley, 1967) informed me of one of the first major champions of civil rights in San Francisco. Various aspects of the struggle for equality in nineteenth-century cities are treated in Francis N. Lortie, Jr., "San Francisco's Black Community, 1870–1890: Dilemmas in the Struggle for Equality" (M.A. thesis, San Francisco State University, 1970); and Larry George Murphy, "Equality Before the Law: The Struggle of Nineteenth-Century Black Californians for Social and Political Justice" (Ph.D. diss., Graduate Theological Union, 1973); Philip M. Montesano's dissertation has been noted. Civil rights issues affected the exodus from California to Canada; this is analyzed in James William Pilton, "Negro Settlement in British Columbia, 1858–1871" (M.A. thesis, University of British Columbia, 1951). A Black San Francisco community of the 1960s is studied in Neil Arthur Eddington, "The Urban Plantation: the Ethnography of an Oral Tradition in a Negro Community" (Ph.D. diss., University of California, Berkeley, 1967).

Among published materials, the federal census has much statistical material and innumerable comparisons, but sometimes lacks the information sought by the scholar interested in a particular Afro-American community. Because the procedure is subject to change every ten years, censuses cannot always easily be compared. As noted, San Francisco's civic officials were not likely to gather material on Negroes—they were far more interested in and fearful of the Chinese. The San Francisco Board of Supervisors *Municipal Reports*, however, include a breakdown on diseases and causes of death by race. Although the number reported may be too small to be statistically significant for the Afro-San Franciscans, scholars may find this useful for assessing the health of the city's Black population.

Henry G. Langley, comp., *San Francisco Directory, 1860–1879* (compiled by others in subsequent years) offers much information. Also, see Charles F. Tilghman, comp., *Colored Directory of the Leading Cities of Northern California, 1916–1917* (Oakland, 1917). In addition to listing names, addresses, and occupations of heads of households, it includes advertisements, photographs of homes and of officers of social clubs, and some statistical information. One of the few remaining copies is at the East Bay Negro Historical Society in Oakland. A generation later, Workers of the Writers' Program of the Works Project Administration in Northern California compiled *San Francisco: The Bay and Its Cities* (New York, 1947); they noted the growing Black population, its geographical origins, and the nature of its social life.

Because much of San Francisco's manuscript and published history was destroyed by the fires of the 1850s and the earthquake and fire of 1906, the material that survived is precious and needs to be carefully mined to recreate an accurate multi-ethnic history of one of the nation's most fascinating cities. Histories, reminiscences, and published collections of letters shed some light on the Afro-American population of the Bay Area. Frank Soulé, John H. Gihon, and James Nisbet, *The Annals of San Francisco* (New York, 1855) provides a colorful portrait of the pioneer period, including a number of references to Negroes. Hinton Rowan Helper, *The Land of Gold: Reality Versus Fiction* (Baltimore, 1855) gives the new state a critical examination and notes the poverty of the Black folk. More typically, John S. Hittell, *A History of the City of San Francisco and Incidentally of the State of California* (San Francisco, 1878), and John P. Young, *San Francisco: A History of the Pacific Coast Metropolis,* 2 vols. (San Francisco, 1912) rarely mention Blacks, except when discussing slavery.

Benjamin E. Lloyd, *Lights and Shades of San Francisco* (San Francisco, 1876), and Anthony Trollope, *A Letter From Anthony Trollope Describing A Visit to California in 1875* (San Francisco, 1876) illuminate several aspects of the city's social life. Other late nineteenth-century visitors left their thoughts. See Rudyard Kipling, *Letters From San Francisco* (San Francisco, 1949); George R. Stewart and Edwin S. Fussell, eds., *San Francisco in 1866,* by Bret Harte (San Francisco, 1951); and Edwin S. Morby, trans. and ed., *San Francisco in the Seventies: The City As Viewed by A Mexican Political Exile,* by Guillermo Prieto (San Francisco, 1938).

Other reminiscences occasionally mention Afro-Americans. Turn-of-the-century San Francisco is portrayed in Evelyn Wells, *Champagne Days of San Francisco* (New York, 1947); Charles Keeler, *San Francisco and Thereabout* (San Francisco, 1902); and Amelia Neville, *The Fantastic City: Memoirs of the Social and Romantic Life of Old San Francisco* (Boston, 1932). More recently, the University of California's place in the East Bay's history has been presented from the perspective of alumni, including well-known Afro-Americans, in Irving Stone, ed., *And Then There Was Light: An Autobiography of a University, Berkeley, 1868-1968* (Garden City, N.Y., 1973).

A few memoirs shed light on the entertainment milieu and vice districts of old San Francisco. There is Clifton Rather, *Here's How: An Autobiography* (Oakland, 1968-1970); Sally Stanford, *The Lady of the House: The Autobiography of Sally Stanford* (New York, 1962); and Ruben V. Vaughan, *The Print of My Reminiscence* (Hollywood, 1955).

The autobiographies and reminiscences of Afro-Americans and articles by Samuel L. Clemens offer insights into Black San Francisco life. An early pioneer, Mifflin W. Gibbs, related the San Francisco civil rights struggles of the 1850s in *Shadow and Light: An Autobiography* (New York, 1968 ed.). Bishop Alexander

Walters, *My Life and Work* (New York, 1917) devotes a chapter to Walters's San Francisco residency.

Another visitor to San Francisco was James Weldon Johnson; see *Along This Way: The Autobiography of James Weldon Johnson* (New York, 1933). While he gives only scant mention to San Francisco, Horace Cayton, in his autobiography, *Long Old Road* (Seattle, 1963), describes a family, its success, and its decline as a result of militant politics, an influx of Black migrants, and the resulting intensification of race hatred. This account sheds some light on what may have been a typical experience for nineteenth-century far western urbanites.

The successes of a Negro playwright, Garland Anderson, a San Franciscan, are recounted in a singular reminiscence, *From Newsboy and Bellhop to Playwright* (San Francisco, 1927). Anderson's play, *Appearances,* brought him fame in New York City. Another remarkable account of Black San Francisco life is included in the journalistic efforts of the young Samuel L. Clemens, in Edgar M. Branch, ed., *Clemens of the Call: Mark Twain in San Francisco* (Berkeley, 1969).

Unfortunately, only one Black resident's account of modern San Francisco and the changes of the 1940s has been published. Maya Angelou, who migrated from Arkansas as a teenager during World War II, gives a vivid description of the booming city in her autobiography, *I Know Why the Caged Bird Sings* (New York, 1970).

Black newspapers constitute a rich source of information, if only because the residents took them so seriously. Only one copy of the first Black newspaper on the Pacific slope, the *Mirror of the Times* (Dec. 12, 1857) was available to the author, though at least one other is known to exist. The San Francisco *Pacific Appeal* (1862–1879) and the *Elevator* (1865–1898) are excellent for the 1860s but vary in number and quality in the 1870s; a few copies of the *Elevator* exist for the next two decades. A handful of issues of the San Francisco *Vindicator* and the San Francisco *Sentinel* illuminate some areas of Black urban life in the 1880s and early 1890s.

Twentieth-century newspapers improve in number and quality through the first three decades. The San Francisco *Pacific Coast Appeal* (1898–1925), which combined with the *Elevator,* is excellent for the first few years of the century. Like many other Negro newspapers, approximately half of each issue consisted of non-racial material from other journals. This highlights the duality of Black life. While I focused on the ethnic dimension, it might be worthwhile to compare this material with that in white newspapers.

Like the *Pacific Coast Appeal,* copies of the Oakland *Western Outlook* (1894–1924) are not as numerous as the dates suggest. As Oakland emerged as a city in its own right, its enterprising Black population published the *Sunshine* (1900–1923), the *California Voice* (1919–), the *Times* (1923–1930), the *Western American* (1926–1929), and the *Independent* (1929–1931). At the same time Black San Franciscans launched the *Western Appeal* (1918?–1927) and the *Spokesman* (1931–1935).

The other daily and weekly newspapers were not reviewed unless I was interested in a specific event I knew had occurred at a particular time. Using the especially useful newspaper index of the California State Library and the microfilm index of the San Francisco *Call* (1894–1904), I found several informative articles. These aids helped fill in the years during which Black newspapers were rare. They were also valuable for notes on such well-known personalities as Peter Jackson and Mary Ellen "Mammy" Pleasant, and some less famous citizens.

These articles were among the most useful: "Thrifty Colored Folk" (*Examiner*, June 16, 1889, p. 10) on successful individuals; "San Francisco Has No Regular Negro Quarter, But She Has A Peculiar Negro Colony" (*Chronicle*, Feb. 7, 1904, p. 7), which may have been written by J. S. Francis, a Black newspaperman; and Oscar Hudson, a lawyer and consul for Liberia, "Negro Citizens of State Show Enviable Race Record" (*Chronicle*, Jan. 18, 1922, p. 14); the historian-journalist Delilah L. Beasley wrote some articles for the Oakland *Tribune* during the Panama Pacific Exposition (1915), but I was unable to locate them.

For labor problems in the Palace Hotel, discrimination in hotels at the turn of the century, Black businesses, and passing as white, I relied upon "A Palace Lock-Out" (*Chronicle*, Nov. 9, 1889, p. 6); "Famous Colored Servants to Go" (*Call*, Nov. 3, 1896, p. 14); "Jackson Feels the Color Line" (*Call*, Sept. 28, 1897, p. 1); "Hotel Men and the Color Line" (*Call*, Sept. 29, 1897, p. 4); "Oakland Business Men" (*The Colored American Magazine* [New York] IX [Nov. 1905], 648–50); and in the same periodical, "A Successful Business Venture" (XIII [Dec. 1907], 269–72); and Fannie Barrier Williams, "Perils of the White Negro" (XIII [Dec. 1907], 21–23).

Oral histories were consulted when they were available. Interviews with several well-known Black Bay Area residents are part of the Earl Warren Oral History Project of the University of California, Berkeley, and they have been transcribed. The Oakland Museum also interviewed several prominent Black residents; Mary Perry Smith permitted me access to nearly two dozen taped interviews. They substantiated some of the ideas I formulated after reviewing the written documents and interviewing a number of residents on my own. Eighteen urbanites allowed me to interview them for several hours in their homes and to revisit them on subsequent occasions.

The informants also led me to their photograph collections. While some nineteenth- and early twentieth-century photos of Black pioneers are available in the California Historical Society Library, the Bancroft Library (University of California, Berkeley), and the East Bay Negro Historical Society, the discovery of the family albums, studio portraits, and snapshots in respondents' homes was much more meaningful to me. They were then part of the context in which the residents used them, and the informants identified individuals when they could and depended on these documents to sharpen their recollections. Walter L. Gibson, Freddie McWilliams, Royal E. Towns, and Eleanor Carroll Watkins have preserved a number of photographs of varying age and in good condition, and other citizens also possessed some of these precious images.

The secondary literature is not particularly rich for the urban scene in the far west or for Blacks in the region. A few biographies of well-known San Franciscans occasionally mention Negro employees. C. B. Glasscock, *Lucky Baldwin: The Story of An Unconventional Success* (Indianapolis, 1933); and Marion M. Marberry, *The Golden Voice: A Biography of Isaac Kalloch* (New York, 1947) give brief but well-drawn portraits of two Afro-American employees.

Aside from Helen Holdredge's controversial *Mammy Pleasant* (New York, 1953), no Black San Franciscan has been treated in a biography. Ann Charters, *Nobody: The Story of "Bert" Williams* (New York, 1970) gives a sketch of Williams and George Walker's lean years on the west coast. Alan Lomax, *Mister Jelly Roll: The Fortunes of Jelly Roll Morton, New Orleans Creole and "Inventor of Jazz"* (New York, 1950) includes a glimpse of Morton's San Francisco sojourn and his travels on the west coast.

Some nineteenth-century Black histories, efforts of Black men of letters, contain brief descriptions of San Franciscans. Examples are: Martin Robison Delany, *The Condition, Elevation, Emigration, and Destiny of the Colored People of the United States* (New York, 1968 ed.); William J. Simmons, *Men of Mark* (Chicago, 1970 ed.); and William Wells Brown, *The Black Man, His Ante? His Genius, and His Achievements* (New York, 1863). Also, I. Garland P? *Afro-American Press and Its Editors* (Springfield, Mass., 1891); and Richard R. Wright, Jr., *The Bishops of the African Methodist Episcop?* (Nashville, Tenn., 1956 and 1957) sketch out the careers and achievemen? San Francisco Negroes, often before migration.

Various chronicles of San Francisco life illuminate this specific urban? the Black presence in it. Herbert Asbury, in *The Barbary Coast: An Inform? History of the San Francisco Underworld* (New York, 1933), has explored this side of the city much as he treated New Orleans, Chicago, and New York. Oscar Lewis covered the city's rich in: *The Big Four* (New York, 1938); *Silver Kings: The Lives and Times of Mackay, Fair, Floor, and O'Brien, Lords of the Nevada Comstock Lode* (New York, 1947); and, with Carroll D. Hall, *Bonanza Inn: America's First Luxury Hotel* (New York, 1937); the last is the history of the Palace Hotel. Other aspects of the city's history are treated in William Martin Camp, *San Francisco, Port of Gold* (Garden City, N.Y., 1947); Samuel Dickson, *San Francisco Kaleidoscope* (Stanford, Calif., 1949); and Joseph A. Baird, *Time's Wondrous Changes: San Francisco's Architecture, 1776-1915* (San Francisco, 1962).

Two published works focus on the Black San Franciscans. Elizabeth L. Parker and James Abajian, *A Walking Tour of the Black Presence in San Francisco During the Nineteenth Century* (San Francisco, 1974) reviews the locations of homes and businesses. Charles S. Johnson, *The Negro War Worker in San Francisco, A Local Self-Survey* (San Francisco, 1944) analyzes the changes in the Black population during World War II; it was supervised by a leading Afro-American sociologist.

Several articles deal with Blacks in San Francisco specifically, or on the Pacific slope generally. E. Berkeley Tompkins, "Black Ahab: William T. Shorey, Whaling Master," *California Historical Quarterly* LI (Spring 1972), 75-84 is based in part on interviews with Tompkins's daughter, Victoria. Rudolph M. Lapp, "Jeremiah B. Sanderson, Early California Negro Leader," *The Journal of Negro History* LIII (Oct. 1968), 321-33 tells the experiences of an early pioneer and school teacher who was also a minister. Philip M. Montesano, "The Amazing Dr. Ezra Johnson," *Urban West* I (Jan.-Feb. 1968), 21-26 examines a Black doctor's role at mid-century; "San Francisco in the Early 1860s: Social and Cultural Life of the Negro Community," *Urban West* I (Nov.-Dec. 1967), 15-16, and "San Francisco Black

Churches in the early 1860s: Political Pressure Group," *California Historical Quarterly* LII (Summer 1973), 145–52 review social and cultural life during the Civil War era.

Slavery in California and Blacks in the Gold Rush and pioneer period are treated in: Delilah L. Beasley, "California Freedom Papers," *The Journal of Negro History* III (Jan. 1918), 33–44; Clyde Duniway, "Slavery in California After 1848," *American Historical Association Annual Reports for the Year 1905* I (1906), 243–48; Howard Holman Bell, "Negroes in California, 1849–1859," *Phylon* X (Summer 1967), 151–60; Rudolph M. Lapp, "The Negro in Gold Rush California," *The Journal of Negro History* XLIV (April 1964), 81–98; James Fisher, "The Struggle for Negro Testimony in California, 1851–1863," *Southern California Quarterly* LI (Dec. 1969), 313–24; and Malcolm Edwards, "'The War of Complexional Distinction': Blacks in Gold Rush California and British Columbia," *California Historical Quarterly* LVI (Spring 1977), 34–45. F. W. Howay, "The Negro Immigration into Vancouver Island in 1858," *British Columbia Historical Quarterly* II (April 1939), 101–13 discusses the reasons behind the California

McEntire and Julia R. Tarnpol, "Postwar Status of Negro Workers in San Francisco," *Monthly Labor Review* LXX (June 1950), 612–17 probe changes in the Black population after World War II. Margaret Johnson, "The Negroes in West Berkeley," *Immigration and Race Problems, 1949–1953* (1953), 865–89 examines this East Bay city at about the same time.

Monographs on Pacific slope topics provide a much-needed historical dimension. Among them are: Earl Pomeroy, *The Pacific Slope: A History of California, Washington, Idaho, Utah, and Nevada* (New York, 1965), which alerted me to the significance of cities in western settlement; and Pomeroy, *In Search of the Golden West: The Tourist in Western America* (New York, 1957), which did the same for tourism. Gunther Barth, *Bitter Strength: A History of the Chinese in the United States, 1850–1870* (Cambridge, Mass., 1964) chronicles the experiences of the largest non-white foreign-born contingent on the west coast; Barth's *Instant Cities: Urbanization and the Rise of San Francisco and Denver* (New York, 1975) highlights the unusual histories and roles of these two western cities.

Labor legislation and relations are the topic of Lucille Eaves, *History of California Labor Legislation* (Berkeley, 1910) and Ira B. Cross, *A History of the Labor Movement in California* (Berkeley, 1935). Like many older histories, they offer little information on Negroes, but are valuable for their examination of the context in which white laborers and the few Black slaves worked.

The histories of Black California were written by newcomers. Delilah L. Beasley, *The Negro Trail Blazers of California* (Los Angeles, 1919), was the first state history of a racial group. This work, along with Sue Bailey Thurman, *Pioneers of Negro Origin in California* (San Francisco, 1949), lacks the sophistication and accuracy of some university-sponsored histories, but contains information that contemporary academics considered unimportant and that otherwise would be lost.

Rudolph M. Lapp, *Blacks in Gold Rush California* (New Haven, Conn., 1977) analyzes the Afro-American presence, political and civil rights struggles, and social life during the early years. Charles Wollenburg, *All Deliberate Speed: Segregation and Race Exclusion in California Schools* (Berkeley, 1976) is excellent. It chronicles the history of race discrimination in a state which has quickly forgotten this aspect of its heritage. Elmer R. Rusco, *"Good Time Coming?": Black Nevadans in the Nineteenth Century* (Westport, Conn., 1975), and Eugene Berwanger, *The Frontier Against Slavery: Western Anti-Negro Prejudice and the Slavery Extension Controversy* (Urbana, Ill., 1967) represent the trend toward state studies and analysis of race relations, respectively.

James de T. Abajian, comp., *Blacks and Their Contributions to the American West: A Bibliography and Union List of Library Holdings Through 1970* (Boston, 1974) contains a wealth of valuable information.

Urban Afro-America has not received as much scholarly attention as slavery, possibly because the latter institution lasted so long. Also, slavery's very remoteness makes it possible for scholars to consider it more readily than a subject which impinges so closely on their basic assumptions. The first study to focus on the condition of Blacks in an American city is W. E. B. Du Bois's classic in sociology and history, *The Philadelphia Negro* (1899). (Before this scholarly work there were reports on the conditions of Negroes in certain cities compiled by antislavery and religious societies.)

Early in this century, the growth of cities and of their Black populations resulted in several sociological studies, as well as works by settlement house and social workers. W. E. B. Du Bois, *The Black North in 1901: A Social Study* (New York, 1969 ed.) reviewed Black life in several northeastern cities. Mary White Ovington, who worked with Du Bois in the NAACP, wrote one of the first studies of Negroes in the major eastern city: *Half A Man: The Status of the Negro in New York* (New York, 1911). George Edmund Haynes, *The Negro at Work in New York City, A Study in Economic Progress* (New York, 1912) probes the economic life of the city's citizens. Black Boston is surveyed in John Daniels, *In Freedom's Birthplace: A Study of the Boston Negroes* (Boston, 1914); Daniels focused on the antislavery heritage and social institutions. Thomas J. Woofter, *Negro Problems in Cities* (New York, 1928) examines the mass migration and its impact upon the cities. A group of New England Negroes were the topic of Robert Warner's *New Haven Negroes: A Social History* (New Haven, Conn., 1940).

More recently, St. Clair Drake and Horace Cayton, *Black Metropolis: A Study of Negro Life in a Northern City* (New York, 1945) set new standards in the use of history, sociology, and anthropology to study modern Black city dwellers. Few scholars have matched Drake and Cayton in depth, breadth, and clarity, or in their sympathy with their subjects, which added an impressive humanistic dimension to their scholarship.

Most monographs focus on twentieth-century Black residents of northeastern cities. Aside from the early efforts of Du Bois, Ovington, and Daniels, James Weldon Johnson's *Black Manhattan* (New York, 1930) treats social and cultural life in Negro New York from the late eighteenth century. This cosmopolitan scholar brought an interest in the sporting world to his study of Black urban life, and he refrained from the pious moralizing that mars other studies. Claude McKay, *Harlem: Negro Metropolis* (New York, 1940) treats such topics as the numbers racket, cultists and occultists, and Father Divine, while Richard Wright and Edwin Rosskam, *Twelve Million Black Voices: A Folk History of the Negro in the United States* (New York, 1941) depicts the modern ghetto. Constance M. Green, *Washington: Capital City* (Princeton, N.J., 1963) and Letitia Woods Brown, *Free Negroes in the District of Columbia, 1790-1846* (New York, 1972) are concerned with race relations and civil rights.

Richard Wade, *Slavery in the Cities: The South, 1820-1860* (New York, 1964) lays bare the close connections between slavery and southern cities. John Blassingame, *Black New Orleans, 1860-1880* (Chicago, 1973) is among the first monographs on Afro-Americans in a specific southern city; it is primarily concerned with traditional topics such as the end of slavery, the freedmen, and Reconstruction.

A number of works on the ghetto accompanied the civil rights struggles of the 1950s and 1960s. Black New York is examined in Seth M. Scheiner, *Negro Mecca: A History of the Negro in New York City, 1865-1920* (New York, 1965), and Gilbert Osofsky, *Harlem: The Making of A Ghetto, Negro New York, 1890-1930* (New York, 1965). Allan H. Spear, *Black Chicago: The Making of A Negro Ghetto* (Chicago, 1967) is one of the better accounts of the development of the modern ghetto. David M. Katzman, *Before the Ghetto: Black Detroit in the Nineteenth Century* (Urbana, Ill., 1973), and Kenneth Kusmer, *A Ghetto Takes Shape: Black Cleveland, 1870-1930* (Urbana, Ill., 1976) examine civil rights, race relations, and class-related issues in two midwestern cities. Ethnic neighborhoods, housing, racism, and reform are analyzed in Thomas Lee Philpott, *The Slum and the Ghetto: Neighborhood Deterioration and Middle-Class Reform, Chicago, 1880-1930* (New York, 1978). Scholarly study of the quality of life in nineteenth- and twentieth-century cities in the upper south, the deep south, the Great Plains, and the far west still awaits the attention of younger generations.

# Index

*223*